GUIDE TO
OUTDOOR CAREERS

GUIDE TO
OUTDOOR
CAREERS

Martha Thomas

STACKPOLE BOOKS

Published by
STACKPOLE BOOKS
Cameron and Kelker Streets
P.O. Box 1831
Harrisburg, Pa. 17105

First printing, October 1981
Second printing, April 1982

Printed in the U.S.A.

Library of Congress Cataloging in Publication Data

Thomas, Martha.
  Guide to outdoor careers.

  Includes index.
  1. Vocational guidance. 2. Outdoor life. I. Title.
II. Title: Outdoor careers.
HF5381.T49   331.7′02   81-16677
ISBN 0-8117-1047-5   AACR2

Contents

Foreword

As a career counselor, I am embarrassed. I had never imagined that the world of outdoor careers had such depth and variety. I now realize that I have been shortchanging my clientele for years, assuming that work outdoors pertains only to a rather narrow category of people. This book has changed all that. Like Jacques Cousteau, Martha Thomas has brought it all into my living room.

Guide to Outdoor Careers is an effective mixture of content and process. Through it, Martha tells the reader what is out there and how to play the various games necessary to get his hands on it. The sections on decision-making and getting ready are rooted in the best principles that anyone can use to move successfully toward a career or job. Furthermore, Martha is sensitive to the unpredictability in job markets and the length of the job search process. The reader will feel amply warned, yet optimistic as he applies these strategies of career development.

The book's immense strength is in its scope and careful detail of content. The job chapters offer a dazzling array of career titles, complete with concise yet appealing descriptions. Wisely, Martha does not limit her emphasis to forest rangers, oil geologists, and the few other outdoor careers most popularly imagined. She includes such diverse categories as environmental protection scientists, anthropologists, seed analysts, limnologists, maple sugar producers, herb culturists, and livestock service workers. These chapters are so encyclopedic and detailed that most anyone will be able to find enough information to stimulate both exploration of possibilities and tentative choices.

Martha uncovers here a rich, remarkable underworld support system for the outdoor professions. The truth is indoor and outdoor professions are inherently connected. Those who work outdoors to provide an indoor environment for other workers—community planners, for example—remind us that the separation is an artificial one, and that many people are hard at work to make the indoor-outdoor relationship more fluid. In the chapter "Indoor Skills—Outdoor Fun," Martha discusses what career counselors have long known —that any two career fields can be combined through the use of imagination and creative marketing of an idea. Those whose careers flow between the indoors and outdoors have the most fun, while the psychological bridges they build enable the rest of us to maintain a relationship to both worlds.

This book will be a tremendous asset to all career counselors, their clientele, and all individuals who seek information and insight without the aid of a counselor. It will be especially helpful in three ways:

1) It is a stellar collection and description of outdoor career fields that truly reveals the breadth and variety of what is *out there* and ways to gain entry. It leaves the reader feeling that he does not need any other resource to get started in the search process.

2) It creates a mandate for the promotion of outdoor careers. I have the feeling it is a critical juncture for the future of outdoor work, and counselors cannot be neutral about the topic.

3) It sensitizes me, as I am sure it will other readers, to our natural heritage, and reminds me that people have not beaten nature; they have just made it less visible.

Up to now, outdoor careers have not been on equal footing with business, law, or medicine. *Guide to Outdoor Careers* will help restore the proper balance and will make it abundantly clear that our superstructure of indoor careers depends upon an equally intricate framework of outdoor careers that have greater intrinsic meaning, personal reward, and community importance than most office creatures may ever know.

Dr. Howard Figler
Director of Counseling and Placement
Dickinson University

Acknowledgments

Within the text, I have identified many career counseling experts and educators and their writings. In addition, I want to credit United States government publications that were invaluable, particularly materials from the Office of Personnel Management and the Small Business Administration (used in Chapter 6), and the U. S. Department of Labor's *Employment Opportunities Handbook* (used throughout the book, but especially in Chapters 7 through 14). I repeatedly drew on U. S. Department of Labor statistics.

I am particularly grateful to Charles Townley, Director of Library Services, and Peg O'Hara, Director of Placement, The Pennsylvania State University, Capitol Campus, and Howard Figler, Director of Counseling and Placement at Dickinson College, for suggesting resource materials; to Ruth Dennison-TeDesco, my editor, for her editorial assistance; and to my husband, Walter Sheppard, who helped with special research problems and with manuscript typing.

I went to live in the woods because I wished to live deliber-
ately, to face only the essential facts of life, and see if I could
not learn what it had to teach, and not, when I came to die,
discover that I had not lived.

                                        Henry David Thoreau

1

From Eden to Antarctica:
Rationale for Outdoor Careers

Outdoor careers. An ambiguous term. What exactly does it mean?
Digging ditches? Or agricultural engineering? Picking fruit? Or forest
management? Outdoor careers are all of these and more, and the
differences in the descriptions are important ones to understand for
your future. Digging ditches or picking fruit is a job. Agricultural
engineering or farm management is a career. A job is a task, or
as *Webster's New Collegiate* says, "a small miscellaneous piece of
work . . ." A career, the same dictionary records, is "a profession for
which one trains and which is undertaken as a permanent calling."
So a job is a short-term chore, perhaps not calling for great skills,
while a career demands not only training but also commitment. A
job is also a position that you will embark upon as part of your
career. You may—indeed, surely will—undertake many jobs.

   This book covers careers that for the most part take place outdoors. In a few cases, the nature of the work also involves some

indoor work; that is, office or research time. But the basic focus is work in the open—careers relating to the environment, the hundreds of ways to earn a living outdoors, ranging from farming to agribusiness to ecology to earth science to conservation to recreation and much, much more.

For those who thrive on outdoor life, there is no greater attraction than spending the working day under the open skies. The discomforts—the rigors of blustery winds and zero temperatures or sticky midsummer heat—pale beside the pleasures. Any nature lover will trade a little discomfort for the privilege of being free to enjoy the good days, the exhilaration of balmy spring or crisp fall weather.

There's more to any outdoor career than this, of course. The personal rewards attached to the idea of outdoor work count heavily. The main one is probably the satisfaction of accomplishment that comes with the melding of skills of head and hands. With most outdoor work also comes the feeling of being at one with the universe, of protecting.

A great attraction of outdoor careers for many people is that they seem to provide a panacea for so much of what is perceived to be wrong in today's society: the blind acceptance of the Judeo-Christian work ethic; the futile search for security in response to fear of a repetition of the Great Depression; the mad pursuit of work for power and prestige; jaded consumerism, the tedious running of the "rat race" to acquire "necessities," which to earlier generations might have been called "luxuries." Outdoor work, as one young woman put it, "seems more honest. The ends justify the means. It seems to be worth doing."

Work worth doing. That young woman put her finger on what seems to be for most people the guiding force in choosing an outdoor career. They care about what they are doing. The great environmental movement of the mid-1960s and '70s created a new public awareness of the troubled state of our environment. Today, in the 1980's, awareness is no longer enough. Awareness must now be tied to action on the part of environmentalists to enhance and protect the world in which we all live. This challenge invigorates some people. If it invigorates you, then an outdoor career may be your calling.

Just because work is worth doing does not exempt it from difficulties. The truth is that the choice of an outdoor career may create many problems for you. For example, finding a niche for yourself may take time and ingenuity. It's not the most wide-open, secure way to earn a living in today's economy. Of the more than 26,000 ways you could pick, the several hundred in the outdoor category may call for special career strategies. The competition in the field is tough. Even more serious is the cutback in governmental funding and the relaxing of many environmental controls. Government—federal, state, and local—is by far the largest employer in the outdoor field, and environmental control has created many jobs, dozens of them unheard of before the past two decades. These are facts and they are discouraging. People should spend their lives working in a field in which they will be happy, but they should also assess situations realistically, set goals, and make plans. After all, one job is all you need to begin a career and make dreams come true.

Working outdoors is nothing new. People have been doing it forever. It was the very first kind of work. Perhaps this fact is one more reason so many contemporary men and women are interested in outdoor careers; they have the feeling of returning to their roots.

People survived for hundreds of thousands of years by the most primitive outdoor work. Their constant, and almost only, quest was for food—gathering roots, nuts, berries, and insects; fishing; hunting. It was only about 10,000 years ago that they discovered how to cultivate plants and harvest them. About this time, too, they domesticated animals, training them to work in the fields and raising them for food.

Sometime between 7000 and 9000 B.C. they invented digging sticks and scratch plows and were able to cultivate the light soils in the great river basins of the Middle East, northwest India, northern China, and the Americas. Sickles and harrows came into use and helped increase production even more.

With this growing sophistication in food production came the growth of population and civilization, advances in the arts and in science and technology, and the dilemma of balancing expansion against conservation of natural resources. From the beginning of time, people faced this predicament, or did not face it. Most often change came slowly, but every giant step in technological advancement ravaged the land. Every field cleared meant the destruction of trees, which led in turn to erosion. Every additional innovation, while labeled as progress, struck a mortal blow at the earth's natural resources. The inexorable advance toward the Industrial Revolution seems, in retrospect, almost like a death march.

The development of irrigation, the discovery of the laws controlling plant and animal genetics, the development of artificial fertilizers, the harnessing of wind and water, the building of roads and bridges, the construction of buildings, the discovery of fossil fuels, the invention of the internal combustion engine—all of these are miracles of human ingenuity. At the same time, they became instruments to make the destruction of the environment easier. People aspiring to riches and progress could proceed with less thought and caution. The world seemed limitless, especially when the New World was opened up to exploration, settlement, and development.

The natural resources in North America—the fertile soil, the hundreds of miles of streams and rivers, the thousands of millions of acres of forest, the rich concentrations of minerals—were the building blocks of a materialistic society unlike any that has ever existed on earth. This was a land of opportunity, the place where anyone could make a fortune. Everything was free, or almost free. Only hard work was called for. Literally, the sky was the limit.

The area was wide open to this conquest because it was unprotected by the restraints of international codes and laws. First came the Spanish and Portuguese, searching for riches and slaves. They destroyed whole cities and civilizations in Central and South America. Moving on to North America, they hacked their way across the virgin wilderness from southeast to southwest without finding what they were looking for.

The next wave of immigrants, while still Spanish, were colonizers rather than marauders. They were the priests and noblemen who settled Texas, New Mexico, Arizona, and California, living in harmony with the land and with the Indians, destroying little and making friends.

The English colonists were another matter. There were more of them and they were more aggressive although, in fairness to them, one must acknowledge that they arrived only with the basic necessities and had to live off the land in order to survive. They cut down forests to make fields to grow food; for wood to build houses, furniture, tools, wagons, and boats; for fuel for warmth and cooking; and for industry to support a struggling economy.

The movement inland and westward was inexorable, with the more ambitious and more adventurous pushing over the Appalachians, through the Ohio and Mississippi valleys to the Great Plains, and ultimately across the Rocky Mountains to the Pacific. Explorers, adventurers, fur trappers, hunters, farmers, ranchers, miners, speculators, canal and railroad builders, and politicians surged over the land like plagues of biblical locusts denuding the country of its forests, its grasslands, its minerals, its water. It took only until the year 1770 to clear the Tidewater country and the Appalachian foothills of forests. By 1889, the buffalo were almost exterminated. By this time, too, the great theft of the Indian lands was complete. In a little less than three centuries, the natural resources of the United States were squandered without thought of the needs of future generations.

A small minority did speak out against this wanton destruction. One of the loudest voices was that of diplomat and scholar George Perkins Marsh (1801–1882). In 1864, he published *Man and Nature,* a pioneering effort in conservation, "to suggest the possibility and the importance of the restoration of disturbed harmonies and the material improvement of wasted and exhausted regions." He cited the pillage of the world from biblical times on, noting the price mankind has had to pay was the reduction of bountiful lands to deserts. "What happened to those ancient countries might also happen to America unless immediate steps are taken to put an end to wanton destruction of our natural resources," he wrote. "People must be made to realize that the strength of our nation is based upon the wise use and careful perpetuation of its natural resources."

Marsh's persuasive arguments became the foundation on which American conservation education was built, and they also promoted a mid-nineteenth-century consciousness of the problem. The seeds were sown for reform and slowly people began to recognize that America's resources were both limited and exhaustible.

Other voices joined Marsh's. Some, like Henry David Thoreau (1817–1862), had little effect in their own time. Others, like John Muir (1834–1914), became leaders of the conservation movement.

While Thoreau was ignored by his own generation, he is often thought of today as the "first environmentalist." His essays about living in the wilds with nature in the area around Walden's Pond near Concord, Massachusetts, have become required reading for anyone who purports to care about people and the universe. He was also an amateur naturalist, doing pioneer work in limnology, dendro-chronology, ecology, and phenology. One of his biographers, Philip Van Doren Stern, calls him "a perceptive observer and first-rate notetaker, far better than most professionals in his field, then and now." He also points out that Thoreau was "an active field-worker at a time when the natural sciences were still being shaped."

The New England writer-naturalist has a particular appeal for rebels and nature lovers because he believed the status quo could—and should—be changed. The message of his writing is as relevant today as it was more than a century ago.

The same is true of poet and essayist John Muir, who led the fight to preserve California's wilderness, helping to establish Yosem-ite National Park. Born in Scotland, he immigrated as a child with his family to Wisconsin, where he helped to wrest a farm out of the wilderness. After working his way through the University of Wis-consin, he made the study of nature his career, contributing pioneer ecological observation to the annals of the infant science. He dis-covered plants and insects, some of which bear his name, as do schools, lakes, mountains, trails, wildlife preserves, and other out-door outposts in California and across the nation.

Muir was an original thinker, and his ultimate philosophy could be summed up in one word: freedom. "I have not yet in all my wanderings found a single person as free as myself," he once told a friend. To him, time was more valuable than money.

He believed that nature, particularly the California wilderness, should be preserved in its pristine loveliness and that if you become a real part of the wilderness, you expand your horizons. "I go to the mountains as a particle of dust in the wind," he wrote. He used his poetry and essays to sway public opinion and develop nature projects to support his beliefs. Aside from Yosemite National Park, these writings led to the creation of Sequoia, Rainier, and Grand Canyon National Parks and to the preservation of thousands of additional acres of forest.

Muir's love of wilderness prompted him to endless exploration, including an Alaskan expedition to Glacier Bay. His zealot's enthu-siasms led him to help form the Sierra Club, which became the spearhead of the western conservation movement. (See chapter nine.)

The work of men like Muir around the world has been responsible for international cooperation to preserve the environment. The most notable recent example may be the United Nations agreement that the Antarctic may be left free for scientific study and as a wildlife sanctuary.

Without a doubt, the conservationists are among the most vocal and visible of the outdoor careerists, but they are not the only people who provide a legacy and a model to present day workers. Indeed, this second list is even longer, so long it is impossible to offer an inclusive catalogue. Leading it are men like two Quakers, John and William Bartram, a father and son team in colonial America. John Bartram was probably America's first naturalist. A generation later, William Bartram followed in his father's footsteps to become a pioneer American ornithologist and traveler extraordinaire.

From early youth, John Bartram's life was given over to plant study and farming. On his large farm near Philaldelphia, he grew crops with record yields. He also developed what was considered in his time the best collection of native plants in America and shipped almost 200 species of American plants to Europe. Additionally, he established the first North American botanical garden, which still survives. He was a forester, a geologist, and an ecologist, studying these disciplines in tandem with plant collecting and propagation. He hiked throughout the eastern United States from Lake Ontario to Florida to study the American nature world, recording his adventures in both words and drawings. Among his more interesting works is a classic essay on tree farming.

Like his father, William Bartram was a passionate explorer and recorded his adventures. The best known is *Bartram's Travels,* which was published in Europe as well as America. He also compiled the first scientific list of eastern birds and did similar work with insects. In addition, he was an accomplished painter and an outstanding teacher. Among his students was Thomas Say, the "Father of American Entomology." Scholars believe that *Materia Medica*, written in 1798 by the eminent botanist Benjamin Smith Barton, was really Bartram's work.

Another artist-naturalist who captured the public imagination and who is considered the greatest American wildlife painter is John James Audubon (1785–1851), or Jean Jacques Audubon, as he was baptized. He is generally accepted as a native, but he may have been born in Haiti. He spent his childhood in France and came to this country as a young adult to live briefly on the family estate in Pennsylvania before finally settling in Henderson, Kentucky, where he opened a trading post. From earliest childhood, he was an observer and lover of nature. This interest asserted itself after his move to Kentucky, so much so that he ignored his business to pursue his studies, and it failed. He spent the rest of his life creating exquisitely detailed watercolor drawings of wildlife, particularly birds, and writing about pioneer America and its wildlife. His name and drawings helped form one of the first naturalist societies in the United States.

In more recent times, there are models like Rachel Carson, biologist and author of *Silent Spring*. She is a prime example of how a typical indoor career—writing—can be combined with an outdoor career—biology. When she entered the Pennsylvania State College for Women, she planned to be a writer. There she was introduced to science, especially biology, and changed her career direction. She worked for her master's degree at Johns Hopkins University and at the Woods Hole Oceanographic Institute and then began to teach, possibly with the idea of working for her Ph.D. The 1930s depression intervened, however, and instead she went to work for the federal government in the Fish and Wildlife Service, where she eventually edited various publications. This, in turn, led to writing about the environment. Her articles and books, especially *Silent Spring*, alerted the people of the United States to the evils of the indiscriminate use of such chemicals as DDT. Ironically, she died of cancer, perhaps a victim of the very ills she denounced.

Another contemporary outdoor careerist is the French oceanographer Jacques-Yves Cousteau. He directs the Office Française de Récherches Sous-marines, one of the leading experimenters in marine engineering. His basic work involves studying how human beings can descend into the ocean's depth, live and work there, and return safely to the surface. He designed the first modern aqualung and initiated a series of daring experiments in underwater living and working. His work has been popularized by a number of television programs and books. The current popularity of oceanography as a career is probably due to his influence.

The prognosis for the Carsons and Cousteaus of the immediate future is uncertain. One statement can be made: it will be different from today. The United States Department of Labor notes that "constant change is one of the most significant aspects of the United

States job market. Changes in the population, the introduction of new technology or business practices, and changes in the needs and tastes of the public continually alter the economy and affect employment in all occupations."

One factor influencing outdoor careers is the development of two technological tools: the electronic computer and the satellite. The first allows the analysis of vast quantities of facts competently and quickly. The second provides data of every kind. Weather satellites send daily weather pictures that show and track destructive storms and other weather systems. Other satellite systems with applications in many fields—including agriculture, cartography, forestry, geology, geography, hydrology, and oceanography—do a similar job for other problems.

Two other major factors influencing outdoor careers in the next two decades are population and government spending. By 1990, the population of the United States is expected to increase to 244 million. Nearly one-third of the total population will be between the ages of twenty-five and forty-four, the result of the "baby boom" that followed World War II. In contrast, because of the relatively low birth rate in the 1960s and early 1970s, the number of people between the ages of fourteen and twenty-four will decline gradually, and the number of people over sixty-five will grow, but more slowly than in recent years.

The effect on the job market of these population statistics should be apparent. As the number of young people declines, the need for educational services will fall and teaching jobs will be scarce. As the "baby boom" people marry and have children, the need for housing and related products and services will increase. Also, the competition for jobs will be stiffer because the number of workers sixteen to twenty-four years old—the ages when most people enter the labor force—will continue to grow in the 1980s, although not as rapidly in the second half of the decade as in the first.

Another point of interest to the outdoor careerist is that, through 1990, replacement job needs as a result of death or retirement are expected to be twice those from the establishment of new jobs. Even more important, research findings indicate that career changes and temporary labor force separations (for example, women leaving their jobs to have babies) will be a larger source of job openings than growth, deaths, and retirements combined.

One of the major changes in the availability of outdoor jobs will come in the environmental protection field. Stringent government regulations, followed by the rush of industry to comply with them, created many new jobs in the 1960s and 1970s. Government agencies, especially the Environmental Protection Agency, made funds available for education and specialized training for people to fill the new jobs. Now, suddenly, at the beginning of the 1980s, inflation, accompanied by radical cuts in government spending, has brought major changes. Jobs in this particular area will undoubtedly be very tight in the next decade. Because of the reduction in government spending, many other traditional entry-level jobs in the outdoor field may be very tight also, for example, conservation, where the majority of jobs are with federal agencies.

None of this means that you should turn your back on a career in an outdoor field if you believe this is the right match for your interests and abilities. What it does mean is that you should be aware of the problems that you may encounter and be prepared to deal with them with competitive job strategies.

So, is there a Henry David Thoreau, a John Muir, or a Rachel Carson among you? Are any of you longing to be farmers, foresters, ecologists, meteorologists, or any one of thousands of other workers in the outdoor field? Would you like the satisfaction of making a real contribution to society through a commitment to an outdoor job? Do you long for an invigorating life living and working outdoors? If your answer to these questions is "yes," read on. This book will help you give yourself—and us—a future.

2

Choice or Chance:
Lessons in Decision-Making

To some people "work" is the ugliest word in the language. It conjures up drudgery and is synonymous with exhaustion, servitude, and punishment. To still others, work is the mainspring of existence. It connotes revitalization, privilege, and pleasure. In between these two extremes are the resigned millions to whom work is nothing more than a passport to the basic necessities—food, shelter, and clothing—as well as the "good things in life."

What does work mean to you? Your answer is important to the rest of your life. Do you have a clear picture of how you want to spend your years? Have you worked? Or have you been exclusively a student? Who are your models? Listen to these students talking about workers in their families.

Angela, the daughter of a miner: "My dad was killed in a cave-in—literally buried alive. I doubt if he was surprised. Mine accidents were an open worry in the family. You could see it in my mom's eyes every day. Why did my dad go on with it, with that daily threat of disaster? My mom says he couldn't do anything else, that with all of us kids to support he didn't have a choice. And now she's working as a maid in a motel. She drives fifty miles a day to and from work. Making other people's beds! She says she doesn't have any choice."

Jim, the son of a doctor: "All my dad does is complain about how the government and insurance companies take all the money he earns. And his schedule is awful. He's up at dawn, and not home until after we're all in bed. He almost never has meals with the family. When he is home, he's cross, and says he's too tired to be bothered with kids' problems. Sure he earns a lot of money. Anyone can tell that from the neighborhood we live in, the cars we drive, the so-called privileges we have. You know, like belonging to the country club, going to camp, taking music lessons, having money to spend on records and dating, eating out . . . stuff like that. And I know he's important in the community. Take school. The teachers treat me differently than the kids from the inner city. They know if I beef they'll get a visit from my parents. My dad gets his name in the papers; he serves on all those boards and committees—or at least my mom does. People ask him for advice all the time, too. But so what? I want time to enjoy life. Why have a swimming pool if you never use it? Why have children if you never spend time with them? Why earn a lot of money if you feel you don't get anything out of it?"

Sarah and Carl, the grandchildren of a retired accountant who worked 50 years in one of the major corporations: "When my grandad retired, they gave him a gold watch. He sits around and looks at the time a lot. Our grandmother says he's underfoot all the time. He used to play golf before he stopped working, but now he says nobody has time for him anymore." The granddaughter: "He's a changed person since retirement. I can't understand how he could change so much in just a few months." The grandson: "He scares me. I think, someday that could be me."

Any one of these situations is common enough. All of them horrify someone trying to make career decisions. Work, no matter how prestigious nor how resolutely pursued, seems futile. The paramount thought becomes, "How can I keep from spending my life like this?" Every generation examines work and tries to provide an answer.

For early man, work was an onerous necessity for survival. Early Greeks and other ancient people thought it degrading and instituted slavery, thus beginning the split between the idle elite and the laboring masses.

Historically, in the Western world, work is tied to religion by both Christians and Jews. The Hebrews of biblical times thought of it as God's punishment for the misdeeds of Adam and Eve in the Garden of Eden. They took seriously his condemnation of Eve: "I will increase your labor and your groaning." To Adam, the censure was even harsher: "Accursed shall be the ground on your account. With labor you shall win your food from it all the days of your life ... You shall gain your bread by the sweat of your brow." In the early sixteenth century, John Calvin and the Puritans took this doctrine even further when they decreed work was the key to life and the path to salvation. Idleness literally became sinfulness.

In the nineteenth century, thinking men began to reject these ideas. Karl Marx, with his theory of Utopian socialism, postulated that men should "live to work" rather than "work to live," to find satisfaction in labor apart from economic reward. Max Weber, the German sociologist, "invented" bureaucracy, with its now familiar features of authority structure based on graded ranks with carefully delineated job descriptions and formal rules and regulations to carry out work. Sigmund Freud was convinced that people worked for hidden sexual pleasure. Other psychologists rejected his ideas and claimed that people worked out of instinct for self-preservation, hence, mankind's effort to try to control the environment.

Latter day behaviorists believe people work for many reasons: for power and the potential for control; for prestige and the gratification of recognition and status; for security and the physical and intellectual satisfaction of comfort; and for a sense of social purpose and the benevolent feeling of service to human kind. This last is perhaps an extension of the Calvinist work ethic that is still strong in the United States, especially among older members of the labor force.

However, the strongest drive behind workers in contemporary society seems to be consumerism. Many people plod through eight hours of routine, even automated, work as a tedious way to acquire luxuries. Then they spend aimless hours before television sets wondering why life seems dull, even hopeless.

As Logan Pearsall Smith, the great Anglo-American essayist and Oxford scholar, wrote, "There are two things to aim at in life: first to get where you want; and after that, to enjoy it. Only the wisest of mankind achieves the second." What you want to know is how you can follow Smith's philosophy.

What do you want? You may not know. Interests are not present at birth and they do not appear spontaneously. They are the result of experience. If you have not had opportunities to meet a wide range of people and see different parts of the world, you may have little to build on. Sometimes youths in the United States lead existences as cloistered as medieval religionists, especially those brought up in middle-class suburbia. They have never been challenged to fend for themselves, and too often their role models are parents with jobs like the one Sarah and Carl's grandfather worked at for fifty years.

Doing what you want in life means you have to cut through your lack of experience and knowledge. You have to make a plan, or you will be like Charles Schultz's superstar Lucy. In the comic strip several years ago, she was having one of her customary conversations with Charlie Brown. "I've made an important decision," she told him. "I'm going to be a nurse when I grow up." Charlie Brown naturally asked why. "Because I like to wear white shoes," Lucy replied. Tastes and fashions change. A passion for white shoes is a slim reason for spending thousands of hours and dollars preparing for a career.

"No one would choose a career like that!" you protest.

Not exactly, perhaps, since exaggeration is part of the stock-in-trade of comic strips, but thinking about career planning is too often limited to something like this: "No, I don't think I'm interested in being a doctor or a dentist. I hate visits to their offices, and I can't stand the smell of hospitals or the sight of blood. I'm not mechanically inclined; that rules out engineering. I'm not a good speaker, so I couldn't be a lawyer. I can't stand unhappy people, so there goes another whole list—minister, psychologist, therapist, you name it. I can't write. What's left? Business. I guess that's it."

One young man entered the business program in a northeastern college after thinking similar to that. He dropped out before his first year ended. He took his motorcycle and traveled around the country. When his father cut off his allowance, he went back to his hometown. Three years later, he is still trying to find his way. He's had jobs in four retail establishments. In each case, he has quit just before he was fired, and this is about to happen again. The only time he is happy is when he is hunting or fishing. It is no wonder.

You may have a similar dismal failure if you choose your life-work with no more preparation than he did. Your search for a career should begin long before high school graduation. Some counselors today consider it is a lifelong process beginning in elementary school. One is Dr. Kathryn L. Towns, Assistant Dean for Research Studies and Continuing Education at The Pennsylvania State University, Capitol Campus. She is the organizer of PROBE (Potential Re-entry Opportunities in Business and Education), an organization devoted to helping women who originally chose marriage and motherhood over a career to find their potential in productive jobs when they decide to return to the work force. Dr. Towns believes that if women had career education early in life so that they understood the options, many would make different decisions.

Another is Dr. James Slick, Assistant Director in charge of Career Information Systems, Career Development and Placement Center, The Pennsylvania State University. "Beginning early is of primary importance," he says. "Timing is what it is all about. Students need time to make mistakes and try out ideas."

Just saying, "Begin early," is not synonymous with getting started, though. "I hear what you're telling me," one young woman says, "but I haven't any idea how to begin."

You begin with yourself, and while it is preferable to start at least by the time you enter high school, it is never too late. There are dozens of techniques to help you. In the last decade—the "me" decade, some sociologists have labeled it—there has been a burgeoning of self-help books, including career direction books by psychologists who have completed substantial research in the field. Several of these books have become the "bibles" of career counselors. The leaders in the field are the books by Richard Nelson Bolles, head of the National Career Development Project of the United Ministries in Higher Education, a coalition of ten major Protestant denominations. They include *What Color Is Your Parachute: A Practical Manual for Job Hunters and Career Changers* (Ten Speed Press, 1972), *The Three Boxes of Life and How to Get Out of Them* (Ten Speed Press, 1978), and, co-authored with John C. Crystal, *Where Do I Go from Here with My Life* (A Continuum Book, Seabury Press, 1974).

These three books are decision-making tools that try to take a lot of the guesswork out of planning a life and a career. They help you analyze your capabilities, accomplishments, and interests and tell you how to apply those in planning a career and a lifestyle. A particularly valuable companion volume is John L. Holland's *Making Vocational Choices: A Theory of Careers* (Prentice-Hall, Inc., 1973). All of these books have led to a number of similar volumes—some excellent and some mediocre. For college age students, one of the best is *The Complete Job-Search Handbook: All the Skills You Need to Get Any Job and Have a Good Time Doing It* by Howard Figler (Holt Rinehart and Winston, 1979). Director of Counseling and Placement at Dickinson College, Figler also wrote *PATH: A Career Workbook for Liberal Arts Students* (Carroll Press, 1975). For the post-college career planner, a good choice is *The Inventurers: Excursions in Life and Career Renewal* by Janet O. Hagberg and Richard J. Leider (Addison-Wesley Publishing Company, 1978), founders and directors of Human Renewal, Inc., a creative and innovative consulting firm specializing in life and career renewal services.

Using a variety of techniques, these books all get you to probe your own life and psyche as a basis for planning a career and lifestyle. In the end, they all ask you to find answers for three questions:

What do you like to do?

What can you do?

What would you like to do?

These three questions are like the magic words in an old fairy tale that release the power of a genie who makes your wishes and dreams come true. Your answers to the questions can make your dreams come true, too.

You need to take the questions very seriously and work very hard at the answers. There are two approaches to the "What do you like to do?" question: writing an autobiography and making a "What I like to do" list. They can be used together or singly.

The autobiography does not have to be a literary masterpiece. All you need is a chronological history of your life and the feelings surrounding the events included. Consider every part of your life—home, school, church, friendships, hobbies, sports, vacations. The list covers the same material. Use whichever technique is easier for you. Or write an autobiography and then develop a list from it.

This exercise is not a test, so don't freeze up. Include anything that has given you joy, from catching your first fish to listening to your favorite music. You will undoubtedly end up with many pages. As your material develops, you will see patterns. They are clues to what you might enjoy doing. But would you be successful at it? This is the job of the second question.

Stick to the list technique for this one. At the top of your work sheet write, "What I can do." Where do you excell? What are your talents and your skills? Do you understand the difference? A talent is a special ability with which you were born. A skill is the development of such abilities. Good eye-hand coordination is a talent. Mounting butterflies is a skill. A pleasant voice is a talent. Public speaking or singing are skills. Everyone has many talents, and too often they are hidden. Identifying them may be difficult.

Janet Hagberg and Richard Leider have a particularly good skills exercise in *The Inventurers*, one of the books previously mentioned. They draw an analogy to a tree, pointing out that the roots of the tree are usable skills, invisible to the eye, but necessary to the support and development of the rest of the tree. A weak root system might mean a scrawny tree, just as weak skills might mean failure. "Root skills are the ones you take with you and use, no matter what job you have, no matter where you are," they write. "You gain them from education, but particularly from experience." They are cognitive skills like reading, writing, calculating, memorizing, and reasoning.

They see the soil in which the tree grows as comparable to survival skills, those which prepare you to adapt yourself to the needs of life and a career, things like flexibility, a sense of humor, a sense of timing, and getting along with people, in what psychologists call coping skills and human skills. "These skills are so important that they are most often prime factors in hiring, firing, demotion, and promotion," Hagberg and Leider declare.

Finally, they look at the specific knowledge you have in a given area, that is, your occupational skills, as similar to the species of the tree. Each area in which you are informed and competent permits you to act and think in different ways just as separate species of trees grow in varying unique places.

If you have trouble identifying your skills, call for help. Ask your family, friends, and teachers to tell you what you do well. As is pointed out many times in this book, false modesty has no place in career planning. Try to end up with an all-inclusive list of your talents and skills. Remember, the list is not set in cement like the footprints of movie stars in the sidewalks of Hollywood. Your list is a guide for growth, as well as an inventory.

Continue with the questions. Make up a page for number three, "What I would like to do." You might also head this page "Things worth doing." In other words, you want to establish what you prefer doing with your life and what is important to you; or, to put a label on it, your *values* and your *preferences*. One of the reasons you may be considering an outdoor career is because you rail against the way many people in contemporary society live. You resent the emphasis on "buy, buy, buy." You see enormous effort being put into mediocre jobs to achieve security and a meaningless way of living. You see an outdoor career as providing you with a lifestyle and workstyle that insulate you against what you view as negative aspects of life. The Work Preferences Quiz may help you clarify your thinking and feelings. It is the clarification that is important. If you find you want to spend your evenings going to the theater or concerts, you will never adjust to the life of a forester or a park ranger. If you prefer making your own decisions and working alone, you will never like being part of a bureaucratic set-up, whether in government or in private industry. If you like winter, snow, and skiing, you will be miserable in California or Florida. This is no time to fool yourself. Be honest. If you have difficulty sorting out your values, all the books suggested above have values clarification exercises. Several hours spent with one of them may make your career decision-making both easier and sounder.

When you complete this search for self-knowledge, you still have two important questions to answer:

What do you know about the world of work in general?

How do you mesh your aptitudes and attitudes with a specific field of work?

Work Preferences Quiz

1. Do you want to be rich?

2. Do you want to be powerful?

3. Do you want to influence people?

4. Do you want prestige? Is status and fashion important to you?

5. Do you want to help people and improve the world around you?

6. Do you want an eight-hour-a-day schedule, or are you willing to commit more time to your working life?

7. Do you like a work schedule that is flexible with great variety, or one that is highly structured with heavy routine?

8. Do you want to work primarily with ideas and words or with tools and machinery? Do you want to use both your head and your hands?

9. Do you want to work alone or with people? Do you enjoy team work?

10. Do you want to be your own boss or work for someone else?

11. Do you like detail work?

12. Do you want to be physically active or sedentary?

13. Do you want to cope with deadlines? Can you handle that kind of stress and ego challenge?

14. Are you a leader or a follower?

15. What kind of work surroundings do you like? Are aesthetic considerations important? Do you needs lots of space?

16. Where do you want to live? State or general region? City, country, or suburbs?

17. Do you like formality or informality in behavior and dress?

18. What kind of recognition do you need to perform consistently?

19. Do you want your working colleagues to be your friends?

20. Do you want excitement and adventure in your work day? What physical risks are you willing to take?

21. Are you worried about security, that is, having a long-term, stable job with growing salary and many fringe benefits? Are you willing to take chances?

22. Do you want to travel?

23. Are you willing to accept the hazards of job transfer imposed by some corporations?

24. Do you like competition? Or vice versa?

25. Do you have leisure time activities that are important to you and that are not compatible with the career field and/or job you are considering?

26. Do you have physical or emotional problems that could affect your ability to work in any particular field?

27. Where do you want to be and what do you want to be doing both personally and professionally five years from now? Ten years from now?

You could look on this stage of your career decision-making as an expedition, perhaps an especially apt analogy to use with outdoor careers. You have already made some of the arrangements. Your provisions—your capabilities, accomplishments, and interests—are ready to be packed and tested. Your big remaining chore is to study the territory and map your trek. In other words, you are beginning to know something about yourself, but you do not know much about the specific careers from which you can choose. If you were to select a field without additional research, your decision would be a little bit like throwing darts and trying to hit the bull's eye without practice.

Go back to the questions just posed. What do you know about the world of work? If you grew up in a household where you were responsible for some of the chores, or if you have spent several summers working at any kind of job, you are on your way to having an answer. You cannot know about work or develop a personal work ethic without working. If you think you can, you will be defeated by false expectations. We discussed earlier various views of work and why people work. Now that you are surer of yourself you may be able to put work in a personal perspective. The words of the late mystery novelist Dorothy L. Sayers may help. "Work is not primarily a thing one does to live, but a thing one lives to do," she believed. "It is, or it should be, a full expression of the worker's faculties, the thing in which he finds spiritual, mental, and bodily satisfaction and the medium in which he offers himself to work."

Think about this statement in conjunction with your answers to the Work Preferences Quiz. You will begin to see your personal work ethic emerge. And as you have a personal work ethic, you will be able to make judgments about work in general. Requirements about commitment of time, energy, and ability will begin to make sense.

The choice of your specific field of work involves weighing all this knowledge, but it also involves finding out about specific fields. This book will discuss some of the major outdoor careers and will suggest additional media resources. Relying on reading about a field is not enough, however. You need to tap two other major resources—workers and work experience.

Begin to talk to people who work, both informally and formally. Ask them questions—the same kind of questions you have been asking yourself. Try to find out exactly what people do on their jobs, how they do, and why they do it. Try to evaluate job satisfaction. Many professional tools for this exist. One that might serve as a guide is a Career Information Questionnaire, published by the National Institute of Career Planning, 521 Fifth Avenue, New York, New York 10017. The sixteen-page guide costs $1.00 and includes a sample letter of introduction to the person being interviewed and forty questions. They cover work experience, career considerations, career preparation, lifestyle considerations, personality and talent requirements, advantages and disadvantages of the specific type of work, and matching personality to job requirements. This is not a questionnaire to be used verbatim. Rather it is a model for setting up interviews and getting answers you need.

It is important for you to make rational judgments about the information you gather from people. Consider the source. For example, information from a man actually working as a park ranger has more validity than that coming from a professor or a retired worker. It is important, too, not to be swayed by either highly positive or negative reports. Take a cool, dispassionate look at all the information you collect, discounting both biases and prejudices.

These interviews give you an opportunity to get acquainted with people in the field and develop mentors. A good mentor is hard to find, but invaluable to you. Such a person will do more than provide you with information. He or she will sponsor you, provide professional know-how, and recommend you for a job. All these actions add up to sometimes unspoken but legitimate support. "I believe in your ability to do what you are trying to do. I know you can succeed." Such subtle support can mean a lot in the rough days of decision making and job hunting.

Finding a mentor is no easier than finding a job. The first step is finding a sympathetic person, as well as a knowledgeable and powerful one. Not everyone will be willing to help you. Some people in top positions in their fields are too insecure. They feel threatened by anyone with ability. Professional organizations are good hunting grounds for mentors. Their members are always ready to aid promising apprentices. Such organizations sometimes give scholarships or prizes for special projects, too.

The very best way to find out about a career field is by working in it, or at least in a related field. A city-bred person has absolutely no chance for an outdoor job unless he or she can demonstrate knowledge and experience in the outdoors. And the more knowledge and experience anyone entering this tight work market has, the better.

Use any ploy to get this experience. Year-around part-time jobs and seasonal jobs are available. You will have to search your own individual field for openings. Work-study programs exist in many areas; chapter three will list some of these. If you cannot find a paying job, and if you can afford to do it, volunteer. Look for established internships. If these are non-existent, create your own. You want to work in the field on a daily basis with a person who knows the job. Be prepared to sweep floors for nothing to get this opportunity.

Gary Newhouse, a manager for the Columbus, Ohio, office of Agri-Associates, Inc., the largest agribusiness employment agency in the United States, reinforces this advice. "Employers are looking for people with experience," he says. "In today's economy, they can't afford any other kind. Recent college grads with ag degrees have limited opportunities. The mere fact that they have degrees doesn't guarantee success. Proven experience does." Take this advice seriously. Start amassing experience as early as you can.

You have had in this chapter, in capsule form, a lesson in de-

cision making slanted especially to the outdoor field. Infinite possibilities for in-depth research remain. You have dozens of books,
people, and jobs to cover. If you concentrate on working with this
information, you will be on your way to developing the competitive
job strategies that are necessary in today's job market.

Formalizing your work will help you even more. Organize a
notebook and label it "My Career Workbook" or something similar.
Divide it into sections. In a "Me" section, include the worksheets
for the getting-to-know-yourself exercises and your autobiography,
if you write one. If you look into the other resources recommended,
include these materials also. In "Education," "Career Field," and
"Work Experience" sections, include all the pertinent data. You will
also want to add a "Job Search" section for the work to come—
preparation of resumes and cover letters, preparation for and results
of interviews, job-decision guidelines, and similar elements. The
more encyclopedic your workbook, the better it will serve you.

Unless you plan your career, it will probably not develop as you
want it to. You cannot believe in luck. You have to take responsibility
for your future. Keeping the kind of written record outlined above
is a good spur. Such a record indicates progress and provides direction. Another good technique is daydreaming. In spite of admoni-
tions against wool-gathering from some parents and educators, daydreaming is considered a problem-solving aid by most psychologists.

Dr. Philip L. Taylor, a Pennsylvania psychologist who did his
doctoral dissertation in daydreaming at New York University, believes that daydreaming refreshes, stimulates, renews, and is "anal-
ogous to relaxation and meditation." He further believes that daydreaming relieves certain kinds of tension. You don't have to perform
an act to receive satisfaction or enjoyment from it. Many people
report that just thinking about something brings the same rewards
as doing it.

His advice to people of any age is to daydream. Your fantasies
may encourage you to set higher goals for yourself by providing
concrete, vivid images of your future, and the process itself may
defuse the highly charged atmosphere in which you exist while you
are in the process of deciding on a career.

Dr. Taylor adds a caution to his advice. While daydreams can
be beneficial, they can also be harmful. If people find themselves so
obsessed with any particular thought that they cannot carry on their

regular activities—their work or care of their bodily needs—they probably need to seek professional help. When daydreaming reaches this obsessional level, it is self-destructive. Keep this admonition in mind. Do not let your daydreaming turn your life into a nightmare.

One of the problems for young people trying to make career decisions is that they may be forced to do so before they are ready. Dr. Howard Figler, Director of Counseling and Placement at Dickinson College (he's also the author of one of the books recommended earlier in this chapter), points out that "decisions are not immutable." He deplores the "railroad train" mentality in which young people "hop on the train and keep going forever, unable to realize when a stop-over or even a new travel plan is needed. No conductor is barring your exit. You are free to make side trips any time in life. Don't be afraid that you're going to get off at the wrong station. There's always another train."

One final piece of advice: don't believe everything you hear, see, and read. Don't let enthusiasm substitute for reasoned thinking. Be skeptical. Ask questions, and keep on asking until you get answers. Keep various facets of your information in perspective; no one part is more important than another. There is no such thing as a perfect career choice. At the end of a difficult day, anyone can find a flaw in a job. The trick is to assess ahead of time the advantages and disadvantages and to be ready to deal with them. Career choice is usually a compromise, but do not compromise without knowing you are doing so. Prepare for every contingency. Then you will not be guilty of thinking about what might have been.

If you have built castles in the air, your work need not be lost; this is where they should be. Now put foundations under them.

Henry David Thoreau

3

Ways and Means:
Preparing Yourself for the Job You Want

You know about yourself—your capabilities, accomplishments, and interests. You have decided on a career field. You know about various employers. You know about the problems. Now you are ready to prepare yourself to take a place in this working world you have been dreaming about.

Ideally, you are reading this book when you are still in high school. Remember the admonition in chapter two: start early. But probably you are in college or even older, a career-changer bent on modifying your work life. Whatever your age, some general facts will help to clarify your thinking and prepare you for the information to come.

This book has little to offer the high school drop-out. In the outdoor fields as in others, the jobs available for untrained youths are as common laborers, helpers, messengers, and the like. A pump attendant in a gasoline station is an outdoor worker, but not the person for whom this book was written unless he or she is ready to do a great deal of work to move up the career ladder. This book is for the person who is interested in acquiring general and/or specialized education in order to work in a variety of different fields, most of which require some kind of technical training. Without this additional education, young people in today's economy stand the chance of being relegated to tedious, poorly paid jobs.

In the mid-1970s, when the job market for college graduates plummeted, arguments against a college education began to surface. Almost anyone can cite one or more instances of a college graduate with no job or a job that fails to utilize his or her training. It is still true, however, that the more years of education a person has, the better are the chances for employment. The odds increase even further when competitive job strategies are used. Data from the United States Department of Labor consistently prove this year after year. In the latest available figures, national unemployment was 9.4 percent, but among four-year college graduates it was only 2.5 percent. Similar statistics show that in many fields, especially technical ones, students with even a two-year associate degree earn double the salary of high school graduates.

Broad education is important for reasons other than economic ones. Educated people find more enjoyment and wider opportunities in life because they are better equipped to appreciate and take advantage of cultural and aesthetic experiences. They also have a better understanding of social issues related to their jobs. This is especially true in the outdoor field, where concern for conservation and environmental control is implicit in the job.

Educated people understand the functions of their jobs better. They are more than mere button-pushers and take pride in their work. This is especially true of the scientific and technological revolution of post–World War II. This has created higher standards of job knowledge and performance and has resulted in additional career opportunities and new training methods and centers.

Another benefit of education will not be reaped for many years by the primary readers of this book, but it is wise to give some thought to retirement even now. You will want to know what retirement benefits are offered by the place where you work, and you should also think about what you will do after retirement. The possibilities are numerous enough for a whole second book, and Arthur Fiedler, the conductor of the famous Boston Pops Orchestra for fifty years, had a favorite adage that he quoted when asked why he kept so busy into his mid-eighties (he conducted his last concert eight weeks before he died): "He who rests, rots."

You may not agree fully with this outlook, but it is a documented fact that individuals who have led busy lives decline rapidly in physical, mental, and emotional well-being if they just sit about watching the world go by. Retirees have varying capacities for physical activity, but individuals with a good basic education are more likely either to develop intellectual interests and activities that continue into retirement years or to find new ones once retired.

Your own educational decisions should be based on self-knowledge and the requirements of the field you have chosen. If you have decided to enter a field where job possibilities are limited, college is even more important. In the current job market, the person with the best credentials usually gets the job. Over the years, the large number of college graduates on the job market has led to upgrading of job requirements. Even so, the United States Department of Labor predicted 140,000 college graduates in 1980 would not be able to find work in the field for which they were trained. By 1985, this figure could grow to 700,000.

Dr. James Slick, Assistant Director in charge of Career Information Systems, Career Development and Placement Center, The Pennsylvania State University, warns against taking job predictions—either negative or positive—at face value. He says generalized predictions are valueless, that every set of statistics "should be examined in light of the assumptions they are built on. Read the newspaper. Keep you ear tuned to the radio. Things can change overnight."

Philip Bucher, Assistant Director for Placement, also at the Career Development and Placement Center of The Pennsylvania State University, has some advice to protect you against unemployment. "Don't be too specialized," he says. "Students tend to prepare themselves for a single job title. This over-specialization can mean disaster if the bottom drops out of the job market. Develop several related skills and you'll stand a better chance." He points out that computer science, business, engineering, and communications are all areas that tie in well with outdoor fields.

Dr. Slick adds to Bucher's advice: "Developing transferable skills is as important as broad skills." He cites the recent practice of many agribusiness firms, which are now hiring engineers as management trainees. The reason: they view engineers as "problem-solvers" who can function in any field. All of the cognitive skills are transferable skills, with technical writing and public speaking right at the top of the list.

A conversation with the personnel officer of a large electronics firm confirms this. "If one job candidate has an edge with writing and speaking skills, that is the one we hire," he says.

When you begin to search for a college and to plan a course of study for yourself, you need to keep this advice in mind. Try to tailor your education to fit your own needs. Most colleges have courses of study in various fields all planned out, with a few electives in and out of the major field of study. These are intended, first, to be sure that every student covers the basic material in the field and, second, to provide direction for students who are unsure of themselves and their choices. Many colleges will be quite willing to rework their planned course of study to fit the needs and interests of individual students as long as there are sound reasons for the changes. Interdisciplinary study has become a common practice, and it is a flat requirement for graduation in some of our leading colleges and universities. Students with short sight sometimes grumble over this, but the value of this requirement is soon apparent to the alert. You may wish to seek out a college with this philosophy.

One question you may have to face is whether to choose a two-year or a four-year institution. In these days of rising costs, your budget may force you into a two-year school, either a community college or a technical school. If this happens, settle for the best training you can get in this time. Circumstances may change, and you may be able to continue for two more years, either right away or at a later time. You may, for instance, be able to go to work at the end of two years and earn enough money to return to school. Or you can take weekend classes. Some large companies help employees who want to get more education. If you really want the education, you can probably work out a way to get it.

Colleges always have some financial help available, even in these days of soaring tuition and living costs. Catalogues and admissions offices have this information. High school guidance counselors can also be helpful. They know local organizations that offer scholarships and can discuss state and federal education grants.

Graduate work is a special problem. "If you have any idea at all that you want to go to graduate school, keep your grades up," Philip Bucher says. "I see dozens of students every year who have wiped out that option because they didn't work hard enough in their undergraduate courses." He thinks a 3.0 grade point average is the lowest possible one acceptable at good schools because "the openings are few and competition is terrific. Schools won't take students who can't handle graduate work."

Just because you graduate or get a job, do not stop learning. Training never ends. You should be developing new skills all your life. "I think people ought to take at least three workshops in new areas every year," says Ann Moffitt, a YWCA executive director. She takes her own advice and, as a result, has worked in every facet of YWCA work from conducting a riding tour through the English moors to raising funds for a $3-million building.

Training is not always easy to get. You can sign up for classes or ask people to show you how to do things, but the responsibility for assimilating the knowledge is yours. You need to make a conscious effort early to set up mechanisms to keep you up to date in your field. Start by reading trade journals and newsletters. Join professional organizations, both local and farther afield. Go to conferences where you can meet other people in your field and discuss common problems and interests.

Planning your education is a dynamic process. You can *block* it in, but you should not *lock* it in. You can follow the traditional plan of four secluded campus years, but you can also train yourself for an outstanding outdoor career by improvising on the conventional *modus operandi*.

The "catch 22" of the job world is that every employer wants job applicants to have experience, and most refuse to hire inexperienced people. Therefore getting that first job—and *experience*—in your field can be difficult. Ingenuity is called for. One of the ways you can begin to solve this problem is by working while you are training for the job. The kind of work you will want to do will vary with your field.

The place to start is your school. There may be opportunities to work as an assistant to a professor or to get a fellowship with a summer research project. Professors, too, may know about part-time openings. Usually, they tell their top students about these possibilities.

Internships or practicums in all fields are becoming more common as employers are increasing their demands for experienced applicants. Even if an internship is unpaid, it may be valuable, especially if it is under the direction of a competent person. Such positions are usually arranged within the student's college department and may carry credit, the amount varying with the length and difficulty of the assignment.

Beyond the school walls, the problem becomes more difficult. You have to make your own luck here. This is where your contacts become invaluable. If you have a mentor, this may be the doorway to a job; so may friends or family. Take help from anyone who offers it. It is best, of course, to work in the career field you have chosen, but any work is better than none. To be successful in your field, you need to develop a work ethic and become accustomed to dealing with people in work situations. Any job can provide those opportunities. Working as a common laborer on a construction job or farm, as a camp counselor, as a play park aide, as an attendant in an amusement park, or a busperson in a resort restaurant are all examples of jobs that will give you your initial work experience.

If you start looking early you might be able to work with the National Park Service, the United States Forest Service, or even the Youth Conservation Service. The openings are limited, but the experience is invaluable. All applicants need to be in prime physical condition because the work is vigorous and the days long. You apply as early as permissible because the competition is fierce. Science and mathematics courses sometimes help get the jobs. So do top grades.

The Youth Conservation Service is modeled after the 1930's Civilian Conservation Corps. It provides paid outdoor jobs and a primitive lifestyle for sixteen- to twenty-five-year-olds. Food and living allowances are included in the contract.

The United States Forest Service employs a limited number of students for rugged jobs as forestry aides, survey helpers, laborers, general maintenance workers, recreation area aides, tree planters, and smoke jumpers. The jobs are available through individual national Forest Service headquarters, of which there are 154 offices throughout the country. Each has its own hiring procedures, but applications for jobs must be made between January 1 and February 15 in the year the summer employment is desired. Salaries vary depending on job title and grade and are low. Sometimes meals are available at minimal cost. Primitive housing is provided, but in most areas workers supply their own sleeping bags and bedding.

According to a Forest Service spokesperson, priority is given to applicants with experience who live in or near the national forests or to college students majoring in forestry and related fields. Sometimes students in accounting, business administration, civil or mechanical engineering, hydrology, landscape architecture, and range management are considered.

Even more limited jobs as engineering aides, surveying aides, clerks, and clerk typists are available with the Forest Service. These are civil service positions and applicants must successfully pass the United States Civil Service Summer Employment Examination given by the United States Office of Personnel Management. Examination schedules are announced in October of each year. Applications to take the test should be made to regional Office of Personnel Management offices in November and December. Testing is done in December, February, and March. The hiring procedures follow standard civil service practice as described in chapter six.

Summer employees in the National Park Service are back-ups for professional staff, and many of them require overtime, including Saturday, Sunday, and evening work. The jobs most students want are as seasonal park rangers, ranger-historians, ranger-naturalists, and ranger-archaeologists. Most of these plums go to teachers or graduate students because of the level of experience and course work required. In addition to excellent health, applicants must take an eye test, have a valid driver's license, and be at least 18 years old. They also must wear National Park Service uniforms.

The National Park Service also hires maintenance workers, firefighters, cooks, carpenters, plumbers, lifeguards, and office workers. Maintenance workers open trails and fire lines, cut timber, and do general repair work. Firefighters maintain equipment, as well as actually locating, identifying, and putting out fires. All of these jobs require two or three seasons of experience, although high school graduation can equal as much as two seasons of experience if the student has enough science and mathematics courses.

See chapter six for instructions for applying for civil service jobs, also the appendix for addresses of various federal agencies.

Another limited but exciting summer job opportunity is that of hut attendant for the nine-hut complex maintained and operated by the Appalachian Mountain Club in the Presidential Range in the White Mountains of New Hampshire. The huts are available to more than 100,000 hikers who converge on the area every summer. They are a convenient day's hike apart and provide sleeping accommodations and meals. The hut attendants cook, clean, and backpack all supplies in to the huts. They also help with trail maintenance.

These jobs may give you an idea of where to look for other summer jobs. Try municipal, state, and local parks, wildlife refuges, playgrounds, resorts, libraries, museums, conservation clubs, camps of all kinds, and organizations like the YMCA, the YWCA, or Jewish Community Centers. Tour camping is a relatively new area in which a few resourceful outdoor careerites like Lori and Andrew Davidson are working. While studying for physical education degrees at the University of Pennsylvania, they acted as tour guides for groups traveling to western national parks and to Mexico. If you live in a resort area and are an experienced camper familiar with local facilities, you might be able to work as a guide or as an assistant to an established local guide. And don't forget about local industry. If you are a forestry student, a summer with a local sawmill might be arranged. If you are an engineering major, the opportunities are endless. Consult the city directory or telephone book yellow pages.

If you cannot find a satisfactory paid job and can afford it, consider a volunteer job. Volunteers are needed by all of the above and by organizations such as the National Audubon Society, the Sierra Club, the National Wildlife Federation, the National Recreation and Park Association, the Izaak Walton League, and the Nature Conservancy. The National Park Service has a Volunteers in Parks Service Program which operates during the summer months. They are interested in volunteers of all ages. For information about qualifications and applications, write to the Park Service. (See appendix for address.)

Another similar program is offered by the Student Conservation

Association. The volunteers can get on-the-job training in exchange for food, travel, and lodging.

Working with Boy Scouts, Girl Scouts, 4-H, Future Farmers of America, and similar groups will help develop leadership ability. The County Extension offices maintained by the United States Department of Agriculture are other places to seek out contacts and ideas.

Job application procedures are the same for part-time jobs as for full time ones. Study the chapters on resumes and cover letters and interviewing with care. Applying for a part-time job is the best practice for getting a full time one.

Part-time jobs, year-around or summer, are limited only by your ingenuity in finding—or creating—them. You have to make your own opportunities.

Organizing your job search is a task that should begin long before the day you want to start earning a salary. The United States Department of Labor estimates that it takes about nine months to get the first job. College placement directors say to give it a year. In these days of tight job markets, it might take even longer. Your search will not be successful unless you set time for it. It is as time-consuming as a college course. Indeed, some schools do offer such a course and if one is available, you might consider taking it. It will clarify all the problems discussed in this book; it will give you support from the instructor and other students; and it will force you to learn to deal with the techniques of searching for a job.

Your first job may not be a dream job. Gary Newhouse, manager of the Columbus, Ohio, office of Agri-Associates, Inc., the country's largest agribusiness employment agency, believes most people work at two jobs prior to settling into the one they want and like. Returning to United States Department of Labor statistics again, most people have eight to ten jobs in a lifetime. If the average working span is forty-five years (twenty to sixty-five years of age), that means you will spend an average of five years on each job. Another set of figures from a private research project says that the average time before a person reaches the top in his/her career is 26 years and that this progress involves at least eleven jobs and seven geographic moves. The point is not which set of statistics is right (anyone can juggle statistics to mean anything), but that job mobility is common in this country. You are going to have more than one job and, realistically, your first job may last only a year or two. You need to find that first job, however. Every worker, every manager, every personnel expert interviewed believes that the first job is the pivotal one of a career and that it is easier to get another job when you already have one. The first job, they say, is the one in which your basic abilities and your work ethic are tested; the better your supervisor, the better your performance. It follows that the security gained in discovering how to hold a job is a plus when looking for another one. Getting that first job is your problem.

A blitz is the best method; that is, set out to cover every possibility so as to give yourself some options. Presumably, by the time you reach the job-search stage, you have narrowed your job choices within your career field. You know your preferences. You have wrestled with your inner self and have established operative values. You have acknowledged your interests. You have worked hard to develop your skills, taking every opportunity to develop contacts.

As pointed out in chapter two, those contacts are among your most important job-search resources. Start with these contacts. Put out the word that you are looking for a job. When you put out these first feelers, you should have your basic resume ready. In chapter four you will find assistance in preparing this and also in adapting it to various job possibilities and in writing the cover letter which must accompany it. Be sure to heed the advice about preparing a separate cover letter for everyone to whom you send your resume. Obviously, your pitch is slightly different when you are asking someone to suggest a job possibility rather than give you a job. Open with the usual personal pleasantries and then get down to the real purpose of your letter. Explain exactly the kind of job you want, reinforcing your ability to handle such a job by referring to your resume. Be sure to mention any limitations on your job search, such as your preferred geographical area. Ask for job leads and recommendations. Do not be coy or even subtle. Only the straightforward approach will make it possible for your contacts—leaders in your career field, mentors, sympathetic professors, friends, and family—to help you.

You cannot afford to stop with this initial step. You need to consider other sources. There is no end to these sources. They are limited only by your ingenuity in developing them, but the traditional ones include: your college placement office; advertisements in newspapers and in trade journals for your field; the newsletters of professional organizations (an item on someone else's promotion or moving is an indirect report of a job opening); governmental agencies; and employment agencies. Running your own "job wanted ad" in trade journals and in newspapers in the geographic area where you want to work sometimes produces results; so does sending your resume with a well-written cover letter to hand-picked organizations for which you would like to work. You can develop such a list from the professional organization in your field, from the telephone book yellow pages, or even from newspaper and magazine advertising. One young man got a job with a cruise ship as a combination recreation director-lecturer by writing to all of the companies advertising in *The New York Times* travel section. He planned activities for adults and children and gave daily talks about marine life and sea adventuring. He was a fledgling oceanographer and used the money earned from two years in this job to return to school and get his master's degree. The master's led to a university fellowship to work on his doctorate.

Statistically, some of these methods are more productive than others; they are listed in the order in which success is most likely. You have to remember, though, that statistics are just that: statistics. You may be one of the minority who get a job through one of the least effective routes. The better you are prepared, the better your chances will be.

In some cases, your chance for success with any one of these methods depends upon your field. For example, large corporations in the agribusiness area looking for engineers, management trainees, and salespeople tend to use campus recruiting to locate entry-level employees. On the other hand, there are almost no available job openings for beginners in this field through employment agencies. Gary Newhouse of Agri-Associates, Inc., quoted earlier in this chapter, says this is "because employers can't afford to pay a fee to hire inexperienced workers. They want a 'sure thing' for their money."

Most first-timers have a mistaken idea of the services of an employment agency. It is not in business to critique your resume or to get you a job. Rather, it is in business to find employees for clients, generally companies trying to fill specific vacancies.

Carolyn Evans, a Philadelphia career counselor, warns that agencies, even big ones, have only a handful of jobs at any one time. "Don't be angry if the agency doesn't have a job for you. It and the world do not owe you a living. Anyone who said the world was fair was kidding."

If you do go to an agency, understand the contract you sign. Make sure you are liable for a fee only if they find you a job. Some contracts are worded in such a way that you must pay the fee even if you uncover the job yourself. Most agencies do not do business this way, but caution is called for when signing a contract of any kind.

Some agencies also play games that can interfere with your job search. They tie up your time by keeping you waiting an inordinate amount of time. They also use "bait and switch" techniques: when you call up, they tell you that your qualifications are perfect for a job which is still open; when you get there, it has been filled, but the agency will be happy to hunt further for you if you'll just fill out and sign this form. . . .

Again, most agencies are honest, but you do not have time to deal with such tactics as these. Refuse to do business with an agency that employs such practices.

You should certainly explore possibilities with your college placement director. Your chances will be best if you start early and if you see as many campus recruiters as possible. Top grades and skills are important here, too; you are competing directly with your peers. Even if you do not get the job, the interviewing experience can be valuable to you. It will get you over the first nervous hurdle of facing the barrage of challenging questions you can expect at interviews. This is a problem taken up in chapter five.

Openings in government—municipal, state, and local—continue to occur in spite of spending reductions. Competition is keener. Almost all of these jobs will be civil service positions; this subject is covered in chapter six and in the Appendix. They will require examinations, sometimes more than one. Again, the admonition is to apply early.

If you want to teach in the outdoor field, your college placement office is the place to start, although you can search out openings yourself. Certification is required for public school positions, and recruiting procedures may vary from state to state. Requirements for private school and college posts vary from institution to institution.

To apply for most teaching positions, you will need—in addition to your resume—a formal credentials form, which will be discussed shortly.

Because of Equal Employment Opportunity Commission and Affirmative Action regulations, most teaching jobs are advertised widely. The best time to look for openings is between March and August. Keep in mind that teaching on any level is one of the most crowded job fields today. Unless you have top credentials, impeccable references, and good contacts, you stand little chance of breaking into teaching.

In your job search, in addition to your resume and cover letter, you may need three other tools—a credentials form (including your transcript), a list of references, and a portfolio of your work. The credentials form is a standard one, available in every college placement office, and most usually utilized by education majors. You should fill out the form and leave it with the placement office. It will be sent out when requested by prospective employers. Authorized transcripts of grades are a part of the credentials information and also can be sent at a small cost to prospective employers with permission of students.

References present a special problem. You never know when they will be needed, but it is wise to have them ready. Usually three names are enough, and ideally they should be long-time personal friends or mentors with high standing in the community. They should not be former employers. Your prospective employer will get in touch with them without your stipulating them as references.

Using a professor as a reference is chancy unless he or she is a particular mentor. A student at a large New England university tells a story about how she and her friends compared notes during three concentrated months of job hunting. A professor, whom they all listed as a reference, sent out the same stock letter for all of them. "And it didn't even say anything specific or good," she says. This practice is all too common; professors admit it freely, claiming that the reason is the Buckley Amendment to the Educational Rights and Privacy Act. This amendment gives students access to their school files. "I can't say anything critical without risking legal action," one professor claims. "So I don't say anything at all. Besides, employers recognize the situation and don't believe anything I write anyway." If the professor is a special mentor, the situation is entirely different.

He or she will usually be willing not only to write a candid, detailed letter about your qualifications, but also to answer lengthy telephone queries as well.

You should always ask permission to use people as references and you should let them know to whom you have sent their names. Whether you get a job or not, you should write thank-you notes for the privilege.

The easiest way to utilize references is to make a separate list of names, addresses, and telephone numbers. Have it ready to present whenever requested. Be sure your own name, address, and telephone number are on the sheet.

"To-Whom-It-May-Concern" letters are of little value. Most prospective employers ignore them. They rely instead on telephone calls to former employers and like to talk to direct supervisors. You should be aware that this happens. Nothing you can do will prevent it, so it is important that your job performance be good. This is one of the many reasons internships, part-time jobs, and volunteer jobs are important. If you do good work in these situations, the people involved with you can say so.

In some fields, you may want to prepare a portfolio of your work. This is especially true if writing, photography, other graphic forms, public speaking, or performance of any kind is a part of your background. You can include samples of reports, memoranda, press releases, advertisements, and printed materials about yourself. If you are an artist, your training will have given you the necessary rudiments for making up such a specialized portfolio. For other fields, a simple folder or notebook in which to display the materials is all that is necessary. Only a small number of perfect examples should be included. No employer will hire you on the basis of your portfolio alone, but if your work is impressive it will give you a better chance to win out over your competitors. Beware of including material that is not yours. Invariably, this tactic will trip you up. If you get the job, you will be expected to perform as well as your portfolio indicates that you can.

Employers want results from employees and they tend to leave as little as possible to chance. Aside from aggressive interview techniques, which are discussed in chapter five, they use tests and trials of all kinds. At one time psychological testing was common. It still is used, but not as much as previously, mainly because of government antidiscrimination guidelines. If tests are used, they must be validated, an expensive procedure. Employers have discovered also that psychological test results are not always conclusive. It is difficult to assess leadership, intelligence, and determination by testing. It is somewhat easier to identify and measure job interests. One common test involves the use of specialized equipment or testing of ability of specialized skills. Most employers will want a demonstration of performance ability in these areas. Anything from a typing test to a trial week or month on the job can be expected.

People react to testing in different ways, but most find it a tension-causing procedure. The trick is to make the tension work for you. It can produce an extra flow of adrenalin that will increase your alertness and help you produce, or it can immobilize you and render you impotent. Try to relax; put your trust in your ability and your solid preparation.

On written tests, the methods you learned in high school and college will help. Look over the complete test (sometimes this is not permitted) and evaluate the problems you face. Read quickly, but analytically. Budget your time, allowing more for difficult sections. Try to answer every question, but skip over questions about which you are not sure after careful reading. Go back to these when you finish everything else. In psychological tests, beware of two problems. On some tests, wrong answers count against you; on others, the same question is posed over and over in different ways, trying to mask the information being sought. The best practice with all tests is to answer honestly and positively. If you are being tested by a conservative organization, you should remember that they are looking for answers that reveal cooperative, outgoing attitudes as opposed to withdrawn, contemplative ones. Except in civil service examinations, you are not fighting a whole war for the coveted job with a test. The test is only a small battle.

If you have particular difficulty with tests, or if you are trying for a job that requires a civil service examination, try practicing. You can get samples in some college placement or counseling centers, and every bookstore has a rack of books full of sample tests of all kinds. Contrary to traditional belief, recent studies show that test preparation *does* improve scores. You will find a list of a few of the most helpful materials in the appendix.

Sometimes facing an actual job situation trial may be easier than taking a written test. You can do nothing to prepare for it that you have not already done in your several years of training in your particular career field. As with written tests, keep cool.

A final word about taking tests: get enough sleep before you take them, and arrange your schedule carefully so that you arrive on time. Even a genius will not perform well under the twin disabilities of fatigue and arriving late.

Understanding the money you can earn is part of your job search equipment. You need to know how much you are worth. To determine a reasonable salary, you need to know what people working in similar jobs are earning. This figure will vary from area to area, depending on the job market. You should ask for the range for particular jobs. Workers can tell you. So can college instructors (sometimes), counselors in your college placement office, a state employment office, or a federal job center. You can study classified advertising in newspapers and trade association publications. Another good reference source is the College Placement Council's annual salary survey which lists the top and bottom salaries in each field. It is available in college placement offices and some libraries. You can also check in the later chapters of this book in specific career fields for salary figures, keeping in mind that they may change with time and with economic conditions.

These "average" or going-rate salary figures can be influenced by a number of factors, including your experience and knowledge. If you are offered a much higher salary than average, look at all the facts closely. There may be no fringe benefits, or the cost of living in the area may be particularly high. Either of these is not necessarily a bad situation, but you should know that they play a part. Take the same careful look at a very low salary. What are the compensations for being underpaid? A grand title? A glamour job? Exceptional fringe benefits?

Fringe benefits in most companies include health insurance, life insurance, retirement benefits, sick leave, and vacations. They may also include commissions, stock purchase plans, expense accounts, tuition-paid training programs or continuing education, recreation and travel opportunities, meals (either free or low cost), low cost housing, clothing, moving expenses, free automobile, discounts on activities or merchandise, and similar services. Health insurance is variable, ranging from complete coverage of medical, psychological, eye, and dental expenses to nothing but simple hospitalization. Some employers spend an amount equal to nearly half of base pay in fringe benefits. Are they important to you? Depending on your personal situation and your goals, they may not be. Certainly, it's never wise to make a job decision based on fringe benefits.

As a beginner in the job market, you have very little bargaining power. However, college graduates and veterans may command slightly higher salaries. A general rule of thumb for first salary negotiations is to decide what you must have to cover your living expenses. Ask for at least 10 percent more than this, and refuse to settle for less. At least this technique will keep you solvent. Salary should not be the most important factor in selecting your first job. You may have to start lower than you want to, to get the job you want.

You need all these pertinent financial facts before you go for an interview, but as advised in the discussion on interviewing in chapter five, do not bring up salary. Try to get prospective employers to take the lead. If you are forced to talk about money, follow the above formula in arriving at a figure.

When you do get around to discussing money, ask about salary reviews. Standard practice is to do them annually on the hiring anniversary, but for new employees, some companies do them every three or six months. You should get a raise within a year. If you do not, you need to find out why. The reason may be that business is bad. It could also be that your boss has either forgotten about a raise or thinks you are satisfied. Usually if you have lasted a year in a job, it is not that you are not doing good work. Ask!

The best way to ask is to put your request in writing to your immediate supervisor, sending a copy to the head of the company, or of your division if it is a very large firm. Stress your performance, pointing out why you feel you deserve a raise. Do not deliver an ultimatum unless you are ready to be out of a job. Be sure of your job footing before you push.

When any kind of financial negotiations are settled, ask for clarification in writing. Most employers will send you such a letter; it constitutes a job contract. It should include starting salary, fringe benefits, starting date of employment, and date of first payroll. Letters about raises or fringe benefits should state the facts clearly.

All your job search activities should be recorded in the job strategies workbook you started in chapter two. Any expenses incurred should also be noted. The purpose is twofold. By examining and evaluating your activities, you can find flaws in what you are doing should your efforts be unproductive. If you seek help from anyone, you will be able to document everything you have tried. Furthermore, job search expenses are deductible. Consult an accountant or a tax preparation guide. You will find several of the latter listed in the appendix.

What can you do if your job search is unsuccessful? Re-evaluation of your capabilities for and preparation in the career field, perhaps with professional help, is called for. If you remain sure that you *can* and *want* to remain in the field, you can take any kind of job just to get that proverbial foot in the door. In professional jargon, this is called underemployment, that is, working at a level below which you are qualified. "Underemployment is one of the best ways to break down job barriers," says Carolyn Evans, the Philadelphia career counselor we met earlier. She believes flexibility, almost more than any other quality, is necessary in today's job market. She does not think this is necessarily bad, especially for a young person, because with flexibility comes knowledge of many different outlooks, procedures, and expectations.

If you have money and ability, you might open a business of your own, but study the entrepreneurial section in chapter six before you make this decision.

You can also volunteer to work for some company. This is the same technique as suggested for part-time jobs. This move will provide additional experience. You may not be able to afford this maneuver, but if you can, it is a good one. If you can prove you are a good worker, you will eventually get a job.

Other options to consider are taking a job in a closely related field, going to graduate school to increase your qualifications, enrolling in an apprenticeship program for the same reason, and enlisting in military service. The latter solution may not appeal to everyone, but the various branches of the military offer splendid opportunities for training for outdoor work. Veterans also have an edge in some jobs, especially civil service positions. As pointed out in several sections of this book, veterans get extra points when applying for civil service jobs; this can be a great help in tight competition for a coveted post. Chapter six gives some basic information about the military.

In some parts of the country, a new wrinkle in job hunting has developed—job clubs. An outstanding example is one in Carbondale, Illinois, organized by a psychologist, Dr. Nathan Azrin, under the auspices of the Illinois Department of Mental Health. Dr. Azrin's club is open to any unemployed person and has a 90 percent success rate in helping members find jobs. A new group of three to twelve members is organized every month. The members work on preparing resumes, making phone calls, lining up contacts, sending out resumes and cover letters, and going to interviews. At every step of the way, they keep individual records and report to the group on their progress. The value of the club is the personal support it provides during this stressful time. If you run into real job hunting trouble, you might try to locate a job club in your area.

Job hunting is hard work. Most people do not realize it. "Hey, did you hear that my roommate got five job offers?" one Elizabethtown College senior asked another while they were going through the cafeteria line. "Yeah, I did," the other answered, "but do you know what he did? He's been working for weeks with resumes and interviews and all that stuff." This is the bottom line, as the accountants say. "Working for weeks" is what it takes and is the only way to achieve success. The old aphorism stands: if at first you don't succeed, try, try again.

"When I use a word," Humpty-Dumpty said, "it means just what I choose it to mean—neither more nor less."

Lewis Carroll

4

In a Nutshell:
Writing Resumes and Letters

"Put it in writing." How often job seekers are given this direction. Every telephone call leads directly to the typewriter. Prospective employers want to see resumes and receive letters about your reasons for wanting to work for them. "I want to be a meterologist, not a male secretary," one job applicant moans. "Why do I have to do all this writing?"

Probably no single skill is more important to your future than writing. In today's competitive job market—yes, even in the outdoor field—it's your ability to express yourself clearly and concisely that will open career doors for you. We're not talking about writing the great American novel or lyrical poetry. We're talking about writing plain English, creating the letters and resumes that will be unique enough to allow prospective employers to pick you out of the masses.

As we have pointed out over and over, as a job seeker, especially an entry level job seeker scouting for outdoor posts, you are in for

a difficult search. Your position may seem about as hopeless as that
of the leprechaun looking for a pot of gold at the end of the rainbow
or a marine explorer hunting the remains of Atlantis. Writing good
letters and resumes can increase these impossible odds against success.

You can all cite examples of jobs gained without going through
this process, but the truth is that the letter and resume remain the
primary tools for introducing yourself to organizations for which you
want to work. In a survey taken by Harold Janes of the University
of Alabama among *Fortune* 500 corporations, 98 percent of the organizations wanted a cover letter and resume from job applicants!
One survey respondent said his company received over 200 job applications a day and that the problem was that too many of *the
resumes and letters used* "canned" formats. Another corporation
representative cited the lack of knowledge by job applicants about
his organization. The cover letters and resumes were judged "run of
the mill," leaving the impression that the applicant "distributed
these indiscriminately like baiting a hook and hoping that some kind
of fish will bite."

These comments should give you a clue to the problem you face.
You have to prepare a resume and write a letter, both of which must
convince prospective employers not only that you have qualifications to do the work you want to do, but also that you have qualities
that set you apart from others looking for the same job. Still another
requirement is that you know something about the organization to
which you are applying. This latter point is discussed generally in
chapter five. There, in talking about preparing for interviews, some
concrete suggestions are given for researching information about specific organizations. The challenge is relating all this to your personality and "putting yourself down on paper."

Your cover letter and resume, properly prepared, will be a picture of you as surely as if you painted a self-portrait. In one job
hunting manual, there's a graphic that particularly illustrates this
point. The designer created an outline of a human head, composed
of the typed material of the resume emerging from an envelope.
Somehow, this is what you must do. When the prospective employer
reads your letter and resume, you must come alive to him or her.
How do you do it? By writing personally and passionately about

yourself. This is the only way you are going to get the interview that will lead to the job you want.

If you have been preparing yourself systematically throughout your college years for the working world, you have surely taken some writing courses. If you have, much of what is said here will be clarification and review. If you haven't, you will see that you are going to be severely handicapped in your job search because you can't be given a complete writing course in a chapter. What can be done is to suggest some ways to approach the problem and some books that will help correct any deficiencies.

Writing resumes and letters is a very personal matter, but the underlying principles are the same as for any other kind of practical writing. There are ten things you can do that will improve your writing at once.

1. Write conversationally. This is assuming you use grammatical English. This means that in your writing, you express yourself in the same informal, relaxed way as you do in speech.

2. Write simply. Writing well does not mean using the longest words in the dictionary or the most pompous constructions. It means saying what you want to say without filling up your sentences with empty words. Some editors call this "fat." William Zinsser, magazine journalist and Harvard writing instructor labels it "clutter" and calls it "the disease of American writing."

3. Write clearly. Say what you mean, avoiding the misuse of words. Watch your grammar, your punctuation, your spelling, and all the "mechanics" of writing. An invaluable tool for clarity is parallelism, that is, expressing similar thoughts in similar form, matching words with words, phrases with phrases, and clauses with clauses. The similar form helps the reader decipher the content more easily. This technique is particularly useful in preparing resumes, or in any writing task where you have many diverse elements. Another friend of clarity is keeping modifiers close to the words they modify. Mastery of these two techniques will clear up vague writing quickly.

4. Write concisely. Avoid involved, confusing sentences and rambling paragraphs. Don't repeat words and ideas needlessly. Take

a well-edited newspaper as your model. Journalists have to learn to communicate with people who have many different levels of reading skills. Good journalists are masters of conciseness. *The Washington Post, The New York Times,* or *The Wall Street Journal* are all good publications to study to see this principle in action.

5. Write specifically. Avoid vague generalizations, using instead concrete terms. For example, don't talk about your outdoor career, or even your career in forestry. Narrow it down to forest management or park ranger. Say what you mean so that you can't possibly be misunderstood.

6. Write logically. Begin with ideas to which your reader can relate. This is especially important when communicating with people you don't know, as in writing a resume or a cover letter.

7. Write with strong words—descriptive nouns and action verbs. Avoid the use of adjectives and adverbs unless they provide additional information.

8. Write with verbs in the active voice. Say "I took riding lessons," not "Riding lessons were taken by me."

9. Write methodically, avoiding shifts of subject, number, tense, voice, or point of view. This is the place where inexperienced writers get into the most trouble. If you concentrate on the first eight rules, this one may not be a problem.

10. Write; then rewrite. Develop self-editing techniques. These will be reviewed shortly when the final steps in preparation of your letter and resume are discussed.

This list is meant as a reminder of principles you've learned in your writing courses. If it strikes you as "new knowledge," you need to spend time with one of the handbooks we suggest in the appendix, especially with *The Elements of Style* by William Strunk, Jr. and E. B. White. Our advice is the same as that of *The New York Times* when a recent revision was published. "Buy it, study it, enjoy it," their reviewer wrote. "It's as timeless as a book can be in our age of volubility." It will help you more than any other volume you might pick up.

Once you review these basics of good writing you are ready to work on your resume and cover letter. There's no mystery about either of them, although to the uninitiated both may sound formidable. The cover letter is exactly that—a letter that is sent along with the resume to "cover" it, that is, to extend and/or protect the information. Its purpose is to get the resume read. The function of the resume and cover letter is to get you an interview; it is nothing more than a marketing tool. What it "sells" is you.

The word "resume" is derived from the French résumer, to summarize, and that is what a resume does. It is an outline of the aspects of your life that are important to your job search, not a biography. It is a brief document, usually one page, rarely more than two. There are exceptions to this. Older workers, with years of experience, especially those in academic fields with many writing credits, might prepare a more comprehensive survey of their backgrounds. However, less experienced workers should concentrate on the preparation of the one- or two-page resume because most prospective employers lack time to read longer ones. If you can make an impression with a brief summary, they will request more detailed information.

There are two general styles of resumes in use today. One, the traditional resume, arranges information chronologically, stressing specific jobs. The other, the functional resume, is a description of skills and talents, many of which might not be related to past job experience. The difference in the two approaches should be apparent immediately. The traditional resume emphasizes experience; the functional resume, skills. Therefore, you can see which form might be best for the job candidate with little experience—the functional resume. The functional resume also allows more opportunity for self-expression since widely varying descriptions and formats are available.

One warning: in your attempt to make your resume unique, don't let it become eccentric or bizarre. A few conservative organizations are still adjusting to the wider use of the functional resume and they are not ready for additional shocks. Do not come up with strange formats or paper in wild colors. Do not be cute or breezy in style.

Some good general guidelines are to use standard-size manuscript paper in white or a neutral color and a simple, legible format. Leave plenty of white space; that is, design a format with lots of space between major sections. Write clear headlines and set them apart, not only with space, but also by using capital letters and by underlining. The completed resume should look professional. That means that if you are a lousy typist, you should get someone else to prepare it for you. You can have a printer set it up, but this really isn't necessary and will cost you more.

The raw materials for your resume are buried in the work you did as you read chapter two. You will find these are the same resources you will use to prepare for the interview, so your work will serve double purpose. Get out your career strategies workbook and review your self-inventory. Also draw on what you learned in chapters three and four. You need to know exactly what abilities you have that will "sell" you to the prospective employer. You also need to know as much as possible about the job for which you are applying.

The best resumes are those written in response to a specific job description. If you know exactly what the job entails, you can write your skills to dovetail to the job requirements. As a young job candidate, looking for your first job, you may find this difficult to do, especially if you are following up many leads. Your best bet is to develop a standard functional resume, reflecting your general career objectives and skills. Once this is done, you can modify it as your sophistication in job hunting techniques grows. You will find you are constantly rewriting portions of your resume.

The sections of the resume are dictated by logic and by the need for specific information as related to the requirements of certain fields. These sections generally include: personal data; employment or career objective; skills and/or work experience; work history; education; special awards and honors; special interests and hobbies; and miscellaneous. Let's consider each of these separately.

Personal Data

Everyone who has ever tried to fill a job vacancy has a story about receiving a resume minus an address or a telephone number—honest! One personnel director interviewed for this book had a sample without a name. Obviously, you must include your name, address, and telephone number. If you are a student, you will need to provide both your home address and your school address. Whether or not you include age, height, weight, state of health, marital status, number of dependents, race, religion, and similar data depends on the job you are applying for. If these factors will help you get the job, include them. If they will hamper you, exclude them. You probably can't hide your sex, but you certainly don't have to advertise anything that will work against you. One point to keep in mind: eventually prospective employers will find out what they want to know. If they feel any of this information is vital to them, they will use the most devious methods to elicit it. The best policy is to be open and provide whatever is requested—not in the resume, but in your initial personal contact.

Employment or Career Objective

If you are a young job candidate, you may find it easier to divide this objective into two parts—immediate employment objective and long-term career objective. A sentence or two is enough. Be specific, but not so specific that you limit your opportunities. Let's say you are graduating with a degree in physical education with a major in aquatics. Your immediate employment objective might be a job as a swimming instructor or swim team coach. Your long term career objective might be aquatics director of a year-round swimming facility. You would not want to say "swimming instructor or swim team coach in a YWCA with a membership of 1000 located in a large midwestern city." You would not add similar restrictions to your long-term objective. Sometimes, especially when you become more experienced, your objective can highlight your major skills. If you were the aquatics major just used as an example, you might eventually write "a position in physical education where my teaching, coaching, and administrative abilities can be utilized in developing a model recreational center." Make sure that what you do say reflects your real abilities and dreams and is backed up by the facts in the rest of your resume.

Skills and/or Work Experience

This is the most flexible section of your resume. In the functional resume you have the option of describing your skills and abilities as work achievement rather than work experience. This provides wide latitude in selling yourself. Let's take the physical education/ aquatics graduate as an example. She might develop the following list:

Personal aquatics skills

Participated in competitive swimming from age six through college, winning major meets during the various levels of the experience. Qualified Senior Red Cross Lifesaver. Also trained in whitewater, dam and flood rescue.

Aquatics Teaching

Handled instruction on every level from children still in diapers to older adults who had never learned to swim. Also taught handicapped children and adults.

Lifeguarding

Served as lifeguard at pools and on lake and ocean beaches.

Other Sports Teaching

Taught various racquet and paddle sports, including tennis, racquetball, squash, and table tennis. Supervised recreational games of volleyball and basketball. Also taught American and European folk dancing.

Camping

Survived lone wilderness camping experience under the aegis of Outward Bound. Served as counselor in camp for handicapped children.

Administration

Supervised "cage" personnel in clubs. Supervised other swim instructors. Prepared budgets and did bookkeeping. Arranged tours, including bus rental, overnight accommodations, and travel schedules.

Writing and Promotion

Organized and promoted swim teams. Wrote and produced flyers soliciting membership in both school and private (YWCA) swim teams. Handled press releases reporting activities and appeared on both radio and television for same purpose.

This kind of list makes it possible to give experience gained from all sources, including volunteer and college intern programs. To develop it, you make a comparative analysis of your abilities and your training, including everything you can do and how you learned to do it. If you have trouble, resort to Rudyard Kipling's "five handy workmen"—who, what, when, where, and why. Write down all the facts. Then break them down into categories as shown in the list. Include only material relating directly to your employment or career objective. Emphasize your outstanding attributes and skills. There is no room for false modesty in resume writing.

Work History

List all the jobs you have held that are *relevant* to the job you're applying for. Include part-time jobs, volunteer jobs, and college internships. For each job, give term of employment, title of position you held, name of the company, location, and telephone number, name of your supervisor, and reason for leaving. Many job seekers now eliminate full addresses and telephone numbers and supervisors' names. They feel it cuts down on the chance that the prospective employer will telephone former employers and get a negative report on previous work. Such a report might mean an interview would not be granted. Of course, the prospective employer may take the trouble to look up the information and call anyway. Indeed, a good interviewer eventually will find a hole in your information if there is one. For this reason, give complete information. If you have a long work history, all *relevant*, select the last four to six *best* jobs. You can list all the others on the job application form if the employer wants them.

Education

This section should cover special courses and workshops as well as formal education if they are relevant. For example, the physical education/aquatics graduate should include all those courses that trained her in special lifesaving techniques.

Scholarships, Special Awards, and Honors

Resume writers always question material for this section. "Do I include all of these?" they ask pointing to a long list of awards and honors. "I feel foolish blowing my own horn." Remember that survey by Harold Jones among the *Fortune* 500 corporations we cited earlier? According to him, 86 percent of the survey respondents wanted to see scholarships, awards, and honors listed on resumes. It was also pointed out earlier that false modesty will never get you a job! So, include these items if they are relevant to the job you want.

Special Interests and Hobbies

Sometimes what you do with your leisure time is important to your employer. Sometimes, too, employers ask this information of you in interviews with an ulterior motive. "Are you so involved with your outside interests that they will interfere with your job?" is the hidden question. You have to weigh the activity or interest against the job. If it is relevant, mention it. For example, if you are applying for a job as a park ranger and have been a volunteer fireman, you would certainly want to list the activity. On the other hand, your passion for golf is of less importance. Or take the physical education/ aquatics student we mentioned earlier. She ice-skates and skis, and also has done a lot of mountain hiking. She should mention these, but leave button-collecting, another hobby, off the list.

Whether to list political or religious activities depends on similar factors. If you have any question about their appropriateness, ignore them, but there might be times when you would find such affiliations useful. For example, if you are trying for a job as a county extension agent in a Bible Belt community, you might want to explain that you teach Sunday School and work with church youth groups as a director of dramatics activities. Relevancy is the deciding factor. Don't discount any interest or activity, but don't feel you have to include it. If you carve willow whistles, grow avocado trees indoors, listen to Baroque music, collect unicorns, or write limericks, know exactly how this relates or keep this information to yourself.

Miscellaneous

This section covers everything from military service to references. Usually military service is important; in state and federal civil service jobs, as a veteran, job applicants get credit that can mean a higher rating for eligibility and/or salary. On the other hand, one woman says her United States Army duty tour worked against her in applying for jobs in civilian life. "Employers thought I was some kind of freak, so I stopped listing it," she says. You will have to make your own judgment here, but for most outdoor careers the kind of experience gained in the military is probably relevant. The following miscellaneous categories are easily handled.

References

Include a line saying, "References available on request." Prepare a separate sheet providing the information and send it when requested. Criteria for selecting references were dealt with in chapter three.

Salary

Never mention it unless you must.

Travel and Relocation

State your willingness, or unwillingness, to do either, listing whatever restrictions are necessary, such as "willing to relocate in Northeast or Southwest," or "Some travel possible, such as occasional trips. No regular weekly travel schedule."

Availability

Simply list the time . . . 30 days, two weeks, or whatever. The time should not be too far in the future. Most employers will not hold jobs for several months. One exception is the first job right out of college. College seniors are sometimes hired in the late winter or early spring with the understanding that they will report to work following graduation. I even heard about a veterinarian taking some additional training in avian physiology who had three job offers going to this course! However, the usual rule is: look for a job when you are ready to go to work—and remember how many chores precede making application for the job.

Should you include a photograph with your resume? The practice is less prevalent than it used to be in the days before Equal Employment Opportunity and Affirmative Action stipulations. At one time, employers demanded photographs and used them as a race discrimination tool. Minority applicants were screened out before they were even interviewed. Like every other decision, the answer is: include a photograph if it will help you. If you are an attractive person, by all means do so. A picture does put a face to all the facts. It might be particularly useful if the job you want would thrust you before the public, as for example with frequent public speaking or television assignments. If you are older and look younger, or vice versa, and you have a problem with this, the photograph might also help you get the interview you want.

Now you have all the information you need to create your own resume. Study the examples included here. Also note the checklist to help you include all the pertinent points. Then get to work. Your first or even your second try may require rewriting, but with effort, you will turn out the resume you need to begin your job hunt.

RESUME AND COVER LETTER CHECKLIST

• Do your resume and cover letter respond to a specific job situation? Are your skills and other information relevant to this situation?

• Have you made your approach personal and unique? Will the prospective employer feel this resume and cover letter could come from you and no one else?

• Have you covered all the necessary information? Check your completed work against the sections listed in this chapter and against your draft.

• Are your dates accurate? Double check both fact and typing.

• Have you included your telephone number and address? If you have more than one number or address, have you included them also?

• Have you reviewed the writing tips in this chapter and applied them to your work?

• Have you struggled through the self-editing techniques we suggested, especially checking spelling, punctuation, and grammar?

• Have you shared your material with a friend or mentor and responded to his or her criticisms?

• Do your resume and cover letter look professional? Neat? Brief? Have an attractive format?

The secret for creating a polished resume—or any piece of good writing—is self-editing, which is nothing more than a systematic self-check on your work to catch errors and improve technique. The first step is to put some distance between you and your work. Try to let a day, or a least a couple of hours, pass between your writing and editing sessions. When you do return to work to begin revising your resume, read it all the way through before you contemplate any changes. Do you like the way it sounds? Are all the facts right? Check figures and spelling. Look for typographical errors. Read through the checklist once again to make sure you have included everything.

Then read again. This time concentrate on the writing. Go back to the first part of this chapter and review the ten rules for improving your writing. Is your writing conversational, simple, clear, concise, specific, logical, and methodical? Have you used the active voice? What about adjectives and adverbs? Are the ones you've used both necessary and effective?

Study the resume format. Is there enough white space so that the various sections look open and are easy to read? Have you utilized capital letters and underlining to accent the important sections?

Before retyping to make all the changes, read the resume through again, this time aloud. Listen to yourself carefully, especially to the Skills and/or Work Experience section. This is where you did the most "creative" writing, and this is where you will probably find the most problems.

At this point, sharing your resume with someone else might help, but be careful. Make sure the person you select is sympathetic and has the knowledge to judge what you are doing. The best people to ask are a friend struggling with a similar task, or a mentor who has been guiding your career decisions. Rewrite only to specific criticism not vague generalities. Do not make changes just because your critic says, "I don't like it." Get a clearly defined reason such as, "That section isn't clear. I don't understand what you mean," or, "The sequence is confusing here."

Finally, retype your resume, making all the changes. Do this even if you are a bad typist and intend to have a professional complete the job. This final typing is your opportunity to catch all the errors.

When your resume is completed, you still have a major task before you are ready to mail it—the cover letter. This cover letter is as important as the resume itself. It is even more personal and persuasive. And even more than the resume, it should be tailored to the individual job application.

Your cover letter does not need to be long, but it does need to be effective. A form letter will not do. Prospective employers have read them all and put them—and the resumes attached—on the discard pile.

You cannot dash off a good cover letter anymore than you can dash off a resume. They both take time. The appearance of the cover letter is as important as the appearance of the resume. It should always follow the accepted layout for business letters. Today, the block form or modified block form are among the most popular choices by organizations and will certainly serve for you. Study the examples of cover letters given. If you have questions about format, consult a standard guide, such as Prentice-Hall's classic *Handbook of Business Letters*, by L. E. Frailey. You should find it in most libraries. Type your letter *with black ribbon on white paper*. Be sure to type your full name below your signature; occasionally letters become separated from resumes and you don't want the opportunity for an interview to be lost because a busy executive cannot read your handwriting.

Your cover letter has three purposes. You want it to get the attention of the man or woman with the job to offer, to grab his or her interest, and to make him or her act, that is, call you for an interview.

Your opening paragraph is of primary importance. Put yourself in the recipient's place. What would capture your attention? Something personal? Exactly. Nothing could be better. Howard Figler, in *The Complete Job-Search Handbook*, has studied this personal approach carefully. He suggests that you start out by commenting about the person to whom you are writing, the organization about which you are writing, and about your own background, as related to the subject about which you are writing. For example, a letter to a fellow at a museum might read: "I saw on television the film you helped make last year, and it inspired me to reactivate my own interest in photography. I think my recent studies of cardinals teaching their nestlings to fly may interest you and show you how serious I am about becoming an ornithologist. I understand that your museum selects a limited number of student interns each summer for field work. I would like to be considered for . . ."

Or, again using Figler's approach: "I am impressed by the advertising campaign your company has been running in the national media. I've seen your ads in the *New York Times*, the *New Yorker*, and *Time*, and I realize I would be proud to think of your organization's philosophy as my long-term professional goal. Please do not think me presumptuous. I am young, and yes, I have limited experience, but my skills, education, and work credits, as listed on the enclosed resume, show that I have prepared well for a career in forestry. In particular, I spent two summers in Canada . . ."

It isn't easy to come up with such an approach, but if you research well enough, you can. If you do your homework as suggested in chapters two, three, and five, you will have enough background to tackle such a project.

The writing of your cover letter may take even more time than the writing of your resume. The rules are the same; the identical self-editing steps apply. Just as with your resume, bad grammar, poor spelling, and amateurish typing could cost you an interview. It should be clear whom a prospective employer will choose if he or she has two candidates with equal qualifications, but one writes a neat, clear letter and one writes a messy, confused letter.

Writing a poor letter or a poor resume is inexcusable for today's job hunters. So much help is available. Draw on it. Consult your mentors. Study the books we suggest. Above all, if you don't achieve the best results on your first efforts, rewrite. Don't feel discouraged if you have to make several attempts. Editors will tell you that almost anything written can be improved by rewriting. Through rewriting, you—like Lewis Carroll's Humpty-Dumpty—will achieve mastery over words, making them work for you, getting you that vital interview, moving you one step closer to the career you dream about.

5

Ac-cent-tchu-ate the Positive:
How to Live Through an
Interview

The job interview is one of the final steps in your job search. It is
also one of the most important. Indeed, it may be the single most
important factor, according to a survey of 196 personnel executives
conducted by the Bureau of National Affairs, Inc., a Washington,
D.C. research firm, much patronized by big corporations and government agencies. Rejections come most often because of the way
job applicants behave during interviews, these survey respondents
say. A good interview can make an employer overlook an applicant's
weaknesses, and a bad one can cancel out all the previous preparation, usually calculated in months and years.

How can you avoid such a catastrophe? There is a one-word
answer: preparation. As in the other stages of getting yourself ready
to pursue an outdoor career, preparation is crucial. Impressive credentials will not excuse a poor face-to-face showing anymore than
superior intellect will compensate for a poorly-prepared term project.

Ac-cent-tchu-ate the Positive lyric: Johnny Mercer; music: Harold Arlen. © 1944
Harwin Music Co. © Renewed 1972 *Harwin Music Co.* International Copyright Se-
cured. All Rights Reserved. Used by permission.

Stressing the importance of the interview is not meant to frighten you. Rather it is to reaffirm that you are in control of your life—the philosophy that we have been supporting throughout this book. If you take the time to get ready for the interview, you will be asserting your independence and ability to take responsibility for your own actions, characteristics we've pointed out before as being absolutely essential in outdoor careers of every kind.

The interview is a multi-purpose job-hunting tactic. And it's one that is as important to you as to your prospective employer. It gives the two of you an opportunity to meet each other. This live contact, usually on the ground where you will work, bridges the gap between correspondence, credentials, and resumes and company brochures, telephone conversations, and library research. Handled properly, the interview can be a winning proposition for both the interviewer and the interviewee.

This point, in fact, gives you the first rule in preparing for the interview process: look at the interview not as a trial or an examination, but as a tool to collect information and expand your own horizons. If you take this attitude, you will stop worrying about the experience. This is important because worry can damage your chances. You need to go into the experience in a positive frame of mind, self-assured and articulate, ready to sell yourself. As with your cover letter, your resume, and all the information skills you have developed, the interview is a marketing technique.

If you were going to sell apples, you would sort out the bad ones, polish the remaining ones, and display them in an appetizing way. If you were going to sell a horse, you would bathe it, groom it, and put it through its paces for several extra training sessions so that it would make the best possible showing during the presentation to the potential buyer. In your exposed position in the interview, you are like the apples or the horse. You use the same sort of steps to prepare yourself for the interview experience.

These analogies are a bit simplistic because you need to do a lot more than groom yourself and choose attractive clothes. These are important, of course, but you need to be thoroughly aware of all your strengths and weaknesses. This calls for homework. You need to return to the career strategies workbook you began in chapter two for intensive review. The raw material for bringing about a successful interview is buried in the self-inventory you made there.

Consider those questions again. What are your major skills . . . your talents . . . your incompetencies . . . your frustrations . . . your preferences . . . your values . . . your priorities . . . your motivations? How do you spend your free time, and why did you choose these particular activities? Why do you think you can do the job for which you are applying? Make sure you can answer all of these questions concisely and authoritatively. If necessary, practice the answers out loud.

You might take a tip from an aspiring Broadway musical comedy star who worked out a technique for dealing with the dreaded auditions performers have to face in order to be chosen for stage roles. "I have only a few minutes, sometimes only seconds, to sell the producer on my talents," she says. "I concentrate on my unique qualities. I ask myself what there is about me that is different from anyone else. Sometimes it's my appearance. Sometimes it's an experience I've had that provides an empathy with the role I'm playing. For example, when I tried out for Maria in *West Side Story*, I drew on my feelings over the loss of my fiancée in Vietnam. Sometimes it's my talent, being able to dance or sing the very best. Always, it's a combination of all of these, although sometimes one aspect is more important than the others, depending on the role I'm trying out for. The thing is, it works. When I think of myself as unique, I become unique."

This actor's technique could help you. You are unique, no doubt about it. No one else is going to have exactly the same combination of skills, talents, personal attributes, and experiences. Just make sure you know what yours are. The kind of attitude that will sway interviewers and win jobs is like the self-confidence of the sixteen-year-old who says: "I have so many abilities to think about when I'm considering the choice of a career. I could do dozens of different things. I just have to decide what I'm going to do."

Equally as important as knowing yourself is knowing your prospective employer. You have broad general knowledge of your career field, but what do you know about the specific employer? Research the question. Say you're trying for a sales slot with a farm equipment manufacturer in a large midwestern city. Your ultimate goal is management, and you've been told sales is one of the best ways to get there. You've never been in the midwest, but you do have a New England farm background. That means you will understand "country" ways. You know about sales and equipment generally because of your college studies in the agribusiness program you've been in for four years. Your job will be to brush up on your geography and the specific company in which you're interested. Consult the encyclopedia and atlas. Write to the chamber of commerce for brochures about the area. Read a local newspaper. Some areas have regional magazines that will be additional help. Send to the public information office of the company for an annual report and flyers about the company's products. Or even visit a salesroom and see the equipment. Consult the *New York Times Index* for the most recent economic surveys of the farm equipment field. If possible, you want to know the history, financial status, problems, products, and services of the employer you are considering. Finally, know the wage or salary generally paid for the job you're thinking about. Now think about what you would like to know that your research hasn't uncovered.

You need to do all this work and to know as much as possible because the interview time will be limited. You will only have time for a couple of questions. And even if you could, you don't want to ask too many and seem to be either stupid or lazy, or both. Invariably, interviewers are impressed with job candidates that have taken the trouble to do this kind of research. To them, such enterprise indicates much more than interest in the field. It means the presence of drive, of ingenuity, of imagination, and of persistence—all qualities desirable in an employee.

Once you've completed the review of your own self-inventory and the research about the company, you're ready to tackle the questions the interviewer will ask you. As you study the sample questions we've included here, you may think they seem easy to answer. You may also wonder what some of them have to do with applying for a job. Be assured, there is a rationale behind the questions. They are more than the bureaucratic need to assemble and assess facts. The questions—or more aptly, the answers to the questions—give clues to how well you express yourself and how well you organize your thinking. They usually fall into four general categories: personal history, educational interests and history, employment history and professional qualifications, and financial goals. We have made up a list of questions for you. They are all actual questions that, at one time or another, have been asked by interviewers of job candidates. Study these questions. Think about your answers. Even write down the answers if that will help you organize your thinking. Don't try to memorize your answers word for word; rather concentrate on key words. You want your responses in the interview to sound spontaneous.

HARD QUESTIONS EMPLOYERS ASK PROSPECTIVE EMPLOYEES

Probably no single interviewer will ask all of these questions, but many of them are sure to turn up in any serious interview. Make sure you have solid answers for all of them.

Personal History

Tell me about your childhood.

How do you think your best friend would describe you?

How do you get along with people?

What kinds of things/people annoy you most?

How do you feel about working with people with backgrounds and interests different from yours?

How do you react to pressure? How does it affect your work?

What is your best time of day?

What are three of your strong points? Three of your weak points?

How do you spend your free time? Hobbies? Volunteer and community work? Have you served on boards or as an officer of any organizations?

What books have you read lately?

Do you attend movies/plays/concerts?

What television programs do you watch?

What is your favorite sport?

Do you have any physical or emotional problems? If so, how would they affect this job?

Whom do you admire most? Who have your mentors been?

Educational Interests and History

What is the highest grade you attended in school?

What is your college grade point average overall? In your major field?

Why did you choose your major field?

If your major field was not your original choice, when and why did you change?

What were your best courses? Your worst?

Did you do the best work you could in school? If not, why?

What courses did you enjoy most?

If you went to graduate school, what was your purpose in getting this advanced degree?

Did you work during college to help pay your expenses? If so, what percentage did you contribute?

Employment History and Professional Qualifications

Why do you want a career in an outdoor field?

How did you happen to apply for this position?

If you were in my shoes, what would you look for in the person applying for this position?

Why do you want to work for our organization? Live in this community?

What other organizations would you want to work for?

Where have you worked before? Summer or part-time jobs? Internships? Volunteer work?

Have you served in the military? If so, what did you do?

What skills do you have that make you feel you will be successful in your field?

What skills have you acquired from previous jobs? From education?

Do you have any special skills or accomplishments not necessarily related to the qualifications for this job. Where did you acquire them? On your own, or in classes? Do you intend to continue to develop them?

What did you like/dislike about previous jobs?

How did previous employers treat you?

Why did you leave your last job?

Do you like routine work?

Right now, what kind of work interests you most?

If you had your druthers, what kind of job would you like to have?

What projects have you completed that demonstrate initiative and willingness to work?

Do you see yourself as a leader or follower?

Have you ever supervised people? If so, describe the circumstances.

Are you an idea person? What ideas have you put into action and how did they work out?

Have you ever been fired? If so, why?

Can you work overtime?

Are you willing to travel? Is there a limitation on how much travel you can do?

What part of the country do you like best? Would you be willing to move if your work demands it?

Do you have objections to psychological tests and/or interviews?

When are you available for additional interviews? For test-taking?

How much money do you have to earn?

If you are offered this position, when can you start work?

What questions can I answer for you?

Special tip: Always take advantage of this last question. Ask as many of the questions on your "hard" list as you possibly can, but be aware of how the interviewer is reacting. If he or she is clock-watching, talk fast!

Future plans and financial goals
What is your career objective?

Where would you like to be professionally five years from now? Ten years?

How much do you expect to be making five years from now? Ten years?

Would you like to go into business for yourself if the opportunity were right?

What are your personal five-year goals? Ten-year goals?

When the actual interview arrives, focus on giving brief, succinct answers. Watch your grammar and diction. Be enthusiastic, and make sure that you let the interviewer know you are willing to work hard. Be calm, pragmatic, diplomatic, and scrupulously honest, but positive, stressing your good points. As the old Bing Crosby standard goes, "Eliminate the negative; latch onto the affirmative . . ."

For example, one of the hard questions for college graduates applying for their first jobs is: "What previous work experience do you have?" You could answer the questions the way one girl did: "I worked my way through school," she told the interviewer. "I was on the federal Work-Study Program all through school, working either in the library or the business office. I spent my summers on my uncle's farm, helping cultivate and harvest crops, and caring for animals. I interned in a dairy research products lab during my senior year. I maintained a 3.7 grade average, carrying up to twenty credits some terms. I also managed to work on the college paper for three years, and in my junior year, I ran for president of the student government. I think this proves I have what it takes to hold a job even if I haven't really earned money in the business world yet." The interviewer agreed with her. She got her job as a dairy technologist with a starting salary of $13,000.

Not all so-called hard questions are as obvious as this one and pose more difficulty for novice interviewees. "How would you describe yourself?" seems innocuous enough. What it really is asking is: "How flexible are you? Are you willing and able to cooperate with other employees?" Or take this one: "Of all the jobs you've had, which one did you enjoy most?" The buried question here is: "What kind of work setting is right for you? What skills really give you satisfaction? What are your weaknesses . . . your strengths."

The list of queries like these is endless and varies from interviewer to interviewer. The best strategy is to consider all questions "hard questions." Trickery is not the intent, although it sometimes may seem to be. Keep in mind that the purpose of the interview for the prospective employer is to flesh out the cover letters, resumes, credential forms, and reference letters, trying to discover your motivations, both stated and unconscious, and your abilities both obvious and unexplored. The organization with the job opening wants to know how mature, compatible, and enthusiastic job candidates are. Furthermore, they are juggling time. They are asking themselves: "How long will any one worker remain on the job? How long can we afford to take to recruit any one employee?" A safe tactic to help deal with answering all questions is to limit your answer to those things about yourself that relate to the job for which you're applying. The interviewer does not want your life story, but does want relevant facts and attitudes that reveal whether or not a particular job candidate is right for a certain job.

How to answer questions "positively" when the truth is "negative" is a particular challenge. For example, suppose you have been fired from a job because you were consistently late. You might say something like this: "I know my inability to be on time in the past has been a problem, but I've learned my lesson. I've changed my entire lifestyle. I go to bed earlier. I always set the alarm. I've learned to leave the house earlier—especially in bad weather. Please let me prove that I have improved."

Or suppose you are asked to describe your major weakness and for you that weakness is spending too much time on the telephone. To answer, describe the ways you have developed to handle this problem, such as not accepting personal calls at work and limiting all calls by setting a stop watch everytime the telephone rings. The trick with questions of this kind, is to be absolutely honest and to demonstrate that you are capable both of making a realistic self-appraisal and accepting criticism.

One question for which there is no good answer is the one about salary. "How much money do you have to earn?" the interviewer blandly asks. What do you say? The subject of salary, you'll recall, was discussed in detail in chapter three. The advice was to know what you're worth and what the job is worth, but to delay the discussion for as late in the job negotiations as possible. Don't mention it in your cover letter. Don't bring it up during the interview. If the interviewer insists that you name a figure, use a formula suggested by a veteran accountant. "Suggest a figure at least 10 percent higher than you're willing to settle for," he says, "and be willing to accept the lesser amount if necessary. Also, set an absolute minimum and refuse to take less than this. This is the only way to keep your sanity."

If you have been so unwise as to go to an interview without doing your homework, you are at the mercy of the interviewer. You may be able to stall with something like, "I don't know what the job is worth in the market; what are other people in comparable jobs getting?" but probably not. An interviewer who asks the question is determined to have the answer. He or she may be trying to hire the job candidate at the lowest possible salary. There's always the chance, as in so many other questions, that it is a test to see how well the candidate is prepared to deal with the job hunting process. Ideally, the prospective employer will make you an offer and you can take negotiations from there. Don't count on too many ideal job interviews or interviewers, though.

You can ask hard questions, too, but remember that tact and good manners are imperative if you want to be considered a job candidate. Temper your curiosity—and sometimes your anger at a particularly aggressive interviewer—with good sense. If you are really offended by interview tactics, you probably are not interested in the job anyway. One of the main reasons for deciding on an outdoor career was because you felt the quality of lifestyle and workstyle offered is better. Don't scrap your values to fight for a job that doesn't measure up to your standards. As we said in the beginning, the interview serves both the interviewer and the interviewee.

HARD QUESTIONS FOR YOU TO ASK PROSPECTIVE EMPLOYERS

You should ask two or three questions that show the prospective employers that you have common knowledge about his organization. These will be easy to pose; your interviewer will be interested to see that you have done your homework. The following questions will be more difficult both to ask and to get answers for, but you do have a right to all of this information. Wait until the interviewer has covered all of his or her questions, then jump right in. Remember you need this information in order to evaluate the job if it is offered to you.

Who had this job before? What is he or she doing now? (If he or she quit, try to discover why.)

Why didn't you fill the vacancy with someone from within the organization?

Who is the immediate supervisor for the job? Will I have a chance to talk with him or her personally? Today? Later?

What exactly will I be doing during my working day? Is there a job description I can study? What people do I work with other than my immediate supervisor?

Where does the job you're considering me for fit into your overall organizational picture?

What are the future plans for your organization? (Especially try to discover plans for the division in which you want to work.)

Is there a chance I will be transferred? (If so, ask when and where.)

Will I be expected to travel? (If so, ask how often and how long the trips will be.)

What is the housing situation in your area? Can you provide help in finding adequate housing? Do you pay moving expenses?

Special Tip: Do not ask salary questions during the initial interview with an organization. Try this tack instead . . . How many new people did you hire last year, and how many of them were college graduates? What was the average starting salary for the college graduates you did hire?

You may face several different styles of interviewing during your job hunting, the most usual being: the preliminary interview; the in-depth interview; the stress interview; the group interview; and the home interview. Both directive and nondirective interview techniques are common.

The *preliminary interview* is a brief session, usually lasting less than a half-hour, designed to help the employer screen candidates for more intensive consideration.

The *in-depth interview* is exactly the opposite, a comprehensive session, lasting more than an hour, and sometimes conducted in several sections. The subject matter is as broad as the job candidate's work experience, aspirations, and personal history.

The *stress interview* is not so much a separate type of interview as a special technique used to push job candidates to see how they react under pressure. Those "hard questions" considered earlier are raw material for this situation.

The *group interview* has two different purposes, one of which may be difficult for the job candidate to handle. This kind of interview is used to teach inexperienced employees how to select new company personnel; if this purpose is obvious, everyone involved feels the strain. The other use makes more sense: a committee works with the job candidate as a team to evaluate his or her suitability for a post. This is most often used for upper level employees and for professional applicants.

The *home interview* is rare and is almost exclusively a tool of large corporations screening upper level employees under consideration for extremely sensitive positions. Its use has declined in recent years.

You should be ready for both directive and nondirective approaches to interviewing. The directive interviewer assumes control and poses open-ended questions. For example, he or she might ask: "What did you like about your college years?" rather than "Did you enjoy your college years?" The nondirective interviewer, who adapts a low key conversational style, puts the question still another way: "Tell me about your college years." The directive technique is by far the most popular because it takes less time.

Still one more technique, rarely used today, is the *patterned interview* in which the interviewer asks a specific list of questions and records the answers in writing. Most personnel experts consider it old-fashioned, but a few employers cling to the idea that it is fairer because it asks the same questions of everyone.

Sometimes job applicants are asked to introduce their spouses to prospective employers. Usually this is true only for upper level job candidates and the meeting situation is strictly a social one, usually a small dinner party. Employers are interested in families of people they want to hire for obvious reasons. The relationship between a husband and wife can affect a worker's job performance.

The manner in which you answer questions is as important as the answers themselves. If you are inexperienced at interviewing, you may react in an unaccustomed way, transmitting via body language, nervousness you would rather conceal. Your first defense against this tension is thorough preparation for the interview. That leaves you comfortable and relaxed about dealing with the problems you will confront. Additional protection is the knowledge that it can happen and an understanding of the give-away signs.

These signs vary from person to person, but you might check this list to see if you react in any of these ways when you find yourself in a tense situation. Do you yawn? Do you use sweeping, uncontrolled gestures? Do you cross your arms tightly across you chest, or make fists of your hands? Do you cross and uncross your legs? Do you stare out the window, refusing to make eye contact with people? This latter is really the most damaging behavior of any mentioned here, suggesting fear and insecurity. Eye contact will help you relate to the person to whom you are talking. As you make this contact, you will relax and be less prone to tension.

While mastering the question-and-answer hurdle is a major step toward a successful interview, there are other problems to consider and conquer, for example, completing application forms and taking psychological tests.

That you should have to make special preparations to fill out forms may seem silly to you, but it really is necessary! Some employers use the exercise of completing application forms as a kind of testing. They want to know how well you read directions and how accurate, neat, and thorough you are, so it is best to take this step very seriously.

You should plan to take several copies of your resume to the interview with you. That way you will have all the data you need. Frequently, interviewers mislay resumes or need extra copies. Sometimes employers send application forms to you ahead of time. This is by far the best way; then you can take all the time you need to do the job carefully.

Testing is a bit more difficult to prepare for. Although fewer employers are utilizing testing than in previous years, it is not unusual for job candidates to be asked to take tests of all kinds. This is probably truer for candidates for outdoor jobs than in almost any other career category, a situation we discussed in chapter three. In

preparing for your job interview, be sure to review all of the suggestions we made for successful test-taking.

Another matter of prime importance is your appearance. First
impressions are very important. As one anonymous wag said, "You
never get a second chance to make a first impression." Poor grooming
and inappropriate clothing could kill your chances. So plan to take
extra care on the day of the interview. Your clothes should be clean
and neatly pressed, and what you wear depends on the kind of job
for which you are applying. Dress like the people who do the work
for which you want to be considered or just a little better. Avoid
extremes because employers are apt to be conservative. Most personnel people recommend that men get a fresh hair cut (shorter hair
is safer) and wear ties and jackets, and that women avoid high fashion, a lot of jewelry, extreme hair styles, and heavy makeup. Clean-
liness is absolutely essential: take a bath and use a deodorant; wash
and brush your hair; clean your fingernails; brush your teeth, And,
of course, men should shave and neatly trim their beards and mus-
taches.

Ideally, what you need to achieve the perfect interview is practice. An hour in front of your mirror is some help, but the best of all
is the real thing. Carolyn Evans, a skilled career counselor and owner
of a major personnel agency in suburban Philadelphia, suggests that
you schedule your first job interviews with potential employers who
rank low on your priority list because "this allows you to make your
mistakes before you have too much to lose."

The late John Boyd, a New York City advertising executive, who
retired to upstate New York, to publish a weekly newspaper and
spend his free time in the mountains photographing wildlife, had
a short check list for first-time interviewees. "The simplest things
can ruin an interview," he said. "Even if you've done your homework, you can blow it if you're not careful." He spoke from experience. During the 1930s, when jobs were really difficult to come by,
he lost four before he learned to obey these dictums. He urged job
applicants to review them the day before an interview.

Show up on time or even ten to fifteen minutes early. Take time before the appointment to find out exactly where you are going and how long it will take you to get there. If you are late, you will be nervous, and you may also disrupt a busy person's schedule. Tardiness creates a negative impression.

Know your interviewer's name and title. If you are not sure, ask the receptionist or even the interviewer himself/herself. Get the spelling, too. You will have thank you notes to write. Address the interviewer by his or her surname, that is Mr., Ms., or Mrs. Martin, not Phil or Phillipa.

Let the interviewer set the pace and control the interview. Follow his or her cues about where to sit and whether or not to shake hands, smoke, and begin talking. He or she will direct the discussion. Limit your conversation to subjects related to the interview. Do not touch on personal topics unless asked. Avoid religion and politics. Never use profanity. Never complain about former employers or professors. The world is, as the old cliche says, a small place. For all you know, the interviewer could know them, their relatives, or friends.

Do not take notes during the interview except at the very end when it is permissible to record names, telephone numbers, or similar data. Notetaking will distract you and could make the interviewer think you cannot handle detail.

Ending an interview is tricky. You should leave the control with the interviewer, but you should be sensitive to signs that it is over and you should know what your next step is. Will the employer call you, or you him, about the outcome of the interview? Are you supposed to take tests, supply additional documents, or return to meet other people to answer more questions? Once you are sure of future action, you should leave promptly. You should take time to say you want the job—if you do—and to say thank you, but then go.

You will probably feel let down after the interview, especially if it is your first. You will be emotionally exhausted because of the strain of the concentrated, artificial emphasis on yourself, and of the inconclusive ending. That, unfortunately, is how most interviews end. Before making a decision, the interviewer may need to see other candidates. He may also need to talk with other people about your qualifications or references.

There are things you have to do, too. If you have been asked to take action of any kind—say, send additional documents or prepare a statement of what you plan to do if you get the job—do it immediately. Don't run the risk of losing a job offer because of lack of follow-through.

You may need to write letters. All the general rules for correspondence given in chapter four apply. Particularly, don't forget to do careful editing. Remember the admonition: make your correspondence work for you, not against you. Every little edge counts all the time, but especially in the crucial final stages of job application negotiations.

You should write a thank-you note, although some personnel experts now disagree. They say do not send such a letter, especially in the case of a woman who has had an interview for a high-level job. The idea, apparently, is that sending a "thank you" for the "courtesy" of the interview is demeaning. Men don't do it, according to them. We think this attitude is a pity because it cuts off a natural opportunity for a follow-up. The best advice is probably to analyze each situation individually, keeping in mind that courtesy is always appreciated. If there is any excuse at all, write a note. You can always find some additional facts you'd like to call to the attention of the interviewer. Many successful job candidates use exactly this tactic. "At the end of the interview," one of them explains, "I bring up a subject that can be clarified only by correspondence. It works every time. It gives me a chance to continue to sell myself."

Sometimes sending a statement of your expenses for reimbursement provides the excuse for the note. In fact, experienced interviewees try to handle such reimbursement in this manner.

Reimbursement for expenses can be tricky. Some prospective employers, usually government agencies or schools, may not pay expenses, but if the interview requires travel, most will underwrite the cost. Be sure you discuss the subject *before* the interview. Find out specifically what expenses will be covered and how they will be reimbursed. You may be given a list of suggested expenses or even sent tickets. You should save receipts and keep careful, itemized records because you may be asked to fill out a special payment form. And remember, too, that job-hunting expenses—and some moving expenses—are tax deductible. Consult a tax preparation handbook, or an accountant about this.

Travel expenses, considered appropriate by most prospective employers and by the Internal Revenue Service, include transportation tickets (any kind), gasoline expenditures based on a prearranged price per mile if an automobile is used, hotel bills, meal costs, and taxi or limousine service from home to airport, train, or bus station to hotel to home again. You should choose moderately priced accommodations, buy tourist-rate transportation tickets, and order from the "middle" of restaurant menus. Most business managers will also accept reasonable tips on expense account renderings. There are no hard and fast rules, but a good word to keep in mind as a guideline is "necessary." Be comfortable, but not luxurious. Your sensible thrift—or your indiscriminate spending—will be duly noted by prospective employers.

Evaluating the interview experience will help you become more comfortable with it. Most likely you will have to go through more than one interview, because almost no one is successful on the first try. You will also have more than one job in your life. To make this evaluation easier, write a brief account of the interview for your career strategies notebook, pointing out for yourself any mistakes you made. Be sure, also, to list any positive aspects of the experience. Your biggest quandary will be wondering whether or not you have a chance at the job for which you apply. Don't be misled by the amiability of the interviewer. Don't mistake the firm handshake and the pleasant "I'll be in touch" of the closing minutes of the interview for a job offer, or even for good faith. You will know a job offer when it comes. Usually you will learn of it via telephone. The conversation will go something like this: "This is Ms. Blank from XX company. We've decided you have the qualifications we need for that job opening we have. We'd like to offer you . . ." The caller will go on to list the salary and fringe benefits, the starting date, when you go on the payroll, and other details, and suggest a deadline for your decision. She should also say, "I will confirm all this by letter immediately." If she does not offer the written confirmation, ask for it. Always get commitments in writing. Know exactly what the acceptance of the job entails. If you are asked to sign a contract, be sure you understand it. Have a lawyer look it over if necessary.

Should you accept the job? Sometimes this is a difficult decision, but it should be made carefully and pragmatically—not in the manner heard recently while having lunch in a community college cafeteria. "I got two job offers," a young man said. "I can't make up my mind . . . guess I'll toss a coin." In chapter six criteria for rating employers will be given. Review this.

Do it in writing: make pro and con columns and compare them. Study the confirmation letter again to be sure there are no loose ends: is the salary specified . . . fringe benefits spelled out . . . starting date indicated . . . responsibilities clearly stated? Remember, you are weighing an investment in your future. Think clearly about the opportunity for advancement. If there isn't any, you need to have other compensations, some of which might include a chance for employer-paid advanced training, long vacations, extensive travel (if you like to travel), short work week, or other similar benefits.

If you are looking for your very first job, think carefully before you turn down a legitimate job offer. You need to get started in your career, and most entry level jobs are just that: entry level jobs. It's not the job that counts; it's what you do with it. And first jobs are just that: first jobs. After a year or more of experience you can try again.

This chapter is by no means the "last word" on developing interviewing skills, although we have tried to cover the most important points. You will get additional help from several of the books mentioned in previous chapters. Howard Figler's books, in particular, may be useful. Consult the appendix for these.

One final word: do not forget all the people who helped you get your job when you finally accept an offer. Thank them and let them enjoy with you the pleasure of success.

God asks no man whether he will accept life. That is not the
choice. You must take it. The only choice is how.
Henry Ward Beecher

6

Bird in Hand:
Who Are the Employers?

Where are you going to work? Who will your employer be? What are
your choices?

In actual fact, although you make the final decision about
whether or not to accept a position when it is offered to you, you do
not choose your employer. Usually, exactly the opposite is true. Your
employer chooses you, especially in these days of a tight job market.
Only a few of you will have the luxury of setting your sights on
specific employers and being successful in your campaign. Most of
you will need to instigate a wide search to come up with a job. To
do this intelligently, you need to understand something about the
various employers.

In the following chapters, more than 100 outdoor and outdoor-
related careers are examined. Some of them, like forestry and oceanography, are traditionally considered outdoor careers. Many more,
like engineering, the biological sciences, and the environmental sciences, have both indoor and outdoor aspects. Still others, like ar-

chitecture, community planning, and agribusiness, are outdoor careers mostly because they relate to environmental concerns. Finally, there are the fields like teaching, law, and communications that can be given an outdoor twist.

In discussing all these careers, many possible employers are considered. These fall into the following categories: private industry; government—federal, state, and local; colleges and universities; other non-profit organizations; and the Armed Forces. The possibility of entrepreneurialism—organizing, operating, and assuming the risks of business ventures—also is covered. Dozens of outdoor fields offer possibilities to the entrepreneur; almost anyone professionally trained can become a consultant—a one-person business—after a few years' experience. In such other areas as law, architecture, and veterinary science, most people who have the training open their own practices. Before turning to chapters about each career field, these employer areas are discussed generally.

Traditionally, government, and particularly the federal government, has been seen as the largest employer in the outdoor career field. No surveys of the total field exist, but this generalization is probably true in conservation and recreation, in some of the engineering fields, such as civil engineering, or in some of the environmental sciences such as oceanography and meteorology. In actual fact, private industry is probably the largest employer in outdoor careers.

Private Industry

Certainly private industry offers the widest of all possibilities for work. The "big money" is also in private industry. But with thousands of companies to which to apply for a job, how does the aspiring applicant narrow the field? In some cases, as with college seniors in some fields, the employers come to the student, particularly agribusiness firms and corporations seeking engineers and scientists. Their representatives conduct on-campus screening interviews and then invite students to corporate headquarters for additional interviews. At some large universities, as many as 20,000 to 25,000 personal interviews are arranged for students. Top students who want the jobs offered are hired promptly with the understanding they will go to work after graduation.

The others—and those who do not choose to participate in campus recruiting—have recourse to many other ways to search out and contact private employers.

One of the best resources is the College Placement Annual, long recognized as a comprehensive source of information about employers and read by 400,000 college students every year. It lists about 1,200 employers and includes convenient occupational cross-reference sections as well as more than 230 full-page display listings. The employers are major corporations who feel their needs are sufficiently large to include in an annual publication.

Another good source of job openings in private industry is association and trade journals, most of which carry classified advertising. A list of these associations is included in the appendix.

The Yellow Pages of the telephone book, city directories, and chamber of commerce directories also provide fertile material for potential employer searches. This was a technique outlined in chapter three. Other good sources of state and local job information are the state occupational coordinating committees. A list of these is included in the appendix.

There is no such thing as a typical private industry employer "profile." The employers will differ widely from one field to another and from one geographic area to another. It will be necessary for job applicants to research each company individually. In recent years, fringe benefits have increased dramatically.

Academia and Non-Profit Organizations

The same is true for colleges and universities and for other non-profit organizations. Working for these two kinds of employers is described in chapter fourteen. Again generalizations are difficult to make. Salaries may be slightly lower than in private industry, especially in the top brackets.

In non-profit organizations, paid employees frequently supervise volunteer employees, a task that calls for patience and tact. They also sometimes have lower budgets and fewer facilities to get jobs done and demand great ingenuity to complete jobs. Not all employees can accept these limitations and should think carefully about this problem before accepting jobs.

Colleges and universities, especially in rural settings, are thought by some people to suffer from the "ivory tower" syndrome. Indeed, the pace is slower and schedules are looser. The red tape of bureaucracy plagues some campuses, which would certainly be a stumbling block for the person who cannot plan ahead and who is not good at watching the budget. Professors do not punch time clocks and have great freedom, although they may on occasion be under great pressure to complete deadline jobs. Institutions do vary widely, depending on administrators. As in private industry, benefits such as health insurance have improved in recent years.

The Armed Forces

In the context of this book, the armed forces as an employer are important in one major way. They often make possible education and training students would be unable to afford in civilian life. In spite of this possibility, some adjustments in thinking are necessary for youths who choose their career track.

The primary objective of the armed forces is the maintenance of national defense. To fulfill this objective, each branch of the armed forces—the army, the navy, the Marine Corps, the air force, and the Coast Guard—performs important functions. The army is primarily concerned with land-based operations, while the navy organizes and trains forces for sea-based activities. The Marine Corps prepares for land and sea actions in support of naval operations. The air force's mission is air and space defense. The Coast Guard, under the Department of Transportation (except in wartime, when it serves the navy), has such maritime responsibilities as conducting rescue of distressed vessels and aircraft, enforcing federal maritime laws, and supervising the cleanup of maritime pollution.

Because of the importance of these missions, the person choosing this career path must realize that even though his occupational specialty designates a particular skill, he or she is a member of an organization geared primarily to defense. Although the person may be highly qualified, the military organization's needs take priority. Oftentimes, additional duties and responsibilities that have nothing to do with the person's occupational field are delegated, and he or she is expected to perform willingly as a soldier, sailor, airman, or marine.

Military personnel—more than two million persons—are stationed throughout the United States and in many countries around the world. In the United States, the largest numbers are in California, followed by Texas, North Carolina, Florida, Georgia, and the Washington, D.C. metropolitan area. Of the approximately 470,000 people outside the United States, 300,000 are stationed in Europe, particularly in Germany; the rest are located in the Western Pacific area.

The range of occupations in the armed forces is almost as wide as in civilian life. Both enlisted personnel and officers can receive education and training that can prepare them for outdoor careers. For example, the Army Corps of Engineers is an excellent training ground. Other fields that offer opportunities include recreation, police science, meteorology, mapping, surveying, scientific and engineering technology, and oceanography.

People planning to apply the skills gained through military training to a civilian career should determine how good the prospects are for civilian employment in jobs related to the military specialty that interests them. They also should know the prerequisites for the related civilian job. Many occupations require licensing certification or a minimum level of education. Those who are interested should find out whether military training is sufficient to enter the field or, if not, what additional training will be required.

But before going any further, there is one very important point. Although the military is an excellent path to an outdoor career, and the training is very often exciting and challenging, there is absolutely no guarantee that a person will receive the training he or she signs up for, and further, no guarantee that he or she will receive a compatible assignment once trained. Keeping this in mind, a person joining the military should investigate enough ahead of time to feel comfortable knowing that he or she will enjoy the military experience as well as the opportunity for training in the outdoor field.

Although specific enlistment requirements for each service or enlistment option within a particular service may vary, all branches have certain general qualifications. Enlistees may be either single or married, but they must be between the ages of 17 and 35. All branches prefer high school graduation or its equivalent and require it for certain enlistment options. Both a written (Armed Services Vocation Aptitude Battery) and a physical examination are required.

A variety of enlistment options, each involving different combinations of active and reserve duty are available. Most active duty

programs range from three to six years, with three or four year en-
listments the most common. Selection depends on the individual's
general and technical aptitudes, personal preference, and the needs
of the service.

Women are now eligible to enter 95 percent of all military specialties. Only fields involving combat duty are excluded.

Enlisted Personnel Training

After basic training, depending on the service branch, most re-
cruits enter formal classroom training to prepare for a specialized
field of work, which is followed by on-the-job training, and subse-
quently by the service assignment. In addition to on-duty training,
military personnel may choose from a wide variety of educational
programs offered during off-duty hours, for which tuition assistance
is available. There are also programs for full-time education in specialized fields that provide full pay, allowances, tuition, and related
fees.

Officer Training

Officer training is provided through the federal service academies (Naval, Air Force, Marine Corps, Army, and Coast Guard), the
Reserve Officer Training Corps (ROTC), Officer Candidate School,
the National Guard (State Officer Candidate School programs), and
several other programs. The federal service academies provide a four-
year college program leading to a bachelor of science degree. The
midshipman or cadet (nomenclature depends on the school) receives
free room and board, tuition, medical care, and a monthly allowance.
When they graduate, they receive regular commissions and have a
five-year active duty obligation. To become a candidate for appointment as a midshipman or cadet to all of the service academies except
the Coast Guard Academy, applicants usually are nominated by a
member of Congress from their home districts. They must have superior academic records and pass certain other qualifications, including a physical examination. Appointments to the Coast Guard
Academy are made on a competitive basis.

The ROTC trains students in about 500 Army, Navy, Marine
Corps, and Air Force units at participating colleges and universities.

Trainees take two to five hours of military instruction a week in addition to regular college courses. Students in the last two years of an ROTC program and all those on ROTC scholarships receive a monthly allowance while attending school and additional pay for summer training. After graduation, they serve as officers on duty for varying, but pre-stipulated, periods of time.

In addition to basic pay, military personnel receive free room and board (or a living allowance), medical and dental care, a military clothing allowance, military supermarket and department store shopping privileges, recreational facilities (which facilities provide dozens of opportunities for recreational job experience for outdoor careerists), thirty paid vacation days a year, and travel opportunities. For pay grades, see Table 1.

Educational benefits also are available to Armed Forces personnel who participate in the Veterans' Educational Assistance Program (VEAP). The government contributes $2.00 for every $1.00 put aside by the service member. This means that service members who save the maximum, $2,700, would have an education fund totaling $8,100.

Information about enlisting in the Armed Forces is available from recruiting officers stationed in every major city in the United States. They are listed under their service name in the Blue Pages of the telephone book. Publications about the military careers and training are available at these offices, at most state employment service offices, and in high school, college, and public libraries. Additional sources of information are listed in the appendix.

The Government

Government, one of the nation's largest employers, provides jobs for about 15.6 million civilians, or about one out of six employed people in the United States. State or local governments (county, city, township, school district, or other special division) employ five out of six government workers. The remainder work for the federal government. As you will see in the coming chapters, substantial numbers of these employees work in the outdoor field.

More than nine out of ten jobs in the federal government are under a federal civil service, or merit, system that has existed for

Table 1

ACTIVE DUTY MILITARY COMPENSATION FOR MEMBERS OF THE ARMED FORCES AS OF OCTOBER 1980.

BASIC PAY

Pay grade	Under 2 yrs.	2 yrs.	3 yrs.
Enlisted members:			
E-1	6,015.60	6,015.60	6,015.60
E-2	6,703.20	6,703.20	6,703.20
E-3	6,966.00	7,347.60	7,642.80
E-4	7,243.20	7,650.00	8,096.40
Commissioned officers:			
0-1	11,091.60	11,545.20	13,957.20
0-2	12,776.40	13,957.20	16,765.20
0-3	14,655.60	16,383.60	17,514.00

BASIC ALLOWANCE FOR QUARTERS

	No dependents Full	Partial	With dependents
E-1	1238.40	82.80	2156.40
E-2	1310.40	86.40	2156.40
E-3	1483.20	93.60	2156.40
E-4	1659.60	97.20	2473.20
0-1	2253.60	158.40	2934.00
0-2	2887.20	212.40	3654.00
0-3	3326.40	266.40	4104.00

almost 100 years. This system, which had become so weighted down with regulations and red tape that it was almost impossible to manage, was reorganized by Congress with the Civil Service Reform Act, which became effective January 1979. Together with these reforms, Congress approved Reorganization Plan No. 2, also effective January 1979, which divided the functions of the old United States Civil Service Commission between two new agencies—the Office of Personnel Management (OPM) and an independent Merit Systems Protection Board (MSPB). The plan also established a new Federal Labor Relations Authority (FLRA) to oversee federal labor management policies and to provide leadership in administering these policies.

The civil service system insures that federal employees are hired on the basis of individual merit and fitness. It provides for competitive examinations and the selection of new employees from the most qualified applicants. As a result of the Civil Service Reform Act:

- Pay increases are now based on quality of performance rather than on length of service.

- Agency managers have more authority over personnel procedures, particularly hiring procedures within their agencies.

- Procedures for firing or demoting nonperforming employees have been simplified, especially providing protection from arbitrary actions of employees.

- "Whistleblowers," who lawfully disclose violations of law or regulations or who are harassed by officials and complain, are protected from reprisals.

- The old system giving ALL veterans lifetime preference over non-veterans in federal hiring and retention situations was rescinded, lessening the advantage which veterans had at the expense of women and minorities. Preference is still given to disabled and recently discharged Vietnam-era veterans, but is limited for other able-bodied veterans and is eliminated entirely for officers retired at the rank of major or higher.

- All agencies conduct minority recruitment programs to help eliminate under-representation of minority groups in the federal work force.

- Nonpaid work by students in connection with educational programs is permitted, provided it does not reduce opportunities for regular employees.

- Employment information about job openings and competitive examination is more available, assuring open competition for jobs. OPM and government agencies now must provide such information to the United States Employment Service, which, in turn, makes sure it is widely circulated.

• Federal agencies are authorized to adopt OPM merit system standards as a personnel requirement for grants to state and local government.

This latter requirement will eventually influence reform of personnel procedures within state and local government and may make personnel policies across the country more uniform. However, for some years to come, state and local hiring procedures will vary widely. The majority of state and local government positions are filled through some type of civil service test, and these positions are also covered by fringe benefits similar to federal benefits that will be described shortly.

For information about positions in state or local government agencies, job seekers should contact the agencies directly. Local offices of state employment services have additional information.

All the federal jobs in the outdoor field are administered by the OPM. Requirements for many of these positions include civil service competitive examinations, which may be taken by the United States citizen. To be eligib le for appointment, an applicant must meet minimum age, training, and experience requirements for the particular job. A physical handicap will not in itself bar a person from a position if it does not interfere with the performance of the required duties. Examinations vary according to the types of positions for which they are held. Some test the applicant's ability to do the jobs applied for. Others test the ability to learn how to do it. Applicants for jobs that do not require a written test are rated on the basis of the experience and training described in their applications and any supporting evidence required.

Applicants are notified as to whether they have achieved eligible or ineligible ratings and the names of eligible applicants are entered on a list in the order of their test scores. When a federal agency requests names of eligible applicants for a job vacancy, the OPM sends the agency the names at the top of the appropriate list. The agency can select any one of the top three. Names of those not selected are restored to the list for consideration for other job openings.

Over half of all federal workers—and all of those working in the jobs described in the outdoor career fields that follow—are paid under the General Schedule (GS), a pay scale for workers in professional, administrative, technical, and clerical jobs, and for workers such as guards and messengers. GS jobs are classified by the OPM in one of 18 grades, according to the difficulty of duties and responsibilities and the knowledge, experience, and skills required of the workers. GS pay rates are set by Congress and apply to government workers nationwide. They are reviewed annually to see whether they are comparable with salaries in private industry.

The maximum salaries for each grade and the amount of each grade's periodic increases are listed in Table 2. Appointments usually are made at the entrance rate for the appropriate grade. However, appointments in hard-to-fill positions may be at a higher rate.

Most employees receive within-grade pay increases at one, two, or three year intervals, if their work is acceptable. Within-grade increases may be given also in recognition of high quality service. Some managers and supervisors receive increases based on their job performance, rather than on time working in a certain grade.

High school graduates, who have no related work experience, usually start in GS-2 grade, but some who have special skills begin at grade GS-3. Graduates of two-year junior colleges and technical schools often can begin at the GS-4 level. Most people with bachelor's degrees appointed to professional jobs can enter at grades GS-5 or GS-7, depending on their academic record. Those who have a master's degree or Ph.D. degree, or the equivalent education or experience, may enter at GS-9 or GS-11 level. Advancement to higher grades generally depends upon ability, work performance, and openings in positions at higher grades.

Federal government employees work a standard 40-hour week. Employees who are required to work overtime may receive premium rates for the additional time or compensatory time off at a later date. Most employees work eight hours a day, five days a week, Monday through Friday, but for many outdoor jobs, the nature of the work requires a different work week.

Federal employees earn thirteen vacation days during their first three years of service; twenty days each year until the end of fifteen years; after fifteen years, twenty-six days each year. Nine paid holidays are observed annually. Workers who are members of military reserve organizations also are granted up to fifteen days of paid military leave a year for training purposes. A federal worker who is laid

Table 2
SCHEDULE OF ANNUAL RATES BY GRADE OF THE GENERAL SCHEDULE FOR FULL-TIME FEDERAL EMPLOYEES, EFFECTIVE OCTOBER 1980

GS GRADE	ENTRY SALARY	AFTER THREE YEARS
1	7960	9954
2	8951	11265
3	9766	12700
4	10963	14248
5	12266	15947
6	13672	17776
7	15193	19747
8	16826	21875
9	18585	24165
10	20467	26605
11	22486	29236
12	26951	35033
13	32048	41660
14	37871	49229
15	44547	57912*
16	52247*	
17	61204*	
18	71734*	

*Basic pay for employees at these rates is limited to $50,112.50 in accordance with 5 U.S.C. 5308 and section 101(c) of Public Law 96-369.

off is entitled to unemployment compensation similar to that provided for employees in private industry.

Other benefits available to most federal employees include: a contributory retirement system, optional participation in low-cost group life and health insurance programs which are partly supported by the government as the employer, and training programs to develop maximum job proficiency and help workers achieve their highest potential.

Information on federal job opportunities is available from state employment service offices, and from OPM regional offices (there are ten of them, for which addresses are given in the appendix) and seventy Federal Job Information Centers in various large cities throughout the country. These centers provide complete one-stop information service on local and nationwide job opportunities in the federal government. To see if you have a center in your area, consult the Blue Pages of the telephone book. If you cannot find a listing, consult one of the regional offices or write directly to the OPM, 1900 E Street, N.W., Washington, D.C. 20415.

Through all the above sources, the OPM announces and conducts the examinations required for various federal government jobs. They evaluate qualifications and refer eligible applicants to employing agencies for their geographic areas.

Sometimes the best information about jobs in specific agencies is available from the agency directly. The addresses of the agencies who traditionally hire workers in the outdoor field are listed in the appendix.

Working for Yourself

The outdoor career field offers many opportunities for entrepreneurialism. When you study the chapters coming up, you will see time after time that starting your own business is the way to make the most of your ability and training. It is also a chancy venture, but not as much so as you may imagine—especially if you are well prepared. United States Department of Labor statistics say you have a 50-50 chance to succeed.

Luck or chance plays a role. For example, the couple that opened a marina and scuba diving school just as the oil embargo struck had a bit of bad luck and are having hard times because vacation travel is down. They should have been successful because they were well capitalized and well prepared. Those two factors, coupled with your own abilities and a little bit of luck, are the keys to success.

Ability for entrepreneurial ventures hinges on many things other than knowing your field—which, of course, is pivotal. Beyond this, four personal traits are important.

Stability

You must be an honest person with the ability to handle stress and responsibility. Surprisingly, being in business for yourself is far more demanding than working for someone else. You will discover that the dreamed-of independence does not materialize. Instead, you will be totally accountable. The "buck" stops with you; there is no one else to whom you can pass it.

Determination

You must believe in yourself and be optimistically committed to your ideas.

Initiative

You must be willing to take chances and assert yourself. You also must be willing to make decisions.

Perseverence

You must be willing to work hard and have the physical stamina and energy to do so.

How do you know whether you have these qualities? Considering ten questions posed by the Small Business Administration (SBA) may help you find the answer. Before reading on, take the quiz "Do You Have What It Takes To Start Your Own Business?"

Capital

You need adequate financial backing and this amount varies with your field. If you are a farmer, you need more capital than you do if you are a consultant in one of the sciences. If the business you have in mind can be run from your home, you need less than if you have to lease other premises.

Sometimes family or friends will loan you money as silent partners in return for stock or for a portion of the profits—to be paid on a delayed basis when the business achieves success. They might also co-sign bank loans.

Bank loans for new ventures may be difficult to get, especially if you have no funds of your own. Most bankers want you to supply

DO YOU HAVE WHAT IT TAKES TO START YOUR OWN BUSINESS?

This test was compiled by the Small Business Administration (SBA) to help people evaluate whether or not they have the talents necessary to go into business for themselves. Answer each of the ten questions by putting a check in the column that best describes you. Check "A" if the answer is a strong yes. Check "B" if your answer is "on the fence." Check "C" if your answer is no.

	A	B	C
1. Do you like to do things on your own without being told?	—	—	—
2. Do you get along with just about everybody?	—	—	—
3. Are you good at getting other people to go along with your ideas?	—	—	—
4. Do you like to take charge of things and see them through?	—	—	—
5. Are you the one who plans all the details when you and your friends decide to do something?	—	—	—
6. When you get started on something, do you keep going until the job is finished?	—	—	—
7. Do you make up your mind in a hurry and find later that you've usually made the right decision?	—	—	—
8. Do you level with people and say what you mean?	—	—	—
9. Is there no stopping you, once you've made up your mind to do something?	—	—	—
10. Do you have good health and lots of energy?	—	—	—

To evaluate your potential as an entrepreneur, count the checks in each column. If you have more A's than anything else, you probably have what it takes to run a business of your own. If you have mostly B's, you may need a partner who is strong in your weak areas. If you have many C's, you will probably have a difficult time operating a business successfully.

If you did well on the SBA test, you will want to consider seriously the other factors involved in starting your own business.

at least a third of the initial capital. They want collateral to guarantee the loan. Stocks, bonds, real estate, or insurance are best, but they might give you the money if you have a co-signer and if your business plan (more about this shortly) is good. They also might consider signed contracts to provide services as sufficient security. Banks loan the money for short periods—about five or six years—and expect regular reviews of your financial situation while the loan is outstanding.

The SBA makes loans to small businesses, but only a small percentage of their funds go to new business. They make direct loans, in which they might loan up to four times the amount you have to invest. The maximum loan is $100,000. They also make a smaller number of guaranty loans, that is, they guarantee 90 percent (or $350,000, whichever is less) of loans made by a commercial bank. They also make Economic Opportunity Loans of up to $50,000 to economically and socially disadvantaged people, and they also provide management assistance. All of these SBA loans have more generous repayment times and a lower interest rate than loans from commercial banks. SBA loans, however, are difficult to get and take a long time to process. To qualify for the loan, you must show a track record of success in your field, invest capital of your own in the business, and have loan rejections from two banks or finance companies. Sometimes your chamber of commerce and/or your representative in Congress can help you.

Credit unions are another source of funding. Interest rates are low and loans are often granted upon your signature alone.

People with ideas worth millions in sales potential might be able to get funds through another group of investors known as *venture capital* groups. They are organized for the specific purpose of buying into businesses. The SBA promotes one such group. Some Wall Street underwriters are attracted by these investments, too. In addition to sales potential, they look for experienced managers with the exclusive rights to the idea behind the projected business.

Planning

Getting financing for your business idea is only part of the complicated process of starting your own business. Careful planning of every aspect is important. In fact, you probably will not be able to secure loans until you have a comprehensive plan. Bankers balance the soundness of your idea and the thoroughness of your planning against the collateral you offer. If all these factors balance, you have a chance.

Research is the first step. You need to find out everything you can about the field you are going into. The best way is to serve an apprenticeship—paid or unpaid. In addition to this approach, draw on the experience of others. Talk to everyone you can locate who has any connection with your field. You can learn from both successful and unsuccessful people.

You need to consult three other experts—lawyers, accountants, and insurance agents. Select each of them with as much care as you would a doctor who was going to treat you for a life-threatening disease. A personal recommendation from a knowledgeable person is best. Lacking this, you can consult professional associations for names of qualified individuals and interview them to establish whether or not they have the credentials to work with you. Insurance agents usually can supply informational booklets outlining their companies' services.

Lawyers help you understand the legal and tax ramifications of your proposed business, making sure that you obey governmental ordinances, particularly those related to registration and zoning. They indicate the form of business—sole proprietorship, partnership, or a corporation—that would be best for your situation and advise the best method of capitalization. They outline your personal liability, assist you with contracts, and make sure you understand bankruptcy laws.

Accountants implement the tax and financial advice of your lawyer, helping you prepare a business plan, including profit-and-loss projections based on revenue estimates. They set up payroll and accounting books and teach you or an employee to keep them. They prepare tax returns and certify financial statements. They also can advise you on setting up a fair salary scale for yourself and your employees.

Insurance agents counsel you about insurance required by law—workers' compensation, social security, state disability, fire, liability, and casualty insurance—and also advise you about providing fringe benefits for your workers (yourself, too). They will suggest the best package you can afford, including medical, hospital, dental, psychiatric, and life insurance coverage. They will also present information about pensions, policies to cover buy-out agreements should there be a death of a partner, and stock option programs.

All this planning takes time. Lawyers and accountants may need as much as six months to do their work. Insurance agents are a little faster. Also remember that bankers may take as long as a month to respond to a loan request. In light of the time-consuming processes involved, be sure you allow enough time.

According to the SBA, business failures are usually caused by bad management, not bad ideas. Your business will be as good as your expertise—your ability to project what revenues will be and what products, services, and every item of overhead will cost, and to keep the actual operating figures in line with these estimates.

Students who see themselves as entrepreneurs should include business courses in their curricula—at the very least, business administration. They should also be sure to take the earlier advice of getting extensive experience in the field.

This chapter is by no means the last word on employers. It merely scratches the surface, giving you some basics to work with and some direction in your own research and providing you with enough background to explore the various career areas in the outdoor field presented in the following chapters. These chapters will provide answers to the following questions:

What skills, education and training are needed for each field?

What are the job opportunities?

What are the advantages and disadvantages of each field?

What are the personal as well as the work satisfactions?

What is the earning potential?

The basic information about these career fields is based on research and statistics from many sources. Some of the major ones include the United States Census Bureau, the Department of Health, Education and Welfare, the Office of Personnel Management, the various departments involved in the career fields, and the United

States Department of Labor, especially from two publications, the *Occupational Outlook Handbook* and the *Dictionary of Occupational Titles*. State personnel manuals were studied as were dozens of pamphlets and books from professional associations. In a few cases, labor union leaders were consulted. Finally, people working in the field were interviewed.

One caution—one which is repeated several times in this book—the conclusions drawn about job availability and salaries are based on the economic situation at this time (1981) and on projections prepared by economic experts. Unpredictable economic, political, and scientific factors could modify these facts substantially. Keep this in mind as you think about your problems and goals and prepare to make your career decisions. Read newspapers, read up-to-date reports from professional associations, talk to professors, talk to people who work in the field, and most of all, read a major metropolitan newspaper like the *New York Times* or the *Washington Post*. These publications report economic trends and can provide good information to help solve your problems.

Finally, before you decide to take a job, go over the positive and negative aspects of the job. The list of questions below will help you to judge employers and the job. Go back to chapter two and review the Work Preferences Quiz. Your answers to these questions also provide criteria for making your decision.

SHOULD YOU TAKE THE JOB?

Here are guidelines for rating a prospective employer and the position which he or she has offered. There are no right or wrong answers, but if you have negative responses to many of the questions, you probably should continue your job hunt.

1. Does the job excite you? Is it work you want to do and work worth doing?

2. What is your intuitive feeling about the job and the employer? Does anything at all make you uncomfortable?

3. How did the workers behave when you visited the company? Did they act like they enjoyed their work or vice versa?

4. Would you like to work with the people already employed?

5. Is the job located in the geographic area where you want to live?

6. Is the community in which the company is located one in which you can live in the manner in which you desire?

7. Is the working area attractive and comfortable? If not, do other aspects of the job compensate for this lack?

8. Is the organization economically sound? This is a fact you should have checked when you researched the company prior to the interview. If you don't know the answer to this question, get it before making a decision.

9. How did the organization handle its initial dealings with you? Did it keep its agreements? Pay your travel expenses? Function in a well-organized manner during the interview and subsequent meetings?

10. Is the salary you are offered enough for you to live on? What did you find out about general salary policies? Do you have an idea about when you can expect a job performance review and a raise?

7

Life and Living:
Biology and Anthropology

One of the most challenging fields for outdoor careerists is life science, the study of living organisms and their life processes. Life scientists are concerned with the origin and preservation of life, from the largest animal to the smallest living cell. They are the Darwins, the Mendels, the Huxleys of the future.

The scope of the field is staggering—and it becomes even more so as modern technology creates problems for all living things. Because the field is so broad, it is usually divided into the three areas—biology, agriculture, and medicine. The areas with which outdoor careerists are concerned are biology and agriculture. Biology will be considered in this chapter and agriculture in chapter eight. Anthropology is also included in this chapter since it is a science devoted to the living and biology is a basic study for all anthropologists.

109

Ecologists

The most popular life science in the outdoor field today is probably ecology, which is also the most widely misunderstood. Many people think the word is synonymous with environment. It is not. It is a separate biological field, founded in 1869 by German naturalist Ernest Haeckel, and it is also called environmental biology or bioomics. It is the science of the relationship between organisms and their environments.

For example, a problem that an ecologist might attack would be evaluating the effect of pollution from a chemical plant on plankton (microscopic plants and animals) in a river into which the plant empties its wastes. Another might be establishing a prairie land park in a midwestern farm field. The question: how long will it take the prairie to re-establish itself?

Ecological problems can be as simple as studying one tiny cell in relationship to one element such as rainfall, temperature, or altitude, or as complex as dealing with an entire city, its physical surroundings, its population, and its social, political, and economic systems.

Ecology is important in contemporary society because man continues to be the great destroyer. Every technological advance brings with it ecological destruction—everything from pollution to water shortages to erosion to the extinction of animals.

Ecology is based on the study of many biological sciences, such as morphology, physiology, and genetics, and other sciences, such as physics, chemistry, earth sciences, and mathematics.

Many classifiers would say that ecology encompasses many jobs not necessarily labeled "ecologist." Forester, for example. Or soil conservationist. Or fish hatchery manager. In this discussion, ecology is considered to be a *part* of the training for these jobs rather than the job.

Other Biological Sciences

This is by no means an inclusive list of the biological sciences. There are dozens of subdivisions classified by the type of organism they study or by the specific activity they perform. These are, however, the main areas of interest to the outdoor careerist.

Botanists

They deal primarily with plants and their environments. Some study all aspects of plant life, while others work in specific areas, such as identifying and classifying plants, or studying the structure of plants and plant cells. Others concentrate on causes and cures of plant diseases.

Zoologists

They study various aspects of animal life: its origin, behavior, and life processes. Some conduct experimental studies with live animals in controlled or natural surroundings, while others dissect animals to study the structure of their parts. Zoologists are usually identified by the animal group studied—ornithologists (birds), entomologists (insects), and mammalogists (mammals).

Anatomists

They study the structure of organisms, from cell structure to the formation of tissues and organs. Many specialize in human anatomy. Research methods may entail dissections or the use of electron microscopes.

Limnologists

They study the life and phenomena of fresh water lakes, ponds, and streams. This field grows more important as water supplies and pollution problems become more critical.

Biological oceanographers

They are biologists, but are generally included under the general field of oceanography. This is explained in chapter ten on the environmental sciences.

Environmental protection scientists

They are not to be confused with environmental or earth scientists, a career field described in detail in chapter ten. In the past, they were known as sanitary scientists. With increasing technological complexity, the scope of the field has broadened and the name has changed in recognition of the growth. The environmental protection scientist can be either a life or an environmental scientist. Usually now, the field is broken down into a number of specialties, including air pollution meteorologist, environmental control chemist, chemical oceanographer, ground water hydrologist, health physicist, and limnologist, some of which have already been listed here and some of which are listed in chapter ten. Whatever the specific field, they are involved in studying the effects of environmental factors in health. They are the researchers who analyze and detect environmental hazards and characterize the various dangers. Take the water supply as an example. They test water samples, making sure the supply is safely stored and safely delivered for use. With engineers, they design new equipment for processing water and sewage, inspecting and testing this equipment. They work with environmental protection engineers, and environmental protection technologists, technicians, and aides.

If you decide on a career in the life sciences, you need an advanced degree. A bachelor's degree is adequate preparation for some beginning jobs, but promotions are limited for those without master's or Ph.D. degrees.

Most colleges and universities offer life science curricula. Different schools may, however, emphasize only certain areas of life science. For example, liberal arts colleges may emphasize the biological sciences, while many state universities and land-grant colleges offer programs in agricultural science. It is important to study catalogues carefully and choose the schools that have the best programs in your field of interest. For example, for zoology you might consider Cornell University, the University of North Carolina, or the University of Washington. Michigan State University and the University of Tennessee specialize in botany. The University of Wisconsin is strong in both botany and zoology. The University of Georgia has the Institute of Radiation Ecology. The University of Minnesota has an outstanding ecology department. For a discussion of agricultural schools, see chapter eight.

Before choosing a school, try to talk to people working in the field, perhaps a professor at a nearby school. Lacking that, write to the professional organizations representing your discipline. Also read the journals in the field—*Science, Ecology* and others.

The best training for careers in the life sciences is the broadest possible undergraduate background in biology and other sciences. You should take courses in biological science, including morphology, physiology, genetics, zoology, and botany. Inorganic, organic, and physical chemistry are necessary. For some fields, biochemistry may be. Physics and mathematics will also be required. So will foreign languages—probably French and German. And computer science will increase your chances in the job market. Courses for advanced study are determined by your specialization.

Prospective life scientists should be able to work independently or as part of a team. They must be familiar with research techniques, including computer science, and laboratory equipment, such as electron microscopes. Communication skills are vital. The ability to write and speak clearly and concisely can bring promotion and higher salary. In the outdoor areas, field research is a pivotal part of training and work. Almost all of these jobs are a combination of indoor and outdoor work. In the move up the career ladder, the jobs split into research and management. The research jobs are the areas that retain the outdoor component.

Good health and physical stamina are important in most areas. Although many jobs offer regular hours and good working conditions, others involve strenuous physical labor and primitive living conditions, as in field work in botany, zoology, or ecology. Animal scientists must be able to manage large animals. Some agricultural research requires long hours outdoors in all kinds of weather.

An estimated 215,000 persons work as life scientists, of which about 110,000 are biological scientists. Nearly three-fifths of the life science jobs are with colleges and universities. The federal government employs about 15,000 life scientists in dozens of agencies, but the largest number work for the Department of Agriculture, the Department of the Interior, the National Institutes of Health, the Smithsonian Institution, and the National Science Foundation. State and local governments have about 22,000 jobs in similar agencies; for example, professional employees in zoos and botanical gardens usually have a life science background.

Probably the largest field in private industry is ecology. Land use management, lumbering, and related industries use ecologists. So do fertilizer and insecticide manufacturers.

The glamour jobs are limited and are with the non-profit research foundations, institutions like the American Museum of Natural History, for example. In some areas, graduate student fellowships may be available on an irregular basis at these institutions. The best source of information is the graduate departments of the colleges and universities having strong life science departments. A few life scientists with wide experience and advanced degrees operate their own consulting firms.

Life scientists work in all fifty states, and job opportunities for life scientists in the outdoor field should be good in the 1980's as a result of the continued emphasis on the preservation of natural environments. Heavy cuts in the federal budget will, however, affect the job market. As in so many other outdoor fields, the prospects are best for those with advanced degrees. The competition will be tough for jobs on all levels. Competitive job strategies, beginning with superior preparation, will be necessary to land the top jobs. Some experts feel ecology offers the best opportunities; others say that was true ten years ago, but that now the field offers about the same possibilities as the other life sciences.

Life scientists receive relatively high salaries. According to the College Placement Council surveys, beginning salaries in private industry averaged $11,500 a year for bachelor degree recipients in agricultural science, and $12,400 for bachelor degree recipients in biological science. Biochemists earned slightly more, about $17,000.

In federal jobs, the salaries are lower, but still good. The entry level salaries are: with a bachelor's degree, $10,963; with a master's degree, $15,193; and with a Ph.D. degree, $18,585. These might be slightly higher, depending on course work and on grades. The average salary of workers in the field is about $23,800.

Salaries paid to college and university life science instructors are comparable to those paid to other faculty members. See chapter fourteen for these figures.

Anthropologists

Perhaps the best known anthropologist in recent decades was the late Margaret Mead. For most of her professional life, she worked with the American Museum of Natural History in New York City, conducting research studies about remote and primitive people. Her reports on this work achieved unusual popularity for scholarly research. She also wrote massive amounts of material for mass media publications and appeared throughout the country as a lecturer. She did more than any other single American to dramatize this profession and to encourage women to enter it and other professional fields.

The problem with anthropology, even more than some of the other outdoor careers that have been discussed, is that it is overcrowded. Jobs are extremely difficult to find. Almost all of them require a Ph.D. degree. Certainly advancement in the field is dependent upon it. But in spite of this, more than 300 colleges and universities have bachelor's degree programs in anthropology, while 160 others offer master's degree programs and about 90, doctoral programs. There is an aura of romance that is irresistible to some students longing for adventure. Just what is the attraction?

It may be the charismatic personality of Margaret Mead and others like her. Or it may be that anthropology is the study of people, one of the most fascinating subjects in the world. The field is broad and covers traditions, beliefs, customs, languages, material possessions, social relationships, and value systems. It is divided into four areas of concentration: ethnology, archeology, linguistics, and physical anthropology.

Ethnologists

They are also called cultural anthropologists (incidentally, Margaret Mead was an ethnologist) and study the customs, culture, and social life of groups. They may, as did Margaret Mead, spend months or years living with a group to learn about its way of life. They may learn another language or adopt new customs while observing and studying a group. Usually, ethnographic research focuses on a particular institution or aspect of group life such as kinship, personality, art, law, religion, economics, or ecological adaption. The field lends itself to comparative studies, such as those on different societies' attitudes towards old age. Recently, ethnologists have begun to study modern urban society and certain segments of populations—ghetto inhabitants, drug addicts, politicians, and business leaders, for example.

Archaeologists

They study human cultures of the past. They dig into ancient ruins, and using scientific techniques for dating and analyzing everything they find, they reconstruct the history and customs of ancient people. The field work takes place wherever people once lived. Their "digs" are found in all parts of the world and span many centuries, from ancient times to the present. Their finds make front page news as well as scholarly treatises. The treasures of Tutankhamen and the Dead Sea Scrolls are two discoveries that captured the public imagination. There are many archaeological sites in the United States. One of the most valuable is an extensive excavation of a twelfth century Cahokia Indian town across the Mississippi River from St. Louis, Missouri. It provides clues to the social and economic life of the Indians who lived there. In recent years, archeological studies have been made of relatively modern communities—American colonial settlements, for example. In Philadelphia, much work has been done to reconstruct sections of the city as it was at the time Benjamin Franklin lived there.

Linguists

They study the role of language in various cultures. They examine the sounds and structure of a society's language and relate these to people's behavior and thought patterns. There are fewer linguists than other anthropologists; however, they have an important role in training educators. Linguistics is a course required for most students planning elementary teaching careers.

Physical anthropologists

They are concerned with humans as biological organisms. They study the evolution of the human body and look for the earliest evidence of human life. They also do research on racial groups and may explore, for example, the effect of heredity and environment on different races. Their work requires extensive training in anatomy, biology, chemistry, genetics, and the study of primates. Frequently they work with animals—for instance, teaching chimpanzees to communicate with sign language.

A growing number of anthropologists work in applied anthropology, that is, they concern themselves with practical applications of research findings. They might consult with architects, designers, and land use experts in planning community development projects. Or they might use their knowledge of ethnic customs and values to help educators improve the effectiveness of classroom teaching and increase parental involvement.

They also prepare cultural environmental impact statements. In many communities, these are required by environmental protection and historic preservation laws to identify and protect historic areas which may be affected by development or renovation plans, such as constructing highways.

Anthropologists' work, like many of the other professions discussed, is of two kinds. They are teachers, writers, consultants, and administrators, all of which confine them to a desk and traditional work pressures. They are also researchers and travel to remote areas and work outside under adverse weather conditions, living in primitive housing, and adjusting to different cultural environments. As in other outdoor fields, physical stamina and good health are vital.

Anthropologists should acquire a broad background in social and physical sciences and in languages. Mathematics, statistics, and computer science are increasingly important research tools.

The choice of a graduate school is very important. Students interested in museum work should select a school associated with a museum that has anthropological collections. Similarly, those interested in archeology either should choose a university that offers opportunities for summer experience in archeological field work, or attend an archeological field school elsewhere during summer vacations.

Anthropology students should have a special interest in natural history and social studies and enjoy reading, research, writing, and the outdoors. Creativity and intellectual curiosity are essential to success in the field. So is objectivity, organization, and perseverance. Archeologists, especially, may spend years accumulating and piecing together artifacts from ancient civilizations and will need a full measure of these talents. The ability to analyze data and think logically also is important. Anthropologists must be able to speak and write well to communicate the results of their work effectively.

About 7,000 anthropologists work in the United States. About four out of five work in colleges and universities. Most of the others work in museums or for the federal government, chiefly in the Departments of Interior, State, Agriculture, and the Army, and in the Smithsonian Institution. A few work for state and local governments, primarily in community development, planning, health planning, archeological research, and historic preservation. A growing trend is for anthropologists to operate their own consulting firms.

One final word about job hunting in this field: students should work out strategies early and utilize every trick in this book and any others they can think of. If they can find jobs, anthropologists with a Ph.D. can expect to earn about $18,000 in entry level jobs. Federal government jobs pay slightly more, about $20,467.

Meanwhile my beans . . . were impatient to be hoed . . . What was the meaning of this so steady and self-respecting, this small Herculean labor, I knew not. I came to love my rows, my beans . . . They attached me to the earth, and so I got strength like Antaeus.

Henry David Thoreau

8

Young MacDonald:
Farming and Agribusiness

Farming, the oldest outdoor career, is today surrounded with an aura of romanticism. It is seen as the perfect way of life, richly rewarding and deeply meaningful. To many young people seeking an alternative to a contemporary lifestyle that is abhorrent, it seems a solution to every problem. Alas, this is not true. Here are the facts.

Farming, a part of the American dream as the idyllic career, is nearly if not completely dead. Current-day economics have killed it. Although the family farm remains an important factor in the total agricultural picture, it presents many problems for any but the most robust and courageous.

Fact: Before World War II, the average size of a farm in the United States was about 175 acres. The capital investment necessary to operate it was $6,200. By the early 1970s, the average size had jumped to 450 acres and the capital investment to $125,000.

This trend, rather than abating, continues. The reasons are twofold, according to a United States Department of Agriculture report. New technology makes it possible to farm more land; the economy makes it imperative. The problem is further complicated by the fact that over a million and a half acres of farmland in the United States are lost each year to suburbanization and, in many areas of the country, farmland for sale is scarce. Only about eighty thousand acres are offered for sale each year. This scarcity means the cost is high and the competition to buy keen. This, in turn, means it is almost impossible for young people interested in farming to buy a farm. The only good way to get started is to inherit a farm. Even then, financing is usually necessary to purchase livestock, seed, feed, fertilizer, and machinery. At current interest rates, the total price is staggering.

Before making a decision to tackle any farm project under these conditions, the prospective farmer should survey the industry. Many job options are open beyond working in farming in the traditional way.

Today, farming is usually referred to as agriculture and the word encompasses much more than just farm production. Incidentally, as used here, agriculture means more than growing enough food for a family. It means dedicating all the economic resources of a family to working land to support all its needs. It is closely related to many other industries—food and fiber processing, marketing and distribution, farm implement production and sales, and feed and fertilizer manufacturing. These industries, considered in the aggregate, have become known as agribusiness. Jobs in agribusiness require agricultural knowledge and skills. In recent years they have increased dramatically. At the same time, technological advances in agricultural production have reduced not only the number of farms, but also the number of jobs available on farms.

Although future growth in agricultural employment will be in agribusiness occupations, over two and a half million workers will continue to be needed in basic agricultural production through 1990. This chapter will discuss the occupations in basic farm production and the factors to consider in making the decision to farm. It also will describe the wide variety of work available in off-farm business utilizing agricultural skills.

The big question is: how can young people who enjoy working outdoors and being their own bosses become farmers?

One way is to rent a farm outright and operate it for both experience and profit. Another is to become a tenant farmer for a land-owner who supplies the machinery, seed, and fertilizer in return for a percentage of the crop. Still one more way is to work as a hired hand. In every case, by saving earnings, eventual ownership might be possible.

There is also still one other way, although not a very hopeful one. A few people try homesteading in the west or Alaska. About a hundred *undeveloped* tracts are released each year for sale or lease by the Bureau of Land Management of the Department of the Interior under the Homestead Act. Note the italics. The land requires the same kind of effort the original pioneers put into wresting farms out of the wilderness. Such a project also requires major financing if it is to become the financial base for family living.

The possibilities for farming in America today are endless. Some of the major—and a few of the minor—kinds of farmers include:

Cattle Raisers

They breed and raise cattle for the meat and leather industries. Most cattle raising operations are large because it is not profitable to raise small herds of cattle. One of the more important operators in the field is the purebred cattle farmer, who breeds registered cows and bulls to sell to other raisers who want to strengthen their own herds. Cattle raisers usually own large ranches, but they also may lease grazing lands from the government or other large landholders. Texas, Missouri, and Oklahoma are important cattle states.

Dairy Farmers

They breed and raise cows to supply milk to the milk and milk products industries. Most dairy farms are family-owned, although in recent years some have been started by large corporations. In either case, milk may be processed and packaged on the farm or sold through farmers' cooperatives. Wisconsin, Minnesota, and New York are major dairy farming states.

Livestock Farmers

They raise swine, sheep, and goats for food or for their hides and hair. They also raise horses, mules, or donkeys as draft animals. Usually, livestock farmers specialize because each animal has different needs.

Small-Animal Breeders

They raise and market fur-bearing animals, animals used in laboratory experiments, and rabbits for food. Fur farmers specialize in mink, chinchillas, foxes, rabbits, and squirrels, and concentrate on developing the quality of the pelt. The breeder has many problems, including selection of ideal breeding times and provision of individual housing. Each animal must have a separate cage because infighting causes fur damage. Laboratory animal breeders raise mice, rats, guinea pigs, cats, chickens, monkeys, and dogs for drug companies, universities, hospitals, and medical laboratories. Rabbits are among the easiest of all livestock to raise; they are also profitable. Each doe in a herd can produce 125 pounds of marketable meat. A herd of 400, whose care would be a full time job, would produce 50,000 pounds of meat.

Horse Raisers

They breed, train, and care for horses of all kinds. Many own their own businesses and specialize in breeding, training, grooming, or riding instruction. Some large farms are owned by investment companies, breeding associations, and leasing companies that specialize in breeding racehorses or pleasure horses of various kinds. Interest in pleasure horses has grown in recent years and this has increased the importance of the horse industry in the total agricultural picture. It means more workers are needed to care for the needs of horses and of amateur horse lovers. Kentucky and Tennessee are the famous horse farming states.

Poultry Raisers

They raise chickens, turkeys, and ducks for eggs and for food. Most poultry farms are located in the East and in California. They may be either family or corporation owned. Usually they specialize in eggs, poultry for food, or poultry for breeding.

Grain Farmers

They grow corn, wheat, rye, grain sorghums, and many others as food for people or feed for animals, usually specializing in two or three types. Grain farms can be as small as 375 acres or as large as 1,500. The big grain farm states are Kansas, Nebraska, Iowa, and Illinois.

Cotton, Tobacco, and Peanut Farmers

Cotton, tobacco, and peanuts are among the major crops in the agricultural industry. As in other parts of the industry, farmers usually specialize in one rather than raising all three. Cotton and peanuts are important for their by-products—oil, for example—as for fiber for cloth and peanuts for nibbling. Cotton and peanuts are Southern crops, but tobacco is grown in Connecticut and Pennsylvania as well as Southern states. Cotton and peanuts have one thing in common: they can be planted, cultivated, and harvested by machine.

Fruit Growers

They specialize in one or two fruits—everything from grapes to nuts to oranges to apples, peaches, berries, and melons. This is a very seasonal industry and also a hazardous one. Both insects and bad weather represent substantial problems. More and more fruit growers are big corporations.

Vegetable Farmers

They raise vegetables for food in all fifty states and in every climate. Every kind of vegetable is available fresh in all seasons throughout the United States, but food processing remains an important adjunct to vegetable farming. Organic vegetable farming—growing vegetables without using chemical fertilizers—is a small, but lucrative part of the industry.

Maple Sugar Producers

Earnings for these farmers are among the highest in agriculture, but it takes time to develop groves of sugar maples—*Acre saccharum* or *Acre nigrum*. The heart of the industry is New England, but the trees grow as far south as Maryland and as far west as Minnesota. This is definitely a part-time industry; the production season is limited to late winter, usually portions of February and March.

Beekeepers

Beekeeping evidently is one of the few foolproof farming pursuits. Production and marketing of honey is easy. According to the United States Department of Agriculture more than $50 million worth of honey is sold every year. In spite of this, the demand exceeds the supply.

Herb Culturists

They constitute a small but growing band of farmers in the country. Many of them produce herbs for restaurants. Others grow medicinal herbs for an expanding health cult market.

Fish Farmers

As with maple sugar production, fish farming offers high profits. The initial cost is high because of the necessity of having shallow ponds that can be drained and of installation of automatic feeders. Fish farming can be a one-person operation except at harvest time.

Which kinds of farming are the best on a shoestring? Those that require small acreage (less than 100 acres) and can be operated with a minimum labor force. These are small animal or poultry farmers, or farming crops that use intensified farming methods, such as tomatoes, strawberries, melons, potatoes, sugar beets, sugar cane, peanuts, rice, or dry beans. Because many of these crops require only seasonal attention to farming, there is also another advantage. Small farm owners could hold another job while farming—say as teachers—which might still leave time to farm. Such farms are usually found in the East or the South.

And what if there's no land and no money and working on a farm is the choice for a job? Here is a rundown of the kinds of jobs available on farms.

Farm Operators

Three out of every four farms are operated by an owner or renter. The remainder are run by hired farm managers or partners and often have 100 or more full-time workers. The specific tasks of a farm operator are determined by the type of farm but, in general, farmers are responsible for planning, tilling, planting, fertilizing, cultivating, harvesting, and marketing crops. Those who raise livestock must feed and care for their animals and keep barns, pens, milking parlors, and other farm buildings clean. Farmers also perform various other tasks, ranging from setting up and operating machinery to erecting fences and sheds. The size of the farm often determines which of these tasks operators will handle themselves. Operators of large farms have employees to do much of the physical work that small farm operators do themselves.

In addition to the physical work, farm operators must make the management decisions required for modern agricultural production including budgeting and financial arrangements.

Farm Laborers and Farm Labor Supervisors

Very few farms today can be run by only one person, so at the end of the 1970s, approximately 975,000 hired workers, 300,000 family workers, and 40,000 farm labor supervisors were employed on farms. On many of them, especially those that rely on a few family workers or hired employees, farm laborers perform a variety of duties. For example, farm hands on a farm with diversified agriculture may care for livestock and crops as well as maintain buildings and equipment.

Other farm laborers may perform specialized duties depending on the location of the farm. In areas where rain is insufficient, irrigators water crops by controlling the flow of water from irrigation ditches through gates or portholes to the fields. They also operate portable sprinkling systems that pump water through pipes spread on the ground and move the pipes from one area to another.

Farms producing fruit and vegetables often need large numbers of workers to harvest their crops. These farms employ laborers with more specialized duties. For instance, if produce is packed on the farm for shipment, then produce sorters and packers will be employed. Other laborers may spend most of their time operating a particular piece of machinery. Still others may be full time maintenance workers.

While many workers are employed in specialized jobs, farm labor supervisors are needed to coordinate work activity. They schedule the work of crews and may hire additional hands, especially during the harvesting season. Farm labor supervisors also teach new employees how to use machinery and tools and keep records of production and crop conditions.

There is a gray area between actual farm labor and agribusiness. Covered by 250,000 workers, it is generally covered by the term "agricultural service occupations." These are the workers who provide crop and animal services to farmers and farm cooperatives. They are both laborers and professionals ranging from mechanics and machine operators to agricultural technicians, veterinarians, and agricultural scientists. This is the area which offers great opportunities for people who want to go into business for themselves, but cannot afford to—or perhaps do not want to—farm.

Animal Breeders

They use their knowledge of genetics and ranch or dairy management to develop improved breeds of animals that will be more productive. They conduct tests on new breeds of livestock to determine growth rates for beef cattle and milk production for dairy cattle. Breeders also maintain records on offspring of new breeds with an animal breeding association of their own.

Artificial Breeding Technicians

This field includes artificial inseminators. They collect semen from male livestock such as bulls and rams, and artificially impregnate cows and ewes. These workers may be employed by animal breeding associations or by artificial breeding distributors who manage insemination distributorships.

Livestock Services Workers

Several occupations in livestock services may be learned easily. Cow testers employed by dairy herd improvement associations travel from farm to farm to test the milk from each cow in a herd for acidity and butterfat content and record the results. Cattle dehorners remove the horns from cattle to prevent injuries to other animals in the herd and often provide castrating and vaccinating services. Poultry hatcheries employ several types of animal caretakers to vaccinate poultry, place eggs in trays in incubators, and take care of baby chicks being used in experimental tests.

Crop Service Workers

They provide custom crop services or general crop services, often on a contractual basis. Although most crop services are provided by self-employed individuals or small businesses with ten or fewer employees, larger service businesses employ people with professional and technical skills, as well as laborers and machine operators. Professional managers are needed to direct the work of employees, as well as manage the business. Also, professional farm managers, who are generally college trained, provide farm management services for absentee landowners and their tenants. They schedule the plowing, fertilizing, planting, cultivating, and harvesting of fields and the marketing of crops and livestock. Other occupations in this field require specialized equipment or technical skills that can be learned through technical or on-the-job training. For example, agricultural pilots and their assistants mix agricultural chemicals and apply them while flying airplanes or helicopters over fields at low altitudes. They also seed an increasing number of fields from the air. In addition, some airplane mechanics are employed to repair and maintain agricultural aircraft.

General Services Workers

Usually special equipment is needed to work in this field. For example, grain elevator operators who have grain drying equipment may provide grain drying and storage service, and agricultural chemical dealers may provide fertilizer hauling and spreading and crop dusting services. Farmers who own special equipment sometimes may supplement their income by providing such services as corn shelling, hay baling, and threshing to farmers in their area. Employees of seasonal service businesses often must work long hours and six or seven days a week during the busy season.

Farm Labor Contractors and Crew Leaders

These workers need no special training. They must establish contacts, however, with farmers and farm managers to whom they supply farm laborers, especially harvest laborers, on a contractual basis at specified times of the year. Farm laborers employed by contractors and crew leaders receive better social security coverage by having only one employer.

There are dozens of agribusiness jobs that, as defined earlier, are in off-farm settings that demand agricultural knowledge or skills. Some can be learned in a few days by persons who have lived or worked in rural areas or on farms. Others require training in technical schools, junior colleges, colleges, and universities for periods of time varying from a few months to as long as several years. Although all industries offer some agribusiness jobs, they tend to be concentrated in the manufacturing, trade, agricultural services, and government sectors.

Since agribusiness occupations are so varied and numerous, it is impossible to cover them all. The concentration will be on professional and technical occupations. Here are some of the major ones:

Agricultural Accountants

They prepare and analyze financial reports that managers use to make important decisions. They may specialize in tax matters, such as preparing income tax forms and advising about tax advantages and disadvantages of certain business decisions. Accountants employed by hardware and farm supply retail businesses, such as dairy equipment stores and farm machinery stores, often need a knowledge of agriculture.

Agricultural Marketing Specialists

They survey wholesalers, retailers, and consumers; analyze data on products and sales; and prepare sales forecasts that businesses use to make decisions relating to product design and advertising. The results of their research are used by food processing companies to create food products that consumers will buy, and by agricultural suppliers to develop products for agribusiness and industrial firms. Marketing specialists also work for commodity brokerage firms, farm organizations, cooperative marketing and purchasing organizations, and research divisions of the federal government.

Agricultural Economists

They deal with problems related to producing, financing, pricing, and marketing farm products. They provide information to policymakers, agribusinesses, farmers, and other sectors of the agriculture industry. Many work for the United States Department of Agriculture, developing cost-benefit analyses for evaluating farm programs at the national, state, and local levels. As part of their analyses, economists study the effects of mechanization and technological advances on, for example, the supply of and demand for farm products and the resulting impact on costs and prices. Others work for farm lending institutions, such as rural banks, the Farmers Home Administration, the Federal Land Bank, and insurance companies that make loans to farmers, determining the feasibility of loan programs and individual loans. Many agricultural economists also work for businesses that manufacture products and provide services for farmers, such as farm equipment. Still others work for agribusiness firms that market agricultural products at both retail and wholesale levels. Agricultural economists who have advanced degrees may teach at colleges and universities. There are also opportunities for agricultural economists in the Foreign Service, conducting research to improve the productivity of agriculture abroad.

Agricultural Communicators

This is a more recent and already overcrowded field. It has been affected, as have all the communications fields, by the increased interest in the media that followed the Watergate scandals in the early 1970s. Agricultural communicators keep farmers, consumers, and others concerned with agricultural industry abreast of current developments in farm technology, research, and consumer products. Crop reporters and market news reporters are employed by the United States Department of Agriculture in field offices throughout the United States. They gather information on crop production through the growing season and on the movement of produce from farm to market. Agricultural journalists collect farm news and data for publication in farm journals, magazines, and bulletins. They also are employed as farm directors at radio and television stations in farming areas to report on prices, sales, crop conditions, and other agricultural information of importance to farm communities. Still others work in communications departments of agribusiness firms to develop advertisements and public relations bulletins. (See chapter fourteen for more information about communicators.)

Agricultural Educators

They teach at all levels in all subjects, including farm management, agricultural production, agricultural supplies and services, operation and repair of farm equipment and structures, inspection and processing of farm products, and ornamental horticulture. Professors of agriculture at colleges and universities do research and write as well as teach. This is a growing area of employment of professional workers in the field of agriculture because of the constant changes in production processes and technological innovations in farming.

Cooperative Extension Service Workers

They do educational work in such fields as agricultural production and home economics and may conduct agricultural educational programs through youth groups, such as 4-H clubs. They do a lot of traveling and public speaking and may be frequent guests on radio and television programs. They also give how-to demonstrations and teach classes.

Rural Sociologists

They study the structure and functions of social institutions—customs, practices, and laws—that are a part of rural society and thus affect farm residents.

Agricultural Engineers

They develop the physical layouts of farms—the placement of barns, sheds, irrigation systems, and other facilities used to carry out production. They also may work for manufacturers of farm implements and machinery, designing equipment that enables farmers to increase their production. Others design improved farm structures, or work for electric utility companies developing efficient methods of utilizing electric power on farms and in food processing. This field is discussed more fully in chapter eleven on engineering.

Agricultural and Biological Technicians

They are para-professionals, working with engineers and scientists in research, development, control, and testing. These fields are discussed in chapter thirteen on engineering and scientific technicians.

Agricultural Commodity Graders

They inspect samples of agricultural products to determine their quality and grade and then issue grading certificates. They generally specialize in the inspection and grading of one particular commodity, such as eggs, vegetables, fresh fruits, dairy products, or grain. Grain inspectors inspect large quantities of grain for the presence of parasites, spoilage, or impurities, such as weeds. They also inspect ships for sanitation prior to loading for transport. Most grain inspectors are employed by federal and state agencies, but some are employed by large buyers of grain, such as breweries. Meat and poultry inspectors are employed by the United States Department of Agriculture and by many state departments of agriculture. They work under the supervision of veterinarians and inspect meat and poultry slaughtering, processing, and packaging operations to insure that proper sanitation is maintained in all phases of processing. They also inspect meat additives and make sure that processed meats are labeled correctly.

Cotton Classers

They use the standards for various grades of cotton established by the United States Department of Agriculture to classify cotton samples on the basis of color, fiber length, and presence of impurities.

Tobacco Graders

They examine the size, color, and texture of tobacco at auctions and certify the quality according to the federal classification system.

Cooperative Workers

They work in local or regional cooperatives where farmers can buy many of their supplies, such as seed, feed, and fertilizer, as well as household goods in large volume and thus at lower retail prices. In addition, cooperatives provide marketing services so that individual farmers do not need to locate buyers for their products. Some also operate local stores. Local branches of cooperatives are found in nearly every rural community and in many small and medium-sized cities, although regional offices of large cooperatives often are located in large metropolitan areas.

Cooperatives employ persons with many different skills. Stock clerks and feedstore managers are employed in local stores. Cooperatives also employ college-trained business managers to operate the cooperatives. Regional cooperatives employ sales representatives, wholesalers, and brokers to contact buyers for large grocery chains, food processing firms, and agricultural exporters to arrange contracts for the sale of agricultural products. They also employ purchasing agents and buyers to arrange volume purchases of seed, feed, fertilizers, and other supplies.

Farm Equipment Dealership Workers

They must know the needs of farmers in their area and stock the latest equipment and machinery to meet those needs. They demonstrate and sell equipment, and service and repair the machinery that is sold. Dealerships often have parts departments and thus employ parts sales workers. In addition, large dealerships often employ secretarial and other clerical workers.

Agricultural Chemical Industry Workers

They are professional and technical workers with agricultural training who are involved with the manufacture, distribution, and application of chemical products. These are covered in chapter eleven on engineering and in chapter thirteen on engineering technology.

One of the most important fields in agriculture is that of agricultural science. These are the life scientists who conduct research vital to the development of more productive plants and animals and better food products for consumers. There are many specialties within this field, some of which include:

Agronomists

They conduct experiments in field crop problems and develop new methods of growing crops to make farming more efficient, obtain higher yields, and improve quality. They study methods of planting, cultivating, and harvesting field crops such as cereals, grains, legumes, grasses, cotton, and tobacco. They also study the effect of various climates on crop production.

Plant Pathologists

They study the causes of plant diseases to develop methods to control noxious weeds, insects, and plant diseases.

Plant Physiologists

They study structure of plants and factors which affect their growth, such as respiration, metabolism, and reproduction. They also are concerned with methods of improving the storage life of fruits and vegetables.

Horticulturists

They work with orchard and garden plants, such as fruit and nut trees, vegetables, and flowers. They seek to improve plant culture methods for the beautification of communities, homes, parks, and other areas as well as increasing crop quality and yields.

Geneticists

They try to develop strains, varieties, breeds, and hybrids of plants and animals that are better suited than those presently available for the production of food and fiber.

Microbiologists

They study bacteria and other micro-organisms to understand better their relation to human, plant, and animal health, and to learn how these micro-organisms function in the production of vitamins, antibiotics, amino acids, alcohols, and sugars.

Animal Physiologists

They study the functions of various parts of the bodies of livestock.

Animal Scientists

They are concerned with production and management of farm animals. They conduct research in the selection, breeding, feeding, and marketing of farm animals and develop improved methods of housing, sanitation, and parasite and disease control. Some are called animal nutritionists and specialize in finding feed requirements that will maximize production and in developing new livestock and poultry feeds.

Entomologists

They study beneficial and harmful insects. They identify the populations and distributions of insects that injure agricultural products during growth, shipping, storage, processing, and distribution. Their research is directed toward finding ways to control harmful insects and manage beneficial ones.

Human Nutritionists

They study the means by which the body utilizes foods and nutrients, and their relation to health and disease. They also study social, economic, and cultural aspects of food to determine how the diets of people may be improved.

Seed Analysts

They conduct tests on samples of seeds to determine their rate of germination, purity, and noxious-weed content.

Veterinarians

They diagnose, treat, and control diseases and injuries among animals. They help prevent the outbreak and spread of animal diseases, many of which can be transmitted to humans. They treat animals in hospitals and clinics or on farms and ranches. They perform surgery on sick and injured animals and prescribe and administer drugs, medicines, and vaccines. There are a number of specialties within the field, which has about 33,500 veterinarians working in it, most of whom are in private practice and specialize. Some treat small animals or pets exclusively. Others work with cattle, poultry, sheep, swine, or horses. Still others inspect meat, poultry, or other foods as part of federal and state public health programs. A smaller group teaches and does research related to animal diseases, foods, and drugs. The kind of practice is dictated by geographic setting, with veterinarians in rural areas working with farm animals and those in urban and suburban areas working with pets. Many young people considering outdoor careers want to be veterinarians, but fail to realize the educational requirements, the minimum for which is six years of college. Veterinary schools have limited enrollments and high entry qualifications. For more information about the specifics of this field, which are very different from most of the other jobs in agriculture and agribusiness, consult the appendix.

Agricultural Chemists

They conduct research to improve crop yield and promote soil conservation. They develop chemical compounds for use in controlling insects, weeds, fungi, and rodents. They also perform experiments to determine proper usage of fertilizers and investigate the problems of nitrogen fixation in soils.

Food Chemists

They are divided by type of food or problem such as dairy products, cereal, food preservation, new foods, etc. They study how various methods of preserving foods affect nutrition content, and taste and test food samples to ensure that they meet government standards for quality and purity.

Pharmacologists and Toxicologists

They conduct tests on animals, such as rats, guinea pigs, and monkeys, to determine the effects of drugs, gases, poisons, dusts, and other substances on the functioning of tissues and organs. Pharmacologists may develop new or improved drugs and medicines.

Soil Scientists

They study the physical, chemical, biological, and behavioral characteristics of soils. These studies have many applications. Sometimes the information is used to prepare maps, usually based on aerial photography, which show soil types throughout an area as well as landscape features, such as streams or hills, and physical features, such as roads. Soil maps are used by urban and regional planners as well as by farmers. Soil scientists may test and develop fertilizers for particular soils and try to find ways to improve less productive soils. They may also investigate and study the effect of plant growth on organic materials in soils. (See also the soil conservation section in chapter nine.)

What are the requirements for an agricultural or agribusiness career? Agribusiness imposes fewer problems than farming because, although farming may be the ideal career for people who enjoy working outdoors and being their own bosses, it is very demanding, and only persons with a great deal of initiative and a sense of responsibility can expect to be successful.

Farmers often must work long hours. A six- or seven-day work week is common during busy seasons and the rule on certain types of farms, such as dairy and livestock farms. Earnings of farmers vary greatly from year to year and by type and size of farm. Prices of farm products fluctuate greatly, depending on weather conditions that determine the amount and quality of products produced. A farm that shows a large profit in one year may show a loss in the following year. Here are some figures for the late 1970s. Dairy farmers with forty cows and an investment of $190,500 earned about $19,800. Ranchers with an investment of about $659,000 earned $34,700. Grain farmers with about 375 acres and an investment of $480,000 earned about $35,500. In each case, the farmers were self-employed and had to provide their own benefits, such as health and life insurance.

Farm laborers are among the lowest paid workers in the field. Average hourly earnings are about $3.07. In comparison, average hourly earnings of all production workers in non-agricultural industries are $5.69. Average wage rates for farm workers range from $2.84 an hour for field and livestock workers to $4.91 an hour for farm labor supervisors. In general, workers paid on a piece-rate basis earn more than those who receive a straight hourly wage. In addition to their wages, some hired farm workers receive room and board allowances. Almost no farm workers receive paid vacations, sick leave, or health benefits.

Earnings in agribusiness and those "gray" occupations between farming and agribusiness are much better than in farming. They correspond to comparable areas in other fields. On the average, entry level salaries are at least $10,500 for positions that require a bachelor's degree. The top jobs in the field range from $25,000 to $35,000. But remember, these figures are generalizations. They could be lower—or higher—for some jobs.

An examination of these figures is not encouraging. Most farmers do not get rich. Certain abilities and skills, however, will improve

their chances for success. They should be willing to try new processes and to adapt to constantly changing technologies to produce
their crops or raise their livestock more efficiently. They must have
enough technical knowledge of crops and growing conditions and
plant and animal diseases to be able to make decisions that insure
the successful operation of their farms. They must have the managerial skills necessary to organize and operate a business. Mechanical
aptitude and the ability to work with tools of all kinds also are
valuable skills for the operator of a small farm who often must maintain and repair his own machinery or structures. A basic knowledge
of accounting and bookkeeping can be helpful in keeping financial
records. Finally, a knowledge of credit sources is essential.

Because of the complexities of modern scientific farming and
the need to keep up with advances in farming methods, an increasing
number of young farmers find it desirable to get additional training
at a two- or four-year college of agriculture. A degree in agriculture
is almost essential for persons who wish to farm, but who have not
had the advantage of living or working on a farm in their youth.
Growing up on a family farm and participating in such farming programs for young people as the Future Farmers of America or the
4-H clubs still is an important source of training for farmers.

Most colleges of agriculture offer major programs of study in
such areas as dairy science, agricultural economics, horticulture,
crop science, and animal science. Colleges also usually offer special
programs of study concerning products important to the area in
which they are located, such as grain science programs at colleges
in plains states. These same schools offer programs in all of the
agribusiness fields.

Some of the areas in agriculture and agribusiness require specialized education, for example, veterinary medicine. Another is agricultural science. Any specialty within this field requires the same
intensive education as the biological sciences, discussed in chapter
seven. Top jobs in this field will require a Ph.D. degree as pointed
out in this chapter.

Agricultural educators, cooperative extension service workers,
and rural sociologists also have slightly different educational demands. The agriculture colleges have or can devise programs in these
fields.

The thing to remember is to research your particular fields of interest thoroughly, including checking out schools in which you are interested to be sure that they have the programs you need.

One final word should be said about agricultural and agribusiness workers. They should be in excellent physical condition. Physical stamina and strength are important, especially to those who do farm work, since they must often work long days, standing on their feet, stooping over under the sun, or lifting heavy items. In addition, some farm-related work can be extremely hazardous.

Each year, many farm workers suffer debilitating injuries from machinery. Also, farm workers are subject to illnesses and diseases from handling and breathing dangerous pesticides and chemicals and from handling crops that have been sprayed with them. In addition to these problems, health care in rural areas sometimes is inadequate or too expensive to meet the needs of farm workers.

We have met the enemy . . . and he is us.
From the cartoon feature *Pogo* by Walt Kelly

9

A Tolerable Planet:
A Place to Work and Play

"What is the use of a house if you haven't got a tolerable planet to put it on?" Henry David Thoreau asked more than a century ago. Today, conservationists are still echoing his question and still fighting the battle Thoreau and others began to save the natural resources of the country.

The conservationists make up one of the major fields of outdoor careerists. They are concerned with the protection and use of our natural resources—the forests, soil, water, minerals, and wildlife. They guard these resources for future generations.

The conservationists are foresters, range managers, soil conservationists, wildlife managers, fisheries managers, and dozens of others in jobs related to these fields. Included in this career field also are the recreation specialists—park rangers, park guards, park police, snow and wilderness rangers, program directors, teachers of individual activities and sports, and hundreds of aides, technicians, and

141

maintenance workers. These recreation specialists help people learn to play sanely, that is, to utilize the resources without destroying them. Recreation actually is considered one of the five basic uses for resources. The others are forage, timber, water, and wildlife.

Most of the jobs in conservation and recreation are under the direction of federal, state, and local governments. By far, the largest employer is the federal government through four agencies administering the major natural lands—the Bureau of Land Management, with 470 million acres; the Forest Service, with 187 million acres; the Fish and Wildlife Service, with 31 million acres; and the National Park Service, with 27 million acres. These lands, with others in the country designated primarily for recreation, make up less than 5 percent of the 2.3 billion acres of land in the fifty states.

It is impossible to cover all of the possible jobs in conservation in this book. In the five main conservation fields alone, more than 100,000 people work. In recreation, where jobs are harder to count, about a million people work, making it one of the largest outdoor career fields today.

Since the major employer is the federal government, these jobs have much in common in terms of job-seeking. Most of them are civil service positions, controlled by the hiring procedures of the Office of Personnel Management. Applying for civil service positions is outlined in chapter six, and people interested in these jobs should study this section carefully.

Salaries within this field are similar also. Entry level employees usually earn about $10,000, although some jobs pay less. Hard work usually pays off in advancement and pay raises, however, and salaries of about $20,000 are the median.

The conservationists all need similar backgrounds. To qualify for college work, high school students should get as broad an educational background as they can, with a heavy concentration in sciences, including chemistry, physics, mathematics, and both environmental and biological sciences. The humanities are important, as is oral and written communication. These studies are continued in college with emphasis on individual specialties. Economics and business administration are important supplementary courses. Computer science is becoming increasingly so.

College is necessary for top level jobs. While entry level positions may require only two years of college or a technical school education, promotion in most areas depends on an advanced degree.

Another important factor in getting entry level jobs is experience. As in so many other outdoor career fields, early experience gives job applicants an edge in being hired for choice positions. The subject is heavily covered in chapter three and should be reviewed in conjunction with this one.

Conservationists and recreation specialists must be able to work well with people. Although they spend much of their time in the wilds, they deal with people constantly—their staffs, other professionals, representatives of special interest groups, and the general public. An understanding of the social and behavioral sciences is vital.

One other thing conservationists and recreational workers have in common is the necessity for being healthy. They spend considerable time outdoors in all kinds of weather, sometimes in remote areas. They should have exceptional physical stamina, good vision, and be willing to contend with snakes, insects, and other hazards of the outdoors. A current driver's license is also usually a requirement.

Each of the conservation fields and recreation will be considered separately.

Foresters

Forests are one of our most important natural resources. About 750 million acres, or one-third of the land in the fifty states, is covered with forests. All of the states have forest lands, even heavily populated, industrial states like New York and New Jersey. And in spite of popular mythology, forests are not declining. For the last three decades, the United States has been replacing trees.

The forests provide trees for building materials, paper, fuel, and a variety of other uses. They help clean the air we breathe and protect our water supplies. They make a home for wildlife. They are a major source of recreational opportunities for people. They are the basis of jobs for more than 300,000 people.

Because of the multiple demands on them, the forests must be managed, developed, and protected, or they simply will not be available for use by future generations. Foresters are trained professionals who help manage, develop, and protect our vital forest resources.

Several men have been responsible for promoting forestry as a career. Foremost was Gifford Pinchot, often called the "father" of professional forestry in America. He was chief of the Forest Service from 1898 until 1910, working with President Theodore Roosevelt to instigate sound conservation practices in American forests. Later he was professor of forestry at Yale University and founder of the Pinchot School of Forestry at Yale. He also served as commissioner of forestry for the state of Pennsylvania and was governor of Pennsylvania twice.

Another great forester was Dr. Bernard E. Fernow, the very first head of the Forest Service. He organized the first collegiate school of professional forestry in the United States at Cornell University.

Foresters today, like Pinchot and Fernow in the past, plan and supervise the growing, protection, and utilization of trees. They make maps of forest areas, estimate the amount of standing timber and future growth, and manage timber sales. They also protect the trees from fire, harmful insects, and disease.

Some foresters may be responsible for other duties ranging from wildlife protection and watershed management to the development and supervision of camps, parks, and grazing lands. Other foresters do research, provide information to forest owners and to the general public (called extension work), and teach in colleges and universities.

Foresters often specialize in one area of work, such as timber management or forest economics. Some of these areas are recognized as distinct professions.

Working conditions for foresters vary considerably according to the type of work they perform. The old image of foresters as solitary horseback riders, single-handedly protecting large areas of land from civilization no longer holds true. Modern foresters spend much of their time working with people. They must deal constantly with landowners, loggers, forestry aides, and a wide variety of other people.

Many experienced foresters advance to jobs in offices, where they use maps and computers to plan and organize the activities of the staff.

Over 25,000 people work as foresters. Two out of five of them work in private industry, mainly for pulp and paper, lumber, logging, and milling companies. About one-quarter work for the federal government, primarily in the Forest Service of the Department of Agriculture. The remainder work for state and local governments, colleges and universities, or consulting firms, or they are self-employed either as consultants or as forest owners.

A bachelor's degree with a major in forestry is a minimum educational requirement for entry level jobs in forestry. As pointed out earlier, advanced degrees are necessary for promotion to top level jobs. Certain jobs, such as teaching and research, require advanced degrees.

Education in forestry leading to a bachelor's degree is offered by fifty colleges and universities, of which forty-three are accredited by the Society of American Foresters. Curricula stress the liberal arts and communications skills, as well as technical forestry subjects. Courses in forest economics and business administration supplement the student's scientific and technical knowledge. Many colleges require students to spend one summer in a field camp operated by the college. All schools encourage summer jobs that give firsthand experience in forest and conservation work.

Foresters are supported by paraprofessionals known as forestry technicians, who sometimes return to school for more education and become foresters. There are about 13,000 forestry technicians working year-around in private industry, mainly for logging, lumber, and paper companies; in reforestation projects of mining, oil, and railroad companies; and in tree nurseries. The federal government employs about 4,000 full-time forestry technicians, primarily in the Forest Service of the United States Department of Agriculture. Two thousand more work for state governments. Another 13,000 forestry technicians are hired every spring and summer, primarily by federal and state governments, to fight forest fires.

Forestry technicians, also sometimes called forestry aides in entry level positions, assist foresters in the care and management of forest lands and their resources. For example, they help estimate present and potential timber production in a certain area. If new roads are needed to make the timber accessible for cutting and removal, technicians may supervise the survey and road-building crews. After the timber has been cut, they measure the logs to determine how much lumber the trees will yield and then assist in the sale of the timber.

Technicians work on many forest improvement projects. They

inspect trees for disease and other problems and record their find-ings. On watershed projects, they work to prevent flood damage and soil erosion and seek ways to preserve the quality of water in the forest. They also help to prevent and control fires. They give fire prevention information to people using the forest and lead fire-fighting crews if a fire occurs. After fires are extinguished, they take inventory of burned areas and supervise the planting of new trees and shrubs to restore the forest.

Recreational use of forests has increased greatly. Technicians maintain forest areas for hunting, camping, hiking, and other rec-reational activities. They also explain forest regulations and policies to visitors and enforce the rules.

Forestry graduates usually work under the supervision of ex-perienced foresters. After gaining experience, they may advance to more responsible positions. In the federal government, an experi-enced forester may supervise an entire forest area, ultimately ad-vancing to regional forest supervisor or to a top administration po-sition. In private industry, foresters start by learning the practical and administrative aspects of the business. Many foresters work their way up to top managerial positions within their companies.

Foresters entering federal government service with a bachelor's degree start at $10,507. Because competition is keen, however, most foresters hired by the federal government hold a master's degree or have some experience and generally start at $13,672 a year. Holders of the Ph.D. generally start at $18,585 a year. The average yearly salary is about $22,000.

Local and state government starting salaries for foresters are about the same as federal salaries, but average yearly salaries are $5,000 to $6,000 lower. College professors with Ph.D.'s start at about $14,000; their average salaries are the same as for federal foresters. In private industry, starting foresters get $12,000; the overall average salary is $21,000.

Starting salaries of forestry technicians range from $8,000 to $10,000 a year. In federal jobs, they are paid $8,951 to $9,766, de-pending on education and experience. Experienced forestry tech-nicians, both in private industry and in federal jobs, average about $13,000.

Range Managers

Rangelands cover more than one billion acres of the United States, mostly in the Western states and Alaska. They contain many natural resources: grass and shrubs for animal grazing, habitats for livestock and wildlife, water from vast watersheds, facilities for water sports and other kinds of recreation, and valuable mineral and energy resources. Rangelands also serve as areas for scientific study of the environment.

Range managers—sometimes called range scientists, range ecologists, or range conservationists—manage, improve, and protect range resources to maximize their use without damaging the environment. For example, range managers help ranchers improve and increase livestock production by determining the number and kind of animals to graze, the grazing system to use, and the best season for grazing. At the same time, however, they conserve the soil and vegetation for other uses, such as wildlife habitat, outdoor recreation, and timber. While in the field, they may evaluate the water supply and types of vegetation available, take soil samples, and estimate the number of deer and other wildlife on the land.

Range managers restore and improve rangelands through controlled burning, reseeding, and biological, chemical, or mechanical control of undesirable plants. For example, some rangelands that have been invaded by sagebrush or other shrubs may be plowed and reseeded with more desirable plants. Range managers also determine the need for, and carry out, range conservation and development plans that provide water for grazing animals, erosion control, and fire prevention.

Range managers usually begin their careers on the range. They often spend considerable time away from home and work outdoors in all kinds of weather. Employers generally supply small planes, cars or, in rough country, four-wheel-drive vehicles or horses for range managers to get around. Occasionally they may walk.

There is much more to the job than simply riding the range, however. Range managers must deal constantly with other people, including the public, ranchers, government agencies, and persons who specialize in other areas of conservation. In some cases, they may work as part of a team.

Not all of a range manager's time is spent outdoors. Office work is not unusual. The range manager may consult with other conservation specialists, prepare written reports, and do administrative work.

About 3,500 persons work as range managers. The majority work for the federal government, principally for the Forest Service and the Soil Conservation Service of the Department of Agriculture, the Bureau of Indian Affairs, and the Bureau of Land Management of the Department of the Interior. Range managers in state government are employed in game and fish departments, state land agencies, and extension services.

An increasing number of range managers work for private industry. Coal and oil companies employ range managers to help restore or reclaim mined areas. Banks and real estate firms employ them to help increase the revenue from their holdings. Other range managers work for private consulting firms and large ranches.

Some range managers who have advanced degrees teach and do research at colleges and universities. Other range managers work overseas with United States and United Nations agencies and with foreign governments. Many foreign countries, however, are now beginning to train their own citizens in range management.

A bachelor's degree is range management or range science is the usual minimum educational requirement, and it is offered by about twenty colleges and universities. A number of other schools offer course work in range management. Graduate degrees in range management generally are required for teaching and research positions and may be helpful for advancement in other jobs.

The specialized courses for range management or range science combine plant, and soil sciences with principles of ecology and resource management. Desirable electives include economics, computer science, forestry, hydrology, wildlife, and recreation.

Federal agencies, primarily the Forest Service, the Soil Conservation Service, and the Bureau of Land Management hire college students for summer jobs in range management. This experience may better qualify these students for jobs when they graduate.

In federal government jobs, range managers with a bachelor's degree start at $10,963. Those having one or two years of graduate work begin at $13,672. Ph.D.'s get $16,826. All may earn slightly more if they have excellent grades. Average yearly salaries are $20,000. Salaries for range managers who work for state governments and private companies are about the same as those paid by the federal government.

Soil Conservationists

Historically, soil conservation was one of the earliest conservation fields developed. All the great ancient agricultural countries practiced it and the Europeans brought it to the New World with them. Northern European farmers as a group were the greatest conservationists, practicing both crop rotation and erosion control. Two colonial presidents, George Washington and Thomas Jefferson, instituted similar programs on their Virginia plantations and urged their neighbors to do the same. Jefferson's journals show that he used gypsum and clover to encourage fertility. He also plowed horizontally to prevent soil erosion. Washington had his slaves lug pails of Potomac River mud to his eroded fields to fill in the gullies.

The real hero of modern soil conservation, though, was Hugh H. Bennett, an Illinois farmer, who became the innovative 1930s director of the Soil Conservation Service. His job was to repair and reclaim more than 300 million acres of farm and ranch land in the drought-plagued midwestern "Dust Bowl." The problem was so severe that red dust fallout colored the snow in New England 2,000 miles away and hid the sun in Washington 1,500 miles away. To win support for his policies, Bennett dramatized the problem to congressmen by proving to them that the dust on their windowsills in the Capitol in Washington, D.C. came from the plains of the midwest. Then, using the funds they appropriated to deal with the problem, he created the Soil Conservation District, a concept which provided advice and technical assistance to land users, but encouraged them to do the bulk of the work themselves. His theory: involvement will make the effort more meaningful and therefore more lasting; it will also be cheaper. He advocated contour plowing, terracing, crop rotation, and strip planting. Although not 100 percent successful, his measures did result in returning much of the damaged land to productivity, either for grazing or growing crops.

Bennett's innovative program is still the backbone of the United States Department of Agriculture's Soil Conservation Service, one of the two agencies where most of the soil conservationists in the United States work.

Soil conservationists have broad duties. They provide technical assistance to farmers, ranchers, and others concerned with the conservation of soil and water. They help farmers and other land managers develop programs that make the most productive use of land without damaging it. Soil conservationists do most of their work in the field. If a farmer is experiencing an erosion problem, the soil conservationist will visit the farm, find the source of the problem, and develop a program to combat the erosion. For example, if the erosion is caused by water runoff on sloped fields, the soil conservationist may recommend ways to terrace the land or construct waterways for the runoff that do not remove soil. If erosion results from wind, the solution might be growing hedges in places that will provide windbreaks, or leaving wheat or corn stalks on the fields after harvesting to provide ground cover.

Soil conservationists inspect rangeland and recommend to farmers areas where ponds can be constructed to provide water for livestock. They also recommend solutions to problems of overgrazing, such as seeding grasslands or placing salt licks in undergrazed areas to keep livestock away from areas that have been overgrazed.

Soil conservationists pay close attention to weather patterns in order to be aware of possible conservation problems before they arise. During the winter months they make periodic snowmobile or ski patrols into the Rockies and other mountainous areas of the West to measure snowfall. This enables them to predict the spring and summer water runoff. In a year when snowfall is light, they alert irrigation districts, farmers, and other water users to possible water shortages and develop appropriate water conservation measures.

In addition to working with individual farmers and ranchers, soil conservationists work as technical advisors to Soil and Water Conservation Districts when solving area-wide land management problems. A Soil and Water Conservation District is made up of farmers and other land users within a county who are concerned with, and responsible for, conservation problems within the area. Soil conservationists working with conservation districts prepare maps of the district, or parts of the district, depicting particular problems of soil and water conservation. They then use the maps to plan and develop a conservation program for the entire area, whether it is only a few farms and ranches or an entire watershed.

Most of the 9,000 soil conservationists in this country are employed by the federal government in the United States Department of Agriculture's Soil Conservation Service or by the Department of the Interior's Bureau of Indian Affairs. Soil conservationists, employed by the Department of Agriculture, work with Soil and Water Conservation Districts in almost every county in the country. Those employed by the Bureau of Indian Affairs generally work on or near Indian reservations.

Smaller numbers of soil conservationists are employed by state and local governments, and some teach at colleges and universities. A few others are employed by rural banks, insurance firms, and mortgage companies that make loans for agricultural lands. Still others work for public utilities and lumber and paper companies that have large holdings of forested lands.

Very few colleges and universities offer degrees with a major in soil conservation. Most soil conservationists, expecially those employed by the Soil Conservation Service, have degrees in agronomy, agricultural education, or general agriculture. A few soil conservationists have degrees in related fields of the natural sciences, such as wildlife biology or forestry or range management. Course work should include thirty semester hours in natural resources or agriculture, including at least three hours in soils.

A background in agricultural engineering is very helpful in soil conservation, as are courses in cartography, or mapmaking.

Opportunities for advancement are somewhat limited. However, conservationists working at the county level can advance to the state level. Also, soil conservationists can transfer to related occupations such as farm management advisors or land appraisers. Those with advanced degrees may find teaching opportunities in colleges and universities.

Soil conservationists, beginning their careers in a federal agency in any of the jobs discussed, who have a bachelor's degree, earn $10,963 a year; those who have a master's degree start at $13,672. Earnings of well-qualified federal soil conservationists with several year's experience range from $19,263 to $32,442.

Wildlife and Fisheries Managers

Wildlife management and fisheries management, while taking place in the same areas, are completely different sciences, each with many different specialties. Sometimes when funding is tight or when an area is small, one person serves both functions.

The Fish and Wildlife Service maintains 384 national wildlife refuges, of which 276 are set aside specifically for 100 million ducks, geese, or swans. They also operate twenty wetland management districts. In all, these refuges encompass 24 million acres. In addition, state and local agencies and private organizations set aside millions of more acres.

Man-made reservoirs as well as farm ponds boost the fish conservation resources of thousands of streams, rivers, and lakes from small trout streams to the Mississippi River to the Great Lakes. There are over ten million acres of reservoirs and over one million farm ponds. More than 1,700 public and private fish hatcheries help stock these areas.

Both wildlife managers and fisheries managers work in wildlife refuges, public forests, and on privately owned lands to preserve, protect, and manage wildlife and fish populations. The professions are relatively new and were created as a result of the work of Aldo Leopold, a forester, who in the early 1930s developed the concept of providing refuge areas with balanced habitats (that is, the right number of animals and their predators in a suitable environment) for specific animals.

Leopold's work led to congressional legislation that improved resources for wildlife management and created many jobs in the field. Basically, the laws levied an excise tax on the sale of guns and ammunition. Funds thus raised were used to create and manage refuges and to set up additional research programs.

Most areas used as wildlife refuges also are used for hunting, fishing, and other recreational purposes as well as commercial activities such as timber production and logging. Wildlife managers juggle all these activities in order to plan conservation programs. They organize surveys and censuses to determine the number of animals and birds in an area. The results are used to set hunting limits and to plan other work, such as restocking of game birds, preventing and controlling diseases in wildlife, and removing diseased wildlife.

In keeping with Leopold's original research, one of the main jobs of wildlife managers is to provide a favorable environment in which desirable species will reproduce. This means making available suitable water, food, and cover while at the same time controlling species that are harmful to wildlife, crops, or timber production.

Fisheries management is even newer than wildlife management. It has benefited from much of the same legislation, but the main funds came as a result of the Dingel-Johnson Act passed in 1950 which provided for matching funds for states to use in fish conservation, including the formulation of new fishing laws and additional research.

Fisheries managers work with fish culture, fisheries management, fish biology, fish nutrition, water pollution control, fish diseases, and fish parasite control.

Wildlife and fisheries managers usually supervise teams of technicians and aides who handle the physical labor involved in habitat development and supervision. With additional training, some of these workers might become managers themselves.

Wildlife and fisheries managers also work closely with wildlife biologists who are involved with research at fish hatcheries and experimental laboratories and whose professions are described in chapter seven on life scientists.

Salaries for wildlife and fisheries managers vary widely with experience and place of employment. The median is probably close to that of federal agency employees who earn starting salaries of $10,000 to $15,000. Technicians and aides earn substantially less.

A job related to that of wildlife and fisheries managers is game warden, who in recent years has been called also game protector or a game management officer. The positions are administered on a national level by The Fish and Wildlife Service and by state Fish and Game Commissions. The work is to enforce hunting and fishing regulations and usually involves heavy public relations, such as educational programs in schools and public speaking before civic and sports organizations. The pay is low—entry level salaries can be less than $8,000 a year—but the competition is keen. Recently, the Pennsylvania Fish and Game Commission had more than 1,000 applications for a handful of jobs.

An important adjunct to The Fish and Wildlife Service is the Youth Conservation Service, which operates 103 camps at refuges and fish hatcheries across the country. These camps, for young men and women 16 to 23, provide a chance to work in many conservation-related projects. The service itself is modeled on the 1930's Civilian Conservation Corps.

During the 1970s, the Youth Conservation Service completed more than $2.5 million worth of projects, including timber management, range management, wildlife habitat improvements, and soil and water conservation projects. This program was pointed out in chapter three, *Ways and Means,* as one of the many excellent ways to get experience and to give wilderness living and working a trial run.

Conservation Agencies

While not many job opportunities exist in private conservation agencies, it is an area in which anyone interested in the conservation field thinks about working. There are dozens of such agencies—some old and some new—with varying aims. Most of them operate with small staffs, sometimes with only one employee. However, the models for all of them are probably the National Audubon Society or the Sierra Club, two of the oldest, largest, and best known conservation agencies.

The National Audubon Society was established in 1906, growing out of a club founded by George Bird Grinnel, the renowned *Field and Stream* editor. It is named for and honors John James Audubon, the great nineteenth century ornithologist. Based in Audubon House in New York City, it serves 100,000 members, who are divided into 200 local chapters. More than 250 garden clubs, community groups, and other organizations are affiliated with the society and help support its aims, which are "to promote the conservation of wildlife and the natural environment, and to educate man regarding his relationship with, and his place within, the natural environment as an ecological system."

The Audubon Society supports twenty-nine bird sanctuaries, several field programs, several educational programs, an 18,000-volume nature reference library, and a nature photography and information service for media. It publishes *Audubon,* a bimonthly conservation magazine, *Audubon Field Notes,* a six-times-a-year birding journal, and *Audubon Leader,* a twice-monthly newsletter. It also produces wildlife films.

About seventy employees work in New York and as many more at sanctuaries and field locations. There are also 40 part-time lecturers and fifty summer camp teachers and administrators. Competition for these jobs is tremendous.

The Sierra Club was founded by naturalist John Muir in 1892 to encourage people to explore, enjoy, and cherish the wilderness and to help rescue certain wilderness areas from commercial development. The club, under Muir, was instrumental in creating the National Park Service and the Forest Service and in establishing several national parks. It also helped set up the Wilderness Preservation System and the Wild and Scenic Rivers System, and lobbied against building dams that would have destroyed Yosemite and Grand Canyon National Parks and the Dinosaur National Monument.

It is based in San Francisco and serves about 100,000 members in thirty-three chapters. It operates six regional offices, including one in Washington, D.C., which is mainly concerned with lobbying for conservation legislation. Of its sixty-five-member staff, only ten are conservation employees. The organization uses many volunteers to implement its various programs in ecology, conservation, and recreation. Like the Audubon Society it has a publishing program. In addition to books and pamphlets, it prints two magazines, *Sierra Club Bulletin* and the *National News Report*.

While most outdoor careerists may not find jobs at either the Audubon Society or the Sierra Club, they will find membership a boon, providing both information about and contacts in the world of conservation. A list of additional conservation organizations is included in the appendix.

Recreation Specialists

Jobs in recreation cover a much broader area than those discussed so far. True, many of them are with the National Park Service and wildlife refuge areas in wilderness locations, but they also are found in urban and suburban locations. Employers, in addition to federal, state, and local governments, are private recreation clubs, country clubs, leisure-oriented communities, commercial recreation areas, organizations like YWCA's, YMCA's, and Girl and Boy Scouts, camps for both children and adults, and the United States Armed

Forces. More than 200,000 professionals and paraprofessionals work in recreation.

In spite of this large number, the National Recreation and Park Association reports that there are not enough trained people to fill the available professional-level jobs. However, competition remains keen for the top jobs, especially those with the National Park Service. Most strategists say the best way to get a recreation job with the park service is to start at the bottom with a season a job and work up through the ranks. If nothing else is available, take a clerical job. This puts you on the inside where you can find out about recreation openings. Almost all park service jobs require civil service examinations. The procedure is described in chapter six. Some of the National Park Service recreation jobs include:

Seasonal Aides and Technicians

They work throughout the system at every park. About 7,000 are hired each year to boost a permanent National Park Service staff of 10,000. They have similar duties, but technicians have better qualifications and earn slightly more money. To work as a technician, job applicants can offer either experience or college. They need one-and-a-half years general experience directly related to park operation, recreation or conservation work, or two years of college in a program stressing natural science, social science, history, archaeology, police science, park and recreation management, community outdoor recreation, or other disciplines related to park management. Lifeguard certification helps an applicant's chances. A valid driver's license is mandatory. Aides need six months experience and a high school diploma or a certificate of equivalency. Aides and technicians collect fees, fight fires, assist in law enforcement, give nature classes, assist in conservation or restoration work, and serve as guides, dispatchers, or receptionists. They are paid an hourly wage ranging from $3.57 to $4.51, depending on background.

Permanent Aides and Technicians

Many of these positions are filled by former seasonal aides and technicians. A few are hired on the basis of satisfactory college work, usually a bachelor's degree stressing the sciences, social science, and mathematics. They work directly under park rangers on a para-professional level helping with preservation and restoration work in historic and archaelogical areas, with campground operations, with guided tours and nature lectures, and with enforcement work such as road patrol and traffic direction. Experienced technicians can earn more than $20,000.

Park Rangers

They can be foresters, historians, naturalists, or archaeologists, depending on the park in which they work. Rangers at small parks are jacks-of-all-trades. Their work covers recreation activity planning, park organization, financial management, supervision of aides, technicians, and other employees, public safety (including law enforcement and public safety), and public education (including lectures, nature walks, and dramatic presentations). Preparation for the job should involve college training in social and behavioral sciences, field-oriented natural science, history, archaeology, and business administration. Police training and experience is helpful. Starting salaries are $13,014, with advancement to $20,000 possible in a short time. Positions as district ranger and park manager are almost always filled from park ranger ranks and may pay as much as $50,000.

Park Guards

They patrol and protect park property on a full-time, year-round basis. Experience is required. Military service or a background in any law enforcement agency is helpful. Entry level salary is $8,951 or $10,963, depending on experience.

Park Police

They work mostly in the District of Columbia and coordinate their activities closely with the District of Columbia Metropolitan Police Department. Starting positions include the usual patrol and desk work assigned to police officers. Experienced officers also may work with community relations and education. Entry level jobs pay $15,193 with a potential of $20,000. In addition to the civil service exam, park police must be 21 to 31 years old when they apply for the job, have excellent vision, and possess a valid driver's license.

Federal agencies other than the National Park Service have recreation jobs—for example, the Fish and Wildlife Service, the Tennessee Valley Authority, the Forest Service, and the Heritage Conservation and Recreation Service. Most of the jobs are similar to those in the Park Service. One of the most exciting is with the Forest Service as a snow ranger, who during the winter months searches out and issues warnings about avalanches and leads ski patrols and rescue teams. During non-snow weather, they are on the lookout for hunters, backpackers, and horseback riders in trouble. The pay scale for this job and for similar ones in other agencies is the same for similar jobs in the Park Service.

State and local governments have recreational jobs similar to the National Park Service, too. They are likely to pay less. Oil companies and other international companies hire recreation specialists to serve their employees who live abroad. These jobs pay well and usually include an extra allowance to cover transportation, cost of living abroad, and home leaves.

Some of the most sought after recreation jobs are in private clubs or at luxury resorts, where duties range from giving lessons in various sports to working as social directors. This latter involves planning recreational programs for many different people with a wide range of interests.

Acting as a tour guide for wilderness camping trips is another recreation job that appeals to a lot of people. So does running whitewater raft trips, canoe trips, hiking trips, and similar activities. They all provide an opportunity for jobs offering individual freedom by exercising a little entrepreneurial ingenuity. Many such opportunities exist, but they depend on the geographical area. The Pacific Northwest suggests chartering salmon fishing trips; the Caribbean, skin or scuba diving classes; the New England coast, windjammer cruises. Operating a marina, a private campground, a camp for children, or a ski lift are other possibilities. The only limitation to such plans is imagination and the expertise and funds to set up a business. As pointed out before, going into business in the outdoor field is expensive and risky.

Certainly, before deciding to start a recreation-related business, study chapter six, reviewing especially the qualifications and pitfalls.

The background and training required for federal, state, and local recreation jobs is good for other recreational areas, too. However, in jobs where teaching or participation in a particular sport is necessary, a bachelor's degree in physical education and recreation is probably more useful. More than 400 colleges and universities, including institutions with both two-year and four-year programs, have recreation and park curricula. The trick in getting such training is to choose a broad-based program, but to specialize in one sport—for example, swimming. It is also important to take courses in economics, business administration, and the social and behavorial sciences.

10

The Good Earth:
The Environmental Sciences

Environmental scientists, also known as earth scientists, make up the smallest group of all the natural scientists in today's work force—about 53,000 scientists in all, about 5 percent of which are women. The field includes geologists, geophysicists, meteorologists, and oceanographers. In turn, each of these is broken down further into many specialties. In the United States, there are approximately 31,000 geologists, 11,000 geophysicists, 7,300 meteorologists, and 3,600 oceanographers.

The environmental scientists are involved with the history, composition, and characteristics of the earth's surface, interior, and atmosphere. They deal with both basic research and practical application of the knowledge gained from research. As ecologists study living things, environmental scientists study nonliving things, although this division is not without some fuzziness. For example, oceanographers are considered environmental scientists, but one division of

161

oceanography is biological oceanography, also sometimes called marine biology, which is the study of plant and animal life in the ocean. So despite their separate names and their areas of specialization, the environmental sciences are thoroughly interrelated, as well as being related to other fields.

Salaries in the entire environmental science field are excellent. Geologists, geophysicists, meteorologists, and oceanographers earn twice as much as other nonsupervisory workers in private industry, excepting farmers. In a study done by the College Placement Council in early 1979, graduates with bachelor's degrees in physical and earth sciences received average starting offers of $15,400. Graduates with master's degrees received average starting offers of $19,000 per year.

In federal jobs, the salaries are lower, but still good. Entry level salaries are: with a bachelor's degree, $10,963; with a master's degree, $15,193; and with a Ph.D. degree, $18,585. Slightly higher salaries may be paid if the applicant has exceptional grades or offers special course work. The average salary is about $25,900.

The employment outlook for environmental scientists is excellent for those with degrees, but probably not as good as during the 1970s. Any substantial growth in the field is dependent upon government funding. Probably the largest growth will come in geology and geophysics because of the necessity for increased domestic exploration activities based on the increased cost of foreign oil and the exhaustion of older sources of minerals. For example, in the 1980s, new jobs may include the search for more efficient mining methods, mineral exploration (especially using sophisticated electronic techniques), and the development of adequate water supplies and waste disposal methods. Research for alternate power sources such as solar energy or geothermal energy may also develop.

In general, in all the fields, at least a bachelor's degree is required for beginning jobs. Advancement up the career ladder is dependent in most jobs—both in the private sector and in federal, state, and local governments—upon advanced degrees. All federal government jobs fall under the jurisdiction of the Office of Personnel Management; examinations may be required before applying for some jobs.

The base science of the environmental sciences is geology, and the "father" of the field is James Hutton (1726-1797), a Scottish scientist who gave up chemical and medical studies when he became

interested in erosion and geological research. As a result of his studies, he formulated theories of the origin of the earth and atmospheric
changes, which he called the doctrine of uniformity of process. Pres-
ent-day scientists shorten this to uniformitarianism. Contrary to the
eighteenth-century contention that the physical features of the earth
were formed by a series of sudden spectacular events, which scientists called "catastrophes," Hutton believed that "the present is
the key to the past." In his greatest work, *Theory of the Earth*, published in 1795, he postulated that geologic processes currently operating on the earth were also active at about the same rate in past
geologic ages. Therefore, he said, the physical features of the earth
could be explained by observing geologic processes at work over
long periods. For example, in Hutton's view, river valleys were not
the result of sudden cracks in the earth's crust, but of time—the
processes of erosion, weathering, and the continual wearing away
of land by river water. His contemporaries viewed his work with
skepticism, but modern environmental scientists still apply his principles to solve their problems. Modern geology and geophysics have
grown out of Hutton's limited studies.

Within the twin divisions of geology and geophysics are dozens
of specialties. Geologists study the structure, composition, and history of the earth's crust, breaking these into three general areas—earth
material, earth processes, and earth history.

Geophysicists are mainly interested in the physical aspect of the
earth and its electric, magnetic, and gravitational fields. They specialize in one of four areas of the science—solid earth, fluid earth,
upper atmosphere, or planetary study.

Geologists

Geologists concerned with earth material include:

Economic geologists

They search for and develop the earth's materials, such as mineral and fuel resources.

Petroleum geologists

They specialize in locating and recovering oil and natural gas
deposits.

Engineering geologists

They apply geologic and engineering principles to the construction of roads, airfields, tunnels, dams, harbors, and other man-made structures.

Mineralogists

They analyze and classify minerals and precious stones according to composition and structure.

Geochemists

They study the chemical composition, character, and changes in minerals and rocks to understand the distribution and migration of elements in the earth's crust.

Geologists concerned with earth processes include:

Sedimentologists

They study sedimentary deposits (matter deposited by water or wind) and try to determine the processes and products involved.

Volcanologists

They study the origins of volcanoes and search for clues to the earth's molten core, working with both active and inactive volcanoes, lava flows, and other eruptive activity.

Geomorphologists

They study landforms and the forces, such as erosion and glaciation, that cause them to change.

Geologists concerned with earth history include:

Paleontologists

They study plant and animal fossils found in geological formations to trace the evolution and development of past life.

Geochronologists

They determine the age of rocks and landforms by the radioactive decay of their elements.

Stratigraphers

They study the distribution and arrangement of sedimentary rock layers by examining their fossil and mineral content.

Petrologists

They deal with the origin, history, occurrence, structure, chemical composition, and classification of rocks.

Some new fields of geology do not fit into any of these categories—astrogeology, for example. Astrogeologists study geological conditions on other planets and on the moon: their discipline has grown along with the space program. Geological oceanographers study the ocean floor and continental shelf, looking for additional clues to the earth's origin and for minerals. This is another example of the interrelation among the environmental sciences. Cross disciplines and new areas undoubtedly will continue to develop.

Geophysicists

The main branches of geophysics include:

Solid earth geophysicists

They search for oil and mineral deposits, map the earth's surface, and study earthquakes.

Exploration geophysicists

They use seismic prospecting techniques to locate oil and mineral deposits and also do research to improve prospecting techniques and instruments.

Seismologists

They study the earth's interior and vibrations caused by earth-quakes and by man-made explosions, trying to perfect prediction and detection respectively. They also provide information for constructing bridges, dams, and buildings.

Geodesists

They study the size, shape, and gravitational field of the earth and other planets in order to make the precise measurements needed for accurate mapping of the earth's surface and to track satellites.

Hydrologists

They study the distribution, circulation, and physical properties of underground and surface waters, including rivers, glaciers, snow, and permafrost. They study rainfall, its rate of infiltration into the soil, and its return to the ocean. Some are concerned with water supplies, irrigation, flood control, and soil erosion. This field is related to that of physical oceanographers, who study the physical properties of the oceans such as waves, tides, and currents. Others work in environmental protection, either in preventing water pollution or in helping build water supply and waste plants.

Geomagneticians

They study the earth's magnetic field.

Paleomagneticians

They learn about past magnetic fields from rocks or lava flows.

Planetologists

They study the composition and atmosphere of the moon, planets, and other bodies in the solar system. They gather data from geophysical instruments placed in interplanetary space probes or from equipment used by astronauts during Apollo missions.

Working conditions for geologists and geophysicists, as in many outdoor fields, are tough, sometimes hazardous. A lot of travel, much of it to remote places and under the most primitive conditions, is involved. Frequently, they are stationed on ships or aircraft. Sometimes living overseas for long periods is required. Much of the work is outdoors or underground. Laboratory and administrative jobs offer more comfort, but less excitement.

More than 31,000 people work as geologists and 11,000 as geophysicists. Private industry is the largest employer, hiring 60 percent of the work force. Petroleum and natural gas companies head the list, followed closely by mining and quarrying companies. Geologists mostly work in five states: Texas, California, Louisiana, Colorado, and Oklahoma. Geophysicists are concentrated around the Gulf Coast. Workers from these fields are posted with American firms overseas for varying periods of time. Some geologists also work for construction firms and as independent consultants in industry and government.

Colleges and universities employ about 10,400 geologists and a much smaller number of geophysicists. Non-profit research institutions and museums offer a few highly prized jobs.

The federal government employs about an equal number in both fields. Most geologists work with the Department of the Interior in the United States Geological Survey, the Bureau of Mines, and the Bureau of Reclamation. Geophysicists find jobs with the United States Geological Survey, the National Oceanic and Atmospheric Administration (NOAA), and the Department of Defense.

A few state agencies employ geologists.

Geologists and geophysicists usually begin their careers in field exploration or laboratory research, both of which require a bachelor's degree. An advanced degree is helpful for promotion as project leaders, program managers, and other management and research positions. It is essential for college teaching and many research positions.

About 350 colleges and universities offer a bachelor's degree and 150 universities award advanced degrees in geology. The number is smaller in the geophysics field—40 for bachelor's degrees and 30 for advanced degrees. Undergraduates in both areas take general academic studies, mathematics, physics, and chemistry, as well as geology courses. About a quarter of their time goes to geology and/or geophysics. Graduate students take advanced geology courses and specialize in one branch of the science.

Meteorologists

The field of meteorology is the study of the atmosphere, that is, the air that surrounds the earth. In fact, it is often referred to as atmospheric science. It dates back at least to Aristotle, who wrote the first treatise on meteorology in the fourth century B.C. Scientific progress began with the development of physics and the invention of basic instruments, including Leonardo da Vinci's wind vane in 1500, Galileo's thermometer in 1593, and Torricelli's mercurial barometer in 1643.

Meteorology developed through the years in response to the requirements of commercial shipping and naval navigation in the early years, and commercial and military aviation in recent years. The French established the first official national weather service in 1855, prompted by the loss of a warship during a storm at sea. The United States did not follow suit until 1891, when they organized the Weather Bureau under the aegis of the Department of Agriculture, although there was an intermediary step in 1870 when the Army Signal Corps was set up to provide weather forecasts for Great Lakes and Atlantic coast shipping. Some changes came in the United States service in the 1930s, but the main ones evolved with the exploration of space in the 1960s.

In its time, the invention of the telegraph was as important as the modern research tools because it improved rapid data collection from remote weather stations. Today, because of such modern research tools as high-altitude airplanes, weather balloons, rockets, earth satellites, and space probes, meteorologists are able to provide more sophisticated understanding and forecasting of weather, their best known function. They also work at solving air pollution problems and studying trends in the earth's climate. Agriculture, transportation, communications, health, defense, business—indeed, all areas of life—are affected by meteorology.

Synoptic meteorologists

They are the weather forecasters and also the largest group of specialists. They study current weather information such as air pressure, temperature, humidity, and wind velocity in order to make both short- and long-range predictions. The data from weather satellites and observers around the world is fed to computers to plot and analyze. A few forecasters still prepare and analyze weather maps.

Physical meteorologists

They study the chemical and electrical properties of the atmosphere, doing research on the transmission of light, sound, and radio waves. They also study factors affecting formation of clouds, rain, snow, and other weather phenomena.

Climatologists

They study long-range changes in climate, analyzing past records on wind, rainfall, sunshine, and temperature in order to predict the general pattern of weather in the future. These studies are used to plan heating and cooling systems, design buildings, and aid in effective land utilization. They are important to agriculture and agribusiness, indeed any industry dependent upon climate.

Paleoclimatologists

They study weather in other geological ages through plant and animal fossils to try to predict future weather patterns.

Industrial meteorologists

They are the weather-makers, producing both snow and rain. They study the relationships between weather and biological processes and human activities. They work in environmental protection, doing studies that have health applications as in such problems as smoke control and air pollution. They also are valuable to industrial and agricultural interests, including insurance companies, resorts, airlines, petroleum companies, and farmers.

Working conditions for meteorologists vary according to their fields. Obviously, the work is rugged at stations like the one on top of Mount Washington in New Hampshire, where the buildings have to be chained to the rock because of the strong winds. Small stations generally have only one employee, so the work can be lonely. The most comfortable situations are probably teaching posts, and the most glamorous are with the few television stations that employ their own meteorologists to forecast the weather for their viewers.

About 7,300 meteorologists work in civilian jobs and probably at least as many more in military assignments. The largest civilian employer is the National Oceanic and Atmospheric Administration (NOAA), where over 1,800 meteorologists fill jobs in the United States and in a small number of foreign areas. The Department of Defense employs about 200 civilian meteorologists. The 3,000 in private industry work for airlines, private weather consulting firms, companies that design and manufacture meteorological instruments, radio and television stations, insurance companies, and aerospace and engineering firms. Colleges and universities employ over 1,300 meteorologists as researchers and teachers. There are very few jobs in state and local government and for non-profit organizations.

Entry level jobs in weather forecasting require a bachelor's degree with a major in meteorology. In other meteorological fields, a bachelor's degree in a related science or engineering combined with meteorology sometimes is acceptable. The same is true of higher level jobs requiring advanced degrees. As in other scientific fields, advanced degrees are necessary for teaching, research, and top management. Both an advanced degree and a business degree and/or experience are necessary to establish weather consulting firms or related businesses.

Meteorology is one area where several helps are available with education. The armed forces provide training for both enlisted personnel and officers. The NOAA sponsors two programs—one provides advanced or specialized training for employees; the other is for college students, providing either summer employment or a work-study program during the academic year. Meteorologists who work for the federal government receive two years of on-the-job training before moving up the career ladder.

Many colleges and universities offer meteorology courses. Only thirty-six offer a bachelor's degree, however, and thirty-nine, advanced degrees. Job candidates without advanced degrees will have tough competition in the 1980s. The field as a whole is not expected to grow dramatically.

Oceanographers

Oceans cover about 71 percent of the earth's surface and have 329 million cubic miles of water! They are a valuable source of food, fossil fuels, and minerals. They also serve as a "highway" for transportation and offer many kinds of recreation. They support fishing and mining industries.

Oceanography is the exploration and scientific study of this fantastic resource and its phenomena. It is not a basic science, but integrates the principles and techniques of mathematics and many sciences—geography, geology, physics, chemistry, biology, astronomy, and meteorology. Aristotle was the first oceanographer, followed by the first navigators to sail the seas. Among the most famous was Captain James Cook, who charted the waters off the Canadian, New Zealand, and Australian coasts and explored the Antarctic Ocean. Benjamin Franklin even made a contribution by studying the Gulf Stream and suggesting it as a speedier route for the eighteenth-century clipper ships. Oceanography did not really develop as a discipline, however, until United States Navy Lieutenant Matthew Fontaine Maury made a systematic study of ocean winds, storm tracks, and surface currents. He compiled all his observations in the first great work of modern oceanography, *Physical Geography of the Sea*, published in 1855. As a result of his work, the Navy issued the first Pilot Charts of the oceans.

Other milestones in early oceanography were the early nineteenth-century marine life studies of Edward Forbes, a British naturalist generally regarded as the founder of marine biology, and the Challenger Expedition, the first scientific study of the world's oceans. The British Navy corvette *HMS Challenger* sailed 70,000 nautical miles in the Atlantic, Pacific, Indian, and Antarctic Oceans between December 7, 1872, and May 24, 1876. It took twenty years to compile the fifty-volume report on the work done during the three and a half years at sea.

In more recent times, the development of pressurized underwater chambers and the modern aqualung have made possible storybook explorations. Jacques Yves Cousteau's work with the office *Français de Récherches Sous-marines* and the United States Navy Sealab experiments have been the subject of numerous articles, books, and television programs. Almost certainly these adventures have affected the popularity of oceanography as a career.

Most major oceanographic research in the United States is conducted by the United States Navy and by several research institutions. The most famous are probably Woods Hole Oceanographic Institute at Woods Hole, Massachusetts, on Cape Cod and the Scripps Institution of Oceanography at La Jolla, California. Woods Hole is associated with the Massachusetts Institute of Technology and Scripps with the University of California.

Woods Hole is an ideal research situation because it offers clean, deep water, with no large rivers emptying into the area. They specialize in Gulf Stream current research and submarine geological investigations, maintaining several research ships, including a submarine. The Bureau of Commercial Fisheries and the United States Marine Biological Laboratory are also located at Woods Hole.

Scripps operates three laboratories and works mostly with problems encountered in the Pacific Ocean. For example, it has done major work with tidal waves caused by underwater earthquakes and with the tuna fishing industry. It has also cooperated with the United States Navy in some phases of the Sealab project.

While the average oceanographer probably cannot expect to be involved in such excitement as this, the work in every area is endlessly fascinating. Most oceanographers specialize in one branch of the science, which includes the following:

Biological oceanographers (marine biologists)

They are the ecologists, studying plant and animal life in the ocean. Their work has many practical applications in improving and controlling commercial and sport fishing, and in determining the effects of pollution on marine life. Many jobs in this area are in the field of environmental protection.

Physical oceanographers (physicists and geophysicists)

They are hydrologists who study the physical properties of the ocean such as waves, tides, current, water density, temperature, salinity, and sound and light transmission through the sea. Their research on the relationships between the sea and the atmosphere may lead to more accurate prediction of the weather.

Geological oceanographers (marine geologists)

They study the ocean's underwater mountain ranges, rocks, and sediments. They also investigate geological phenomena such as continental drift and volcanoes. They are the prospectors of the ocean, looking for minerals, oil, and gas beneath the ocean floor.

Chemical oceanographers

They study the chemical composition of ocean water and sediments, as well as chemical reactions in the sea. They tackle problems like ocean pollution, the effects of oil spills, and the problem of making sea water drinkable.

Oceanographic engineers

They design and build instruments for oceanographic research and operations. They also build bridges, underwater tunnels, dams, piers, and breakwaters.

Archaeological oceanographers

They search for buried treasure or buried cities from ancient civilizations.

Writer, Photographer, and Artist oceanographers

They record the work of others so that it can be shared with other scientists and with the general public.

Oceanographers can work in land-based research laboratories, but many of the jobs require ocean expeditions that take them away from home for weeks or months at a time. This means working and living in cramped areas. It also means working underwater with scuba gear, submersible craft, and other equipment, sometimes a hazardous duty.

Of the 3,600 oceanographers today, more than half work in colleges and universities. Another one-fifth works for the federal government, for the United States Navy, or for the National Oceanic and

Atmospheric Administration (NOAA). The rest work in private industry or for fishery laboratories of state and local governments. Although there are oceanographers in every state, most work in states that border on the oceans.

The minimum requirement for beginning professional jobs in oceanography is a bachelor's degree with a major in oceanography, biology, earth or physical science, mathematics, or engineering. Most other jobs in research and teaching require graduate training. Top-level positions always go to oceanographers with a Ph.D.

About sixty-five colleges and universities offer undergraduate degrees and fifty-five, advanced degrees in oceanography or marine sciences. Undergraduates should study mathematics, physics, chemistry, geophysics, geology, meteorology, and biology. Graduate students should specialize in a particular science pertinent to the intended field of work. For example, students interested in biological or chemical oceanography should study biology or chemistry, respectively.

Graduate students usually do research part-time aboard ship to become familiar with the sea and with research techniques. This work is usually offered as a summer course.

Entry level jobs are as research or laboratory assistants or as clerks doing routine data collection, computation, or analysis. Usually, on-the-job training is necessary. Experienced oceanographers with advanced degrees can look forward to directing surveys and research programs, to administrative or supervisory jobs in research laboratories, or to teaching.

11

The Problem Solvers:
Engineering

Modern technology would collapse without engineers. They are the
problem solvers of the world; their jobs are the link between scientific
discovery and its useful application.

Engineers design machinery, products, systems, and processes
for every industry. They develop electrical power, water supplies,
and waste disposal systems. They design, plan, and supervise the
construction of buildings, highways, and rapid transit systems.

The first engineers are lost in the fog of the past, but some ancient
examples of their art still exist: the Great Wall of China; Egyptian
pyramids and temples; Mayan temples; the Acropolis; Egyptian, Ba-
bylonian, and Mesopotamian irrigation systems; Roman roads,
bridges, and aqueducts; the Hanging Gardens of Babylon . . .

From those early days until the Industrial Revolution, engineering was made up of two branches: military, which embodied the
construction of fortifications, weapons, and machines; and civil,

175

which included the construction of tools, roads, bridges, buildings, and machines. As technology grew more sophisticated, so did the engineering profession.

More than a million engineers work in the United States, making it the largest scientific and technical occupation in the country and the second largest professional occupation, following teaching, which ranks first. Although every engineer does not have an outdoor job, there are outdoor jobs, or combinations of indoor-outdoor jobs, within many of the engineering fields. There are twenty-five engineering specialties recognized by professional societies. Within the major branches are more than eighty-five subdivisions. The primary fields that interest outdoor careerists are aerospace, agricultural, chemical, electrical, civil, industrial, mechanical, mining, and petroleum engineering. There is also one other area, which is discussed elsewhere—the specialized engineering fields in the environmental, or earth sciences field, which include geological and oceanographic engineering. They are covered in chapter ten on environmental scientists because they are closely integrated with other jobs in that field.

One of the problems in the engineering field is that, even more than in other fields, jobs are tied to technology and government spending. If the economy becomes further depressed, or if research and development expenditures do not increase as expected, some engineers will have difficulty in getting jobs. It has happened in the past. This can be a particular problem for older engineers working in specialized fields. In order to find jobs, they may need additional education. A hedge against these problems is continuing education to keep up on the latest technological developments.

Projections show that the number of degrees expected to be granted in engineering in the 1980s is substantially higher than the number graduated recently. This may mean that some graduates will have difficulty finding jobs. This situation calls for the competitive job strategies encouraged in other chapters of this book.

Despite these difficulties, the prognosis for the continued health of the engineering field is excellent. Not only are engineering posts open to them, but in some fields, such as agribusiness, employers actively seek engineers as management trainees because of their problem-solving ability.

The energy crisis of the 1980s makes the mining and petroleum industries of vital importance in today's economy and major employers of outdoor workers. This work force is expected to increase faster than any other industry throughout the 1980s. Obviously, this means mining and petroleum engineers have especially good job potential.

Working conditions for engineers are generally good, but a few fields, such as civil, mining, and petroleum engineering, can be hazardous. These problems are cited in the discussions of the individual fields. Travel, living in remote areas, and overtime work to meet deadlines (usually without additional pay) can be less dangerous hazards.

Pay for engineers is excellent. The College Placement Council provides the following schedule for average starting salaries in some branches of engineering for 1978. Because of inflation, the figures go up slightly every year.

Petroleum engineering	$19,836
Chemical engineering	18,156
Mining engineering	17,964
Mechanical engineering	16,848
Electrical engineering	16,404
Industrial engineering	16,380
Aeronautical engineering	16,248
Civil engineering	15,456

Almost half of all engineers work in manufacturing industries. About 400,000 are employed in non-manufacturing industries, primarily in construction, public utilities, engineering and architectural services, and business and management consulting services. Federal, state, and local governments employ about 150,000 more. Federal jobs are mainly with the Departments of Defense, Interior, Energy, Agriculture, and Transportation, and in the National Aeronautics and Space Administration. Most engineers in state and local government agencies work in highway and public works departments. Another 50,000 engineers teach or do research for colleges and universities. A smaller number work for non-profit research organizations.

Engineers are employed in every state, in small and large cities, and in rural areas. Specific geographical considerations will be discussed in conjunction with each engineering branch.

A bachelor's degree in engineering is the generally accepted education requirement for beginning engineering jobs. College graduates trained in one of the natural sciences or mathematics may also qualify for some beginning jobs. Experienced technicians with some engineering education are occasionally able to advance to some types of engineering jobs.

Many colleges have two- or four-year programs leading to degrees in engineering technology. These programs prepare students for practical design and production work rather than for jobs that require more theoretical scientific knowledge. More information is given for these jobs in chapter thirteen. Graduates of four-year engineering technology programs may get jobs similar to those obtained by engineering bachelor's degree graduates. Some employers do not, however, accept such students as fully trained engineers.

Graduate training is essential for most beginning teaching and research positions, but is not needed for the majority of other entry level engineering jobs. Many engineers obtain master's degrees, however, because an advanced degree often is desirable for promotion or is needed to keep up with new technology. Some specialties, such as nuclear engineering, are taught mainly at the graduate level.

About 240 colleges and universities offer a bachelor's degree in engineering, and almost seventy colleges offer a bachelor's degree in engineering technology. Although programs in the larger branches of engineering are offered in most of these institutions, some small specialties are taught in only a very few. Therefore, students desiring specialized training should investigate curricula before selecting a college.

Admission requirements for undergraduate engineering schools usually include high school courses in advanced mathematics and the physical sciences.

In typical four-year engineering curricula, the first two years are spent studying basic sciences—mathematics, physics, chemistry, and introductory engineering—and the humanities, social sciences, and English. The last two years are devoted to specialized engineering courses. Some programs offer a general engineering curriculum, permitting the student to choose a specialty in graduate school or acquire it on the job.

Some engineering curricula require more than four years to complete. A number of colleges and universities now offer five-year master's degree programs. In addition, several engineering schools have formal arrangements with liberal arts colleges whereby a student spends three years in a liberal arts college studying pre-engineering subjects and two years in an engineering school and receives a bachelor's degree from each.

Some schools have five- or six-year cooperative plans where students coordinate classroom study and practical work experience. In addition to gaining useful experience, students are able to finance part of their educations.

Because of the need to keep up with rapid advances in technology, continuing education is necessary and engineers need to plan for frequent refresher courses.

All fifty states and the District of Columbia require licensing for engineers whose work may affect life, health, or property, or who offer their services to the public. In 1978, there were over 300,000 registered engineers. Generally, registration requirements include a degree from an accredited engineering school, four years of relevant work experience, and the passing of a state examination.

Engineering graduates usually begin work under the supervision of experienced engineers. Some companies have programs to acquaint new engineers with special industrial practices and to determine the specialties for which they are best suited. Some engineers obtain a graduate degree in business administration to improve their advancement opportunities, while still others obtain law degrees and become patent attorneys.

Engineers should be able to work as part of a team. They should be creative, analytical, and have a capacity for detail. In addition to technical skills, they should have superior oral and written communication skills.

Aerospace Engineers

Aerospace engineers design, develop, test, and help produce commercial and military aircraft, missiles, and spacecraft. They usually specialize in one area of work in one type of product—say, navigational guidance of satellites. They are especially concerned with design as it affects environment, as with noise and air pollution caused by jet engines, or with the elimination of water vapor that planes leave in the atmosphere.

About 60,000 aerospace engineers work for federal agencies (primarily the National Aeronautics and Space Administration or the Department of Defense), commercial airlines, consulting firms, and colleges and universities.

Agricultural Engineers

Agricultural engineers design agricultural equipment and develop methods that will improve the production, processing, and distribution of food and other agricultural products. They are also concerned with the conservation and management of energy, soil, and water resources.

There are 14,000 agricultural engineers working in the private sector in research and development, production, sales, or management. Some are employed by manufacturers of farm equipment, electric utility companies, distributors of farm equipment and supplies, agricultural organizations, or agricultural processing plants. Others are consultants who supply services to farmers and farm-related industries.

The federal government has jobs for about 450 agricultural engineers in the Department of Agriculture. A small number work for state and local governments and teach.

Chemical Engineers

Chemical engineers are involved in many phases of the production of chemicals and plants, designing equipment as well as determining manufacturing methods. This branch of engineering is important to outdoor careerists mainly in the area of pollution—for example, solving the problems related to treatment and disposal of industrial waste. Because their work cuts across many fields, they must combine knowledge of mechanical and electrical engineering with chemistry and physics. The work is so diversified and complex that chemical engineers usually specialize in a particular operation, such as oxidation, or a particular product, such as plastics.

Of the 50,000 chemical engineers working, most are employed by manufacturing industries producing chemicals, petroleum, and related products. Some work in government agencies, or teach and do research in colleges and universities. A small number work for independent research institutes and engineering consulting firms.

Civil Engineers

Civil engineers work in the oldest branch of the engineering profession. They design and supervise the construction of roads, harbors, airports, tunnels, bridges, water supplies, sewage systems, and buildings. Major specialties within civil engineering are structural, hydraulic, environmental (sanitary), transportation (including highways and railroads), urban planning, and soil mechanics.

Civil engineers often face difficult and unpleasant working conditions when jobs take them to remote construction sites or to foreign countries. Most of the 150,000 civil engineers work for federal, state, and local government agencies or in the construction industry. Others work for consulting engineering and architectural firms, as independent consulting engineers, or for public utilities, railroads, educational institutions, and manufacturing industries. Their duties cover design, inspection, planning, maintenance, research, and teaching.

Electrical Engineers

Electrical engineers design, develop, test, and supervise the manufacture of electrical and electronic equipment, two fields that are the underpinnings of hundreds of other outdoor jobs today. Electrical engineers who work with electronic equipment are often called electronic engineers. This is a developing field, spurred by technological advances during World War II and by the space exploration program of the last three decades.

Electrical equipment includes power generating and transmission equipment used by electrical utilities, electric motors, machinery controls, and lighting and wiring in buildings, automobiles, and aircraft. Eelctronic equipment includes radar, computers, communication equipment, and consumer goods such as television and stereo sets. Electrical engineers also design and operate facilities for generating and distributing electric power.

As in other engineering fields, electrical engineers usually specialize in a major area such as microwave communication or aviation electronic systems.

Electrical engineering is the largest branch of the engineering field, and most of the 300,000 members of the field work for manufacturers of electrical and electronic equipment of various kinds, including professional and scientific equipment. Others are employed by telephone, telegraph, and electric light and power companies. They are the engineers who design and operate nuclear power plants. They also deal with environmental problems generated by electrical power or electronics. Some are employed by government agencies, by colleges and universities, and by construction firms and engineering consultants. A number open their own engineering consulting firms.

Environmental Protection Engineers

They used to be called sanitary engineers. Their job is to apply engineering principles to the prevention, control, and management of environmental factors that influence people's physical, mental, and social well-being. Generally, they are concerned with air and water pollution, disease vectors, radiation, solid waste disposal, safe milk, food, and water, and community environmental hazards such as rats, unsafe housing, and injury control. They tend to specialize in one of these fields, the most popular being air pollution, industrial hygiene, public health, radiological health, or hospital engineering.

Industrial Engineers

Industrial engineers determine the most effective ways for an organization to use the basic factors of production—people, machines, and materials. They are more concerned with people and methods of business organization than are engineers in other specialties, who are generally more concerned with particular products or processes such as metals, power, or mechanics.

To solve organizational, production, and related problems most efficiently, industrial engineers design data processing systems and apply operations research techniques. They also develop management control systems, design production planning and control systems to coordinate activities and control product quality, and design or improve systems for the physical distribution of goods and services. Industrial engineers also conduct plant location surveys, where they look for the best combination of sources of raw materials, transportation, and taxes, and develop wage and salary administration systems and job evaluation programs. To do all this they spend hours in the field evaluating work and workers.

This is a growing field because of the increasing complexity of industrial operations and the expansion of automated processes. Increased recognition of the importance of scientific management and safety engineering in reducing costs, increasing productivity, and protecting the environment will create additional opportunities.

There are about 185,000 industrial engineers, two-thirds of whom work in manufacturing industries. In the outdoor field, construction and mining firms and public utilities are heavy employers. For example, nuclear power plants, especially, need the help of industrial engineers to combat the "bad press" caused by the Three Mile Island incident in central Pennsylvania in 1979. Experienced industrial engineers have an excellent chance of developing a successful independent consulting firm.

Mechanical Engineers

Mechanical engineers are concerned with the production, transmission, and use of power. They design and develop machines such as internal combustion engines, steam and gas turbines, and jet and rocket engines—in fact, any machine using power.

The work of mechanical engineers varies by industry and function since many specialties have developed within the field. Outdoor careerists might find this a stimulating field because of problems relating to air pollution caused by the internal combustion engines of automobiles, trucks, buses, and other machines. The petroleum and construction industries employ hundreds of mechanical engineers.

Of the 200,000 mechanical engineers working in the field, almost three-fourths are employed in manufacturing. The balance work for government agencies, educational institutions, and consulting engineering firms.

Mining Engineers

Mining engineers plan mining operations, design underground and surface mines and mining equipment, train mining crews, supervise mining, and devise methods for transporting the mined minerals to processing plants. They are responsible for economical and efficient operating of mines and for mine safety, including ventilation, water supply, power, communications, and equipment maintenance. Some mining engineers work with geologists and metallurgical engineers to locate and appraise new ore deposits. They frequently specialize in the mining of one specific mineral such as coal or copper. In recent years with an increased emphasis on protecting the environment, many have become environmental specialists, helping to solve problems relating to the reclamation of mined-land sites and and water and air pollution.

As mentioned earlier, engineers working in coal are in an especially strong position in the 1980s because of the energy crisis of the decade. As shortages develop in any mineral resource, greater effort will go to exploration and development.

Almost all of the 6,000 mining engineers in the United States work directly in the mining industry. These are more hazardous jobs than those in many other engineering fields. More comfortable slots are with firms that produce equipment for the mining industry or in teaching posts in colleges and universities. There are also openings in government agencies and as independent consultants.

Only the petroleum industry is more hazardous than the mining industry. In spite of recent progress in promoting changes in safety and health regulations, mines remain a dangerous place to work. Underground mines are dark, noisy, cold, damp and sometimes wet with several inches of water on tunnel floors. Although mines usually have electric lights, invariably many areas are without illumination. Work space is cramped, too. Miners suffer from industry-related diseases, especially coal miners, who risk developing pneumoconiosis (black lung) from coal dust and silicosis from rock dust generated by the drilling in mines.

Most of the nation's coal is mined in the Appalachian area that extends from Pennsylvania through eastern Ohio, West Virginia, Kentucky, Tennessee, and Alabama. Smaller amounts are mined in Indiana, Illinois, and in the Rocky Mountains. Other ores—including iron, tin, copper, zinc, silver, nickel, chromium, magnesium, aluminum, lead, and gold—are recovered throughout mountain areas, both in the west and east. The area surrounding Lake Superior is iron-mining country. Many American companies have interests in Canada and other foreign countries.

Petroleum Engineers

Petroleum engineers are mainly involved in exploring and drilling for oil and gas. They work to achieve the maximum profitable recovery of oil and gas from a petroleum reservoir by determining and developing the best and most efficient production methods.

About 17,000 petroleum engineers work in the petroleum industry and closely allied fields, including the major oil companies and hundreds of smaller independent oil exploration and production companies. They also work for companies that produce drilling equipment and supplies. Their work is concentrated in the oil-producing states of Texas, Oklahoma, Louisiana, and California. Many American petroleum engineers work overseas in oil-producing companies. As mentioned earlier, petroleum engineers like mining engineers (especially coal mining engineers) can expect a growing job market in the 1980s. Just how strong it will be depends on funds committed by private industry and by the federal government to exploration and development.

Like mining engineers, petroleum engineers have a rugged outdoor life and are required to work through all kinds of weather. Their work places are in remote settings—the western United States, the Gulf of Mexico, the Arctic Circle. Physical strength and stamina are important because the work involves standing most of the time, lifting, climbing, and stooping. Frequent travel is necessary and some petroleum engineers many be lifelong nomads, never really establishing a home base other than the home office.

The field is hazardous, especially oil and gas well drilling and servicing. Statistics from the late 1970s show that the injury rate in the petroleum industry is about four times the rate for all private industry. More than twice as many workdays were lost because of accident or injury. Of course, engineers are not always exposed to dangerous conditions, but they can be.

I think that I shall never see
A billboard lovely as a tree.
Indeed, unless the billboards fall
I'll never see a tree at all.
                    Ogden Nash

12

Doing What Comes Naturally:
Building With the Environment

The late Frank Lloyd Wright always told his architecture students
to search for the perfect building in nature as models for their own
work. They would find it, he said, in the bee's hive, the ant's laby-
rinth, the oriole's nest, and the beaver's dam, but most of all in shells.
He believed that the creatures of the sea were doing that which
human beings seem so often to be unable to do—"living in naturally
inspired, beautiful form." What's more, they did it with great indi-
vidualism. True, all the shells provided shelter, but a clam did it
differently from a scallop, an oyster, a conch, or a chambered nau-
tilus.

Why don't people learn the lesson architect Wright advocated
and that the shell teaches? Why are houses so often an atrocious
liability rather than an extension of natural environments? And why
do the creators of buildings too often destroy that which is beautiful
in the process of building? Why are cities filled with deteriorating

slums? Why have they become giant spider webs of highways that lead no place but into parking garages and to other highways, taking travelers away again? Why are more and more rural areas dotted with egg-carton houses? Why are green belts yielding to industrial parks?

These are questions that the architects and planners of the future will try to answer as they plan their careers and work out a rationale for the time and cost that will go into its preparation. These are questions that make the three careers considered here vital to the outdoor lover. The community planner, sometimes also called a regional or urban planner, the architect, and the landscape architect can control the growth and rebirth of the country. They are the "doctors" who can cure the spiritual paralysis affecting real estate developers, bureaucrats, politicians, investors, and others who are intent on progress and growth at any cost. They can write the "prescriptions" that will turn the course of this lingering illness of stupidity and apathy.

The "treatment" has already begun. Throughout the country, hundreds of communities are drawing on the skills of community planners, architects, and landscape architects who have acknowledged a concern for the environment. They are trying to rescue their old neighborhoods, save their historic buildings, and update zoning codes to protect natural resources. They are trying to develop buildings that are extensions of the environment rather than a denigration of it.

Neighborhood development committees, regional commissions, national task forces—they all are working to halt the decline of inner city neighborhoods, change the structure of over-crowded areas, plan public transportation, and cut down on pollution. This is the challenge for these "planning" professions.

There are many models to follow—Paolo Soleri's Arcosanti *arcology* (a word meaning architecture and ecology) built in the Arizona desert, or Moshe Safdie's Habitat, an apartment complex erected in Montreal for that city's 1967 international exposition, for example. Nothing can be done to change the past. Congress cannot take back the millions of dollars that, through FHA low-interest mortgages, subsidized housing. This move, more than any other, made the suburban dream a reality. Nor can it tear up all the highways built as a result of the National Defense Highways Act of the 1950s, the bill that committed the country to a nation of private automobile ownership rather than to mass transit riding. What *can* happen is that decisions and actions of the future can have a sounder base in environmental concerns.

Like so many outdoor careers discussed in this book, community planners, architects, and landscape architects face a schizophrenic indoor-outdoor work schedule. They have outdoor inspection tours to survey land or buildings under consideration for development, but they also have many administrative duties that keep them at their desks and hours of drafting at their drawing boards. Then, too, they must be prepared to work in the competitive environment of business where leadership and ability to work with others is important. The fields have a common base of an appreciation for nature and creative and artistic talent. All of these fields are primarily concerned with design. Community planners work with the total environment. Architects deal with buildings. Landscape architects employ natural features combined with man-made features to enhance the environment. But they all must think in terms of spatial relationships and visualize the effects of their plans and ideas. They employ lines, colors, textures, spaces, and light to achieve their ends. Safety and function are as important as esthetic appeal.

While the three fields have striking similarities in both talent and training, the actual work is very different, as examination of each shows.

Community Planners

Community planners develop programs to provide for future growth and revitalization of urban, suburban, and rural communities. They help local officials make decisions to solve social, economic, and environmental problems.

Planners examine community facilities such as health clinics and schools to be sure they can meet the demands placed upon them. These planners also keep abreast of legal issues involved in community development and redevelopment and of changes in housing and building codes. Because suburban growth has increased the need for better ways of traveling to the inner city, the planner's job often includes designing new transportation and parking facilities.

Community planners prepare for many situations that are likely to develop as a result of population growth or social and economic change. For example, they estimate the community's long-range needs for housing, transportation, and business and industrial sites. Working within a framework set by the community government, they analyze and propose alternative ways to achieve more efficient and attractive urban areas.

Before preparing plans for long-range community development, community planners prepare detailed studies that show the current use of land for residential, business, and community purposes. The report presents such information as the arrangement of streets, highways, and water and sewer lines, and the location of schools, libraries, and playgrounds. They also provide information on the types of industry in the community, the characteristics of the population, and employment and economic trends. With this information, urban and regional planners propose ways of using undeveloped land. They design the layout of recommended buildings and other facilities, such as subways. They also prepare cost projections and program plans.

Community planners often confer with private land developers, civic leaders, and officials of public agencies that do specialized planning. They may prepare materials for community relations programs, speak at civic meetings, and appear before legislative committees to explain and defend their proposals.

In small organizations, planners must be able to do several kinds of work. In large organizations, planners usually specialize. They may work in such areas as physical design, community relations, or the reconstruction of rundown business districts.

About 17,000 persons work as community planners. Most are employed by city, county, or regional planning agencies. A growing number are with state or federal governments in agencies dealing with housing, transportation, or environmental protection.

Many planners do consulting work, either part-time in addition to a regular job, or full-time for a firm that provides services to private developers and government agencies. Planners also work for large land developers or research organizations and teach in colleges and universities.

After a few years' experience, community planners may advance to more important assignments, such as outlining proposed studies, designing the physical layout of a large development, or recommending policy, program, and budget options. Some are promoted to jobs as planning directors and spend a great deal of time meeting with officials in other organizations, speaking to civic groups, and supervising other professionals. Further advancement is difficult at this level. Often the only solution is a move to a larger city, where the problems are more complex and the responsibilities greater.

Architects

Architects provide a wide variety of professional services to individuals, organizations, corporations, and government agencies planning a building project. Architects are involved in all phases of development of a building or project, from the initial discussion of general ideas through construction. Their duties require a variety of skills—design, engineering, managerial, and supervisory.

The architect and client first discuss the purposes, requirements, and costs of a project. The architect then prepares schematic drawings that show the scale and the structural and mechanical relationships of the building.

If the schematic drawings are accepted, the architect develops a final design showing the floor plans and the structural details of the project. For example, in designing a school, some of the determinations the architect makes include the width of corridors and stairways so that students may move easily from one class to another; the type and arrangement of storage space; and the location and size of classrooms, laboratories, lunchroom or cafeteria, gymnasium, and administrative offices.

Next the architect prepares working drawings showing the exact dimensions of every part of the structure and the location of plumbing, heating units, electrical outlets, and air conditioning.

Architects also specify the building materials and, in some cases, the interior furnishings. In all cases, the architect must ensure that the structure's design and specifications conform to local and state building codes, zoning laws, fire regulations, and other ordinances.

Throughout this time, the architect may make changes to satisfy the client. A client may, for example, decide that the original design is too expensive and ask the architect to make modifications. Or the client may change the project requirements. Redesigning plans to suit the client requires flexibility and patience on the part of the architect.

After all drawings are completed, the architect assists the client in selecting a contractor and negotiating the construction contract. As construction proceeds, the architect visits the building site from time to time to ensure that the contractor is following the design and using the specified materials. The architect also checks to be sure that the work meets the specified standards. The job is not complete until construction is finished, all required tests are made, construction costs are paid, and guarantees are received from the contractor.

Architects design a wide variety of structures, such as houses, churches, hospitals, office buildings, and airports. They also design multi-building complexes for urban renewal projects, college campuses, industrial parks, and new towns. Besides designing structures, architects also may help in selecting building sites, preparing cost and land-use studies, and long-range planning for site development.

When working on large projects or for large architectural firms, architects often specialize in one phase of the work, such as designing or administering construction contracts. This often requires working with engineers, community planners, landscape architects, and others.

About 54,000 architects work in the United States. This figure includes architecture school graduates who have not become registered, that is, licensed, although they may work in the field. They must work under the supervision of licensed architects.

Most architects work for architectural firms or for builders, real estate firms, or other businesses that have large construction programs. Some work for government agencies responsible for housing, planning, or community development. About 1,600 architects work for the federal government, mainly for the Departments of Defense, Interior, Housing and Urban Development, and the General Services Administration.

New graduates usually begin as drafters in architectural firms. where they prepare architectural drawings and make models of structures under the direction of a registered architect. After several years of experience, they may advance to chief or senior drafter responsible for all major details of a set of working drawings and for supervising other drafters. Others may work as designers, construction contract administrators, or specification writers who prepare documents that specify the building materials, their methods of installation, the quality of finishes, required tests, and many other related details. Employees who become associates in their firms may receive, in addition to a salary, a share of the profits. Usually, however, most architects dream of establishing their own businesses.

Landscape Architects

Landscape architects design residential areas, public parks, and commercial zones. They are hired by many types of organizations from real estate firms starting new developments to municipalities constructing airports or parks. They usually plan the arrangement of vegetation, walkways, and other natural features of open spaces. They may also design such areas as fountains, kiosks, and streets that have been modified to improve pedestrian access and limit automobile traffic. They sometimes supervise the construction stages of outdoor projects.

In planning a site, landscape architects first consider the nature and purpose of the project, the funds available, and the proposed elements. Next they study the site and map such features as the slope of the land, the positions of existing buildings, roads, walkways, and trees. They also observe the sunny parts of the site at different times of the day, soil texture, existing utilities, and many other landscape features. Then, working sometimes as the leader of a design team or sometimes in consultation with the project architect or engineer, they draw up plans to develop the site. If the plans are approved, landscape architects prepare working drawings to show all existing and proposed features. They outline in detail the methods of constructing features and draw up lists of building materials. Then they may invite landscape contractors to bid for the work.

Some landscape architects specialize in particular types of projects, such as parks and playgrounds, hotels and resorts, shopping centers, or public housing. Still others limit their business to such services as regional planning and resource management, feasibility and cost studies, and site construction.

About 14,000 persons work as landscape architects. Most have their own businesses or work for architectural, landscape architectural, or engineering firms. Others are employed by government agencies concerned with forest management, water storage, public housing, city planning, urban renewal, highways, parks, and recreation. The federal government employs over 600 landscape architects, mainly in the Departments of Agriculture, Defense, and Interior. Some landscape architects are employed by landscape contractors, and a few teach in colleges and universities. Employment of landscape architects is concentrated around large metropolitan areas, primarily on the East and West coasts. Employment opportunities in the field are growing, however, in the Southwest.

Beginning landscape architects usually start as junior drafters, tracing drawings and doing other simple drafting work. After gaining experience, they help prepare specifications and construction details and handle other aspects of project design. After two or three years, they can carry a design through all stages of development. Highly qualified landscape architects may become associates in private firms, but usually those who progress this far open their own offices.

Community planners, architects, and landscape architects have similar background requirements and training. Interested students should take high school courses in mechanical or geometrical drawing, art, and more mathematics than the minimum required for college entrance. Physics is a good idea. So are both written and oral communication courses. Success in the fields will depend upon the ability to communicate ideas to clients and to make presentations before large groups.

In college, the course load includes English, physics, mathematics, social sciences, economics, drafting, sketching, surveying, construction, design, graphics, engineering, and urban planning. To that list, the aspiring landscape architect should add horticulture and botany.

Actually, a bachelor's degree in either architecture or landscape architecture can be a stepping stone to a career in community planning. Some beginning positions are open to people with those qualifications. In all three fields, however, advanced degrees are necessary.

Employers seeking community planners always want workers who have advanced training. Most entry level jobs in federal, state, and local government agencies require two years of graduate study or at least the equivalent in work experience. In addition, candidates for these jobs usually must pass civil service examinations.

The demands in architecture are even more stringent. All fifty states and the District of Columbia require individuals to be licensed before they may call themselves architects or contract for providing architectural services. To qualify for the licensing exam, a person must have either a Bachelor of Architecture degree followed by three years of acceptable practical experience in an architect's office, or a Master of Architecture degree followed by two years of experience. As a substitute for formal training, most states accept additional experience, usually twelve years, and successful completion of a qualifying test for admission to the licensing examination. Many architecture school graduates work in the field even though they are not licensed. A registered architect is required, however, to take legal responsibility for all work.

A bachelor's degree in landscape architecture, which takes four or five years, is usually the minimum educational requirement for entering the profession. Here, licensing, based on the results of a uniform national licensing examination, is required in thirty-eight states for independent practice. Admission to the examination usually requires a degree from an accredited school of landscape architecture plus two to four years of experience. Lengthy apprenticeship training of six to eight years under an experienced landscape architect sometimes may be substituted for college training.

Many colleges and universities offer excellent programs in these fields. Over seventy schools give a master's degree in urban or regional planning, which usually requires two or three years beyond the work for a bachelor's degree.

The National Architectural Accrediting Board accredits eighty-seven programs of the 101 schools offering professional degrees in architecture. Most of these schools offer either a four- or five-year curriculum leading to a Bachelor of Architecture degree or a six-year curriculum leading to a Master of Architecture degree. Students also may transfer to professional degree programs after completing a two-year junior or community college program in architecture. Many architecture schools also offer graduate education for those who already have their first professional degree. Although such graduate education is not essential for practicing architects, it often is desirable for those in research or teaching.

The American Society of Landscape Architects accredits about forty colleges and universities that offer a bachelor's degree in landscape architecture. About sixty other schools also offer programs or courses in landscape architecture.

Community planners, architects, and landscape architects are expected to face tough competition for jobs through the 1980s because in recent years qualified applicants have exceeded openings. Demand in all three fields is highly dependent upon the growth of non-residential construction, which is expected to be slow. Because of their design skills and familiarity with building materials and techniques, however, workers in these fields can move into related fields such as graphic design, advertising, visual art, product design, construction contracting and supervision, and real estate. Community planners also accept jobs in public administration. The one thing that will help the job market is the public concern about the quality of the environment.

Salaries are good in this planning-architecture field. Community planners earn an average of $20,500. Architects take in a median of over $25,000. Landscape architects range between $15,000 and $25,000. In all three fields, much higher salaries are possible, especially for practitioners who own their own businesses.

Federal jobs for applicants with bachelor's degrees in architecture or landscape architecture pay $10,963 or slightly more, depending on qualifications. For those with master's degrees, the figure jumps to $15,193.

Planners with master's degrees in community planning can start at about $13,000 a year. Sometimes, job applicants with less than two years of graduate training can find jobs with the federal government as interns at $10,963. The average federal salary is $27,450.

Salaries paid by state governments for beginning community planners can vary from about $12,150 to more than $14,000. Salaries for more experienced planners have just as wide a range—from $17,700 to $23,500. Planning directors are paid from $26,000 to $32,000.

City, county, and other local governments pay urban and regional planners median salaries of more than $19,000 a year. Planning directors earn median salaries of $23,000.

13

Stopgap Careers: *Working Your Way Up the Career Ladder*

In chapter three on *Ways and Means,* methods of financing an education if money is a problem were discussed. Working your way through school was suggested. And working as an engineering or science technician is a good way to accomplish this. You work several years, getting basic training in a field that interests you, save money, and continue your education. When you get a degree, you have that winning combination that all employers seem to want—education *plus* experience.

If you do not want a college education but have a strong interest in engineering and science, working as a technician is a good way to earn a reasonable living in a field you can enjoy. Incidentally, the terms "technician" and "technologist" are synonomous. Some people sometimes use "technician" to mean a lower grade worker than a "technologist," but this is a distinction the dictionary does not recognize.

Another field with many of the same characteristics is surveying and surveying technology. Either of these can be a life career, or they, too, can pave the way for a career in the environmental sciences or in the planning field—community planning, architecture, and landscape architecture.

Drafting could serve a similar purpose, but it is not included here because it has no "outdoor" aspect at all. Surveying, without a doubt, is a rugged field. Engineering and science technology fields offer less outdoor opportunity, but a lot of technicians do spend part or all of their time outdoors. If this is important to you—and it probably is, since you are reading this book—choose the field carefully.

If you are interested in working as a technician or surveyor with the idea that you will go on to college, study the chapters on engineering, environmental science, life science, and community planning, architecture, and landscape architecture. They will help orient you to the problems you face and help you expedite your formal education. Consult your employer, too, and the college you think you want to attend. You will find interested counselors who will help you formulate a long-range, manageable plan. Some employers even have continuing education plans for employees that will help you pay for your dreams.

The fields of engineering and science technology and surveying are very different in requirements and work style, so they will be handled separately.

Engineering or Science Technology

Engineering and science technology, according to the American Society of Engineering Education, is "that part of the technological field which requires the application of scientific and engineering knowledge and methods combined with technical skills in support of engineering activities; it lies in the area between the craftsman and the engineer, closest to the engineer." The technician or technologist is a paraprofessional, that is, a professional's helper. He or she works as part of a scientific team, but should also be able to work independently.

Those interested in a career as a technician should have an

aptitude for mathematics and science and enjoy technical work. An ability to do detailed work with a high degree of accuracy is necessary. For design work, creative talent is also desirable.

Engineering and science technicians usually begin work as trainees in routine positions under the direct supervision of an experienced technician, scientist, or engineer. As they gain experience, they receive more responsibility and carry out a particular assignment under only general supervision. Technicians may eventually move into supervisory positions. As pointed out, if they get additional education, they can advance to positions as scientists or engineers.

Although their jobs are more limited in scope and more practically oriented than those of engineers or scientists, technicians often apply the theoretical knowledge developed by engineers and scientists to actual situations. Technicians frequently use complex electronic and mechanical instruments, experimental laboratory equipment, and drafting instruments. Almost all technicians must be able to use technical handbooks and calculators, and some must work with computers.

In research and development, one of the largest areas of employment, technicians set up experiments and calculate the results, sometimes with the aid of computers. They also assist engineers and scientists in developing experimental equipment and models by making drawings and sketches, and frequently by doing routine design work.

In production, technicians usually follow the plans and general directions of engineers and scientists, but often without close supervision. They may prepare specifications for materials, devise tests to insure product quality, or study ways to improve the efficiency of an operation. They often supervise production workers to make sure they follow prescribed plans and procedures. As a product is built, technicians check to see that specifications are followed, keep engineers and scientists informed on progress, and investigate production problems.

As sales workers or field representatives for manufacturers, technicians give advice on installation and maintenance of complex machinery. They also may write specifications and technical manuals, a subject discussed in chapter fourteen.

The specific areas in which technicians work are as wide as the engineering and environmental and life sciences fields. Here are the major ones relating to the outdoor field.

Aeronautical Technology

Technicians in this area work with engineers and scientists to design and produce aircraft, rockets, guided missiles, and spacecraft. Many aid engineers in preparing design layouts and models of structures, control systems, or equipment installations by collecting information, making computations, and performing laboratory tests. For example, a technician might estimate weight factors, centers of gravity, and other items affecting load capacity of an airplane or missile. Other technicians prepare or check drawings for technical accuracy, practicability, and economy. Sometimes technicians also prepare technical information for instruction manuals, bulletins, catalogues, and other literature.

One of the primary jobs involving outdoor work is as a manufacturer's field service representative. These technicians serve as the link between their companies and the military services, commercial airlines, and other customers.

Civil Engineering Technology

Technicians in this area assist civil engineers in planning, designing, and constructing highways, bridges, dams, and other structures. They often specialize in one area, such as highway or structural technology. During the planning stage, they estimate costs, prepare specifications for materials, or participate in surveying, drafting, or designing. Once construction begins, they assist the contractor or superintendent in scheduling construction activities or inspecting the work to assure conformance with blueprints and specifications.

Environmental Protection Technologists

They are more commonly known as sanitarians and actually implement the programs identified and set up by environmental protection scientists and engineers. (See chapters ten and twelve.) The duties might include planning and conducting public health programs, enforcing food processing and serving regulations, collecting and disposing of solid wastes, and treating and disposing of sewage. They might inspect plumbing, recreation areas, hospitals, and other institutions for compliance with health and environmental codes. They also deal with problems relating to noise, pollution, and radiation. Usually the sanitarian is a scientist rather than an engineer. Part of the job is interpreting and promoting environmental health programs and communicating health information. This job is slightly different than the others in this chapter. In most areas it requires more than a two-year college or technical education. It is a state job, usually requiring at least a bachelor's degree. Thirty-two states require licensing although actual requirements vary from state to state. It is included here because the work is similar to most of the others described in this chapter, including environmental technicians and aides described next.

Environmental Technicians and Aides

They also are called sanitarian technicians, sanitary inspectors, or sanitation aides. They investigate public and private establishments to determine either compliance with, or violation of, public sanitation laws and regulations. They take samples of food, water, and air and perform or order tests to determine if contamination is present. If it is, they initiate action to stop it. They also may be concerned with waste control and oversee the treatment and disposal of sewage, refuse, and garbage. In large local and state health and agriculture departments, environmental protection technicians and aides may specialize in such areas as milk and dairy products, food sanitation, air pollution, institutional sanitation, or occupational health. In rural areas and small cities, they may be responsible for a wider range of environmental protection activities.

Industrial Production Technology

Technicians in this area, usually called industrial or production technicians, assist industrial engineers on problems involving the efficient use of personnel, materials, and machines to produce goods or provide services. They prepare layouts of machinery and equipment, plan the flow of work, make statistical studies, and analyze production costs. Industrial technicians also conduct time and motion studies to improve the production methods and procedures in manufacturing plants.

Many industrial technicians acquire experience that enables them to qualify for other jobs. For example, those specializing in machinery and production methods may move into industrial safety. Others in job analysis may set job standards and interview, test, hire, and train personnel. Still others may move into production supervision.

Mechanical Technology

Mechanical technology is a broad term that covers a large number of specialized fields including automotive, diesel, and production technology, and tool and machine design. This is a stimulating field for outdoor careerists because of problems relating to air pollution caused by the internal combustion engine. The petroleum and construction industries also employ mechanical technologists.

Technicians assist engineers in design and development work by making freehand sketches and rough layouts of proposed machinery and other equipment and parts. The work requires knowledge of mechanical principles involving tolerance, stress, strain, friction, and vibration factors. Technicians also analyze the costs and practical value of designs.

In planning and testing experimental machines and equipment for performance, durability, and efficiency, technicians record data, make computations, plot graphs, analyze results, and write reports. They sometimes recommend design changes to improve performance. The job often requires skill in the use of complex instruments, test equipment, and gauges, as well as in the preparation and interpretation of drawings.

When a product is ready for production, technicians help prepare layouts and drawings of the assembly process and of parts to be manufactured. They frequently help estimate labor costs, equipment life, and plant space. Some mechanical technicians test and inspect machines and equipment in manufacturing departments or work with engineers to eliminate production problems. Others are technical sales workers.

Tool designers are among the better known specialists in mechanical engineering technology. Tool designers prepare sketches of designs for cutting tools, jigs, dies, special fixtures, and other devices used in mass production. Frequently, they redesign existing tools to improve their efficiency. They also make, or supervise others who make, detailed drawings of tools and fixtures.

Instrumentation Technology

Automated manufacturing and industrial processes, oceanographic and space exploration, weather forecasting, satellite communication systems, and environmental protection have helped to make instrumentation technology a fast growing field. Technicians help develop and design complex measuring and control devices, such as those in a spacecraft that sense and measure changes in heat or pressure, automatically record data, and make necessary adjustments. These technicians have extensive knowledge of physical science as well as electrical-electronic and mechanical engineering.

Chemical Technology

Chemical technicians work with chemists and chemical engineers to develop, sell, and utilize chemical and related products and equipment. Outdoor careerists will find the area of pollution of the most interest—for example, helping to solve the problems related to treatment and disposal of industrial waste.

Most chemical technicians do research and development, testing, and other laboratory work. They often set up and conduct tests on processes and products being developed or improved. For example, a technician may examine steel for carbon phosphorus and sulphur content or test a lubricating oil by subjecting it to changing temperatures. The technician measures reactions, analyzes the results of experiments, and records data that will be the basis for decisions and future research.

Chemical technicians in production generally put into commercial operation those products or processes developed in research laboratories. They assist in making the final designs, installing equipment, and training and supervising operators on the production line. Technicians in quality control test materials, production processes, and final products to insure that they meet the manufacturer's specifications and quality standards. Many also sell chemicals or chemical products as technical sales personnel. Selling to farmers might appeal to the outdoor careerist.

Many chemical technicians use computers and other instruments. Because the field of chemistry is so broad, chemical technicians frequently specialize in a particular industry, such as fertilizer or pesticides.

Meteorological Technology

Meteorological technicians support meteorologists in the study of atmospheric conditions. Technicians calibrate instruments; observe, record, and report meteorological occurrences; and assist in research projects and the development of scientific instruments.

Geological Technology

Geological technicians assist geologists in evaluating earth processes. Currently much research is being conducted in seismology, petroleum and mineral exploration, and ecology. For example, working in seismology, technicians install and record measurements from seismographic instruments, assist in field evaluations of earthquake damage and surface displacement, or assist geologists in earthquake prediction research. In petroleum and mineral exploration, they help conduct tests and record sound wave data to determine the likelihood of successful drilling, or use radiation detection instruments and collect core samples to help geologists evaluate the economic possibilities of mining a given resource. In an ecological project, they would help set up, operate, and record experiments.

Hydrologic Technology

Hydrologic technicians gather data to help hydrologists predict river stages and water quality levels. They monitor instruments that measure water flow, water table levels, or water quality, record and analyze the data obtained.

Agricultural Technology

Agricultural technicians work with agricultural scientists in food production and food processing. Plant technicians conduct tests and experiments to improve the yield and quality of crops, or to increase resistance to disease, insects, or other hazards. Technicians in soil science analyze the chemical and physical properties of various soils to help determine the best uses for them. Animal husbandry technicians work mainly with the breeding and nutrition of animals. Other agricultural technicians are employed in the food industry as food processing technicians. In quality control or in food science research, they help scientists develop better and more efficient ways of processing food material for human consumption.

Biological Technology

Biological technicians work primarily in laboratories, where they perform tests and experiments under controlled conditions. Microbiological technicians study microscopic organisms and may be involved in immunology or parasitology research. Laboratory animal technicians study and report on the reactions of laboratory animals to certain physical and chemical stimuli. They also study and conduct research to help biologists develop cures for human and animal diseases. A biological technician also might work with insects to study insect control, develop new insecticides, or determine how to use insects to control other insects or undesirable plants.

Technicians also specialize in such fields as atomic energy, where they work with scientists and engineers on problems of radiation safety, inspection, and decontamination. New areas of work include environmental protection, where technicians study the problems of air and water pollution, and industrial safety, a subject covered in chapter thirteen.

Over 600,000 persons work as engineering and science technicians. As pointed out earlier, not all of these technicians are outdoor workers, but many of their jobs are in traditional outdoor fields and they have an opportunity to work part or all of their time outdoors.

About two-thirds of this group work in private industry. In the manufacturing sector, the largest employers are the electrical equipment, chemical, machinery, and aerospace industries, all of which have some connection with the outdoor field. In non-manufacturing, large numbers work in engineering and architectural firms, again outdoor-related fields.

The federal government employs about 90,000 technicians, chiefly as engineering and electronics technicians, geological technicians, cartographic technicians, meteorological technicians, and physical science technicians. The largest number works for the Department of Defense, and most of the others work for the Departments of Transportation, Agriculture, Interior, and Commerce.

State government agencies employ nearly 50,000 engineering and science technicians, and local governments about 11,500. The remainder work for colleges and universities and non-profit organizations.

Although persons can qualify for technician jobs through many combinations of work experience and education, most employers prefer applicants who have had some specialized technical training. Such training is available at technical institutes, junior and community colleges, area vocational-technical schools, extension divisions of colleges and universities, and vocational-technical high schools. Some engineering and science students who have not completed the bachelor's degree and others who have degrees in science and mathematics also are able to qualify for technican positions.

People also can qualify for technician jobs by less formal methods. Workers may learn through on-the-job training, appreticeship programs, or correspondence schools. Some qualify on the basis of experience and training received in the armed forces. Post-secondary training is, however, becoming increasingly necessary for advancement to more responsible jobs.

Some of the types of post-secondary training include:

Technical Institutes

They offer training to qualify students for a job immediately after graduation with a minimum of on-the-job training. In general, students receive intensive technical training, but less theory and general education than in engineering schools or liberal arts colleges. A few technical institutes and community colleges offer cooperative programs in which students spend part of the time in school and part in paid employment related to their studies. Some technical institutes operate as regular or extension divisions of colleges and universities. Other institutions are operated by states and municipalities or by private organizations.

Junior and Community Colleges

Curricula in junior and community colleges that prepare students for technician occupations are similar to those in technical institutes but emphasize more theory and liberal arts. After completing the two-year programs, some graduates qualify for technician jobs while others continue their education at four-year colleges.

Area Vocational-Technical Schools

These secondary public institutions serve students from surrounding areas and emphasize training in skills needed by employers in the local area. Most award a high school degree upon graduation.

Other training

Some large corporations conduct training programs and operate private schools to fill the need for technically trained personnel in specific jobs. Such training rarely includes general studies. Training for some technician occupations is available through formal two- to four-year apprenticeship programs. The apprentice gets on-the-job training under the close supervision of an experienced technician and related technical knowledge in classes, usually after working hours.

The armed forces have trained many technicians. Although military job requirements generally differ from those in the civilian sector, military technicians often find employment with only minimal additional training.

Many private technical and correspondence schools specialize in a single field of technical training. Some of these schools are owned and operated by large corporations that have the resources to provide up-to-date training in a technical field.

In the 1980s, employment opportunities for engineering and science technicians will be best for graduates of post-secondary school technician programs. Industrial expansion and the increasing complexity of modern technology underlie the steady demand for technicians. Automation of industrial processes and continued growth of such new areas of work as environmental protection and energy development will add to the demand for technologists.

According to a survey by the Engineering Manpower Commission, technicians in private industry who complete a two-year post-high school training program earn starting salaries of about $10,500 a year. Those with five years of experience on top of the training earn about $12,800. Workers without training start at about $9,000 a year and with five years of experience, about $11,100. Senior technicians average about $18,700 a year.

Starting salaries for all technicians in the federal government are: high school/no experience, $8,366; associate degree, $9,391; and bachelor's degree, $10,507 to $13,014.

According to a Department of Labor survey, the average annual salary of all engineering technicians employed by the federal government is $19,617; for physical science technicians, $15,935; and for life science technicians, about $11,375.

Surveyors and Surveying Technicians

Surveyors with the assistance of surveying technicians establish official land boundaries, research deeds, write descriptions of land to satisfy legal requirements, assist in setting land valuations, measure construction and mineral sites, and collect information for maps and charts.

Surveys are usually conducted by a survey party which determines the precise measurement of distances, directions, and angles between points, and of elevations, points, lines, and contours on the earth's surface.

Land surveyors, who may head one or more survey parties, are directly responsible for the party's activities and the accuracy of its work. They plan the field work, select survey reference points, and determine the precise location of natural and constructed features of the survey project area. They record the information disclosed by the survey, verify the accuracy of the survey data, and prepare sketches, maps, and reports.

A typical survey party is made up of the party chief and one to six assistants and helpers. The party chief leads the day-to-day work activities of the party. These helpers include:

Instrument assistants

They adjust and operate surveying instruments such as the theodolite, used to measure horizontal and vertical angles, and electronic equipment, used to measure distances. These workers also compile notes, sketch, and record the data obtained from using these instruments.

Surveyor helpers

They use a steel tape to measure distances between surveying points and use a level rod, a stadia rod, range pole, or other equipment to aid instrument assistants in determining elevations, distances, and directions. Surveyor helpers also may clear brush and trees from the survey line and assist in setting survey markers.

Surveyors may specialize in particular types of surveys. Many perform land surveys to locate the boundaries of a given tract of land. They then prepare maps and legal descriptions for deeds, leases, and other documents. Surveyors doing topographic surveys determine elevations, depressions, and contours of an area and indicate the locations of distinguishing surface features, such as farms, buildings, forests, roads, and rivers. Surveyors with specialized skills include:

Geodetic surveyors

They make precise, broad-area measurements that take into account the earth's curvature and its geophysical characteristics.

Geophysical prospecting surveyors

They mark sites for subsurface exploration, usually related to petroleum prospecting.

Marine surveyors

They survey harbors, rivers, and other bodies of water to determine shorelines, topography of the bottom, depth, and other features.

Two professions closely related to surveying are geodesy and photogrammetry. Geodesists study the size, shape, and gravitational field of the earth. They make the measurements and computations necessary for accurate mapping of the earth's surface. This science is a branch of the environmental sciences and is described completely in chapter ten.

Photogrammetrists measure and interpret photographic images to determine the various physical characteristics of natural or constructed features of an area. By applying analytical processes and mathematical techniques to photographs obtained from aerial, space, ground, and underwater locations, photogrammetrists are able to make detailed maps of areas that are inaccessible or difficult to survey by other methods. Control surveys on the ground are made to insure the accuracy of maps derived from photogrammatic techniques.

Surveyors and surveying technicians usually work an eight-hour day, five-day week. Sometimes they work longer hours during the summer months, when weather conditions are apt to be most suitable for surveying.

The work of a survey party is active and sometimes strenuous. Party members often stand for long periods and walk long distances or climb hills with heavy packs of instruments and equipment. They also are exposed to all types of weather. Occasionally they must commute long distances or find temporary housing near the site. They need good eyesight, coordination, and hearing to communicate over great distances by hand or voice signals.

Surveyors spend considerable time performing such office duties as planning surveys, preparing reports and computations, and drawing maps.

About 62,000 persons work as surveyors or surveying technicians. Federal, state, and local government agencies employ about one out of every ten of these workers. Among the federal agencies are the United States Geological Survey, the Bureau of Land Management, the Army Corps of Engineers, the Forest Service, the National Ocean Survey, and the Defense Mapping Agency. Most surveyors and surveying technicians in state and local government agencies work for highway departments and community planning and redevelopment agencies.

Nearly three-quarters of all surveyors and surveying technicians work for construction companies and for engineering and architectural consulting firms. A sizable number either work for or own firms that conduct surveys for a fee. Surveyors and surveying technicians also work for crude petroleum and natural gas companies and for public utilities.

Most people preparing for survey work combine post-secondary school courses in surveying with extensive on-the-job training. Some prepare by obtaining a college degree. Junior and community colleges, technical institutes, and vocational schools offer one-, two-, and three-year programs in surveying. A few four-year colleges offer bachelor's degrees specifically in surveying, while many others offer several courses in the field.

High school students interested in surveying as a career should take courses in algebra, geometry, trigonometry, drafting, and mechanical drawing.

High school graduates with no formal training in surveying usually start as surveyor helpers. After several years of on-the-job experience and some formal training in surveying, it is possible to advance to instrument assistant, then to party chief, and finally to licensed surveyor.

Beginners with post-secondary school training in surveying can generally start as instrument assistants. After gaining experience, they usually advance to party chief and can later, with additional experience, become licensed surveyors. In many instances, promotions to higher level positions are based on written examinations as well as experience.

For those interested in careers as photogrammetrists, a bachelor's degree in engineering or the physical sciences is usually needed. Most photogrammetry technicians must have some specialized post-secondary school training.

All fifty states require licensing of land surveyors. Licensing requirements are generally quite strict, because once licensed, surveyors can be held legally responsible for their work. Requirements for licensure vary among states, but generally the quickest route is a combination of four years of college, two to four years of experience, and passing the state licensing exam. In most states, persons also may qualify to take the licensing exam after five to twelve years of surveying experience. A few states now require a bachelor's degree, emphasizing surveying, as a prerequisite to licensure.

Surveyors and surveying technicians should have the ability to visualize and understand objects, distances, size, and abtract forms. Also, because surveying mistakes can be very costly, surveyors must perform mathematical calculations quickly and accurately and must pay close attention to the smallest details. Leadership qualities also are important as surveyors must supervise the work of others.

The growth of jobs for surveyors and surveying technicians is tied to the growth of all kinds of construction, including single residences, housing developments, apartment buildings, shopping centers, office buildings, recreational areas, and roads and highways. For this reason employment fluctuates from year to year. If the economy remains stable throughout the 1980s, average growth in the field is expected.

In federal jobs, high school graduates with little or no training or experience start as surveyor helpers at $7,960 annually. Those with one year of related post-secondary school training earn $8,951. Those with an associate degree that included courses in surveying generally start as instrument assistants at $9,766. Survey technicians working as party chiefs earn between $11,000 and $15,000 per year. Land surveyors average about $20,000.

Although salaries in private industry vary by geographic area, limited data indicate that salaries generally are comparable to those in federal service.

Everything is connected to everything else.
Barry Commoner

14

The Best of All Possible Worlds: *Indoor Skills—Outdoor Fun*

Any career can be an outdoor career. If you have a strong interest in the outdoors and want to combine this interest with another field, you can probably do it. This chapter is about how to give a few indoor jobs—teaching, law, and communications—an outdoor component to create uniquely individual career fields.

Teaching

Teaching, especially at the college level, is an important aspect of many outdoor careers. For that reason, it seems necessary to discuss the subject separately from the various disciplines covered in this book.

The overall employment outlook for teaching in the decade of the '80s is not a good one. The basic factor underlying the demand for college faculty is enrollment. While the prospect for college enrollments during the 1980s and 1990s is uncertain, they seem likely to decline for two reasons. First, census figures show there are fewer people of college age. Secondly, the cost of a college education is becoming astronomical at the same time that sources of financial aid to college students, especially from the federal government, are drying up.

The conclusion must be, then, that employment for college faculty will decrease. Almost certainly the bulk of the job openings will result from replacement needs, and those needs will vary from institution to institution.

Competition will be keen. Already the number of Ph.D. holders exceeds the number of job openings. The hope of gaining tenure is slim. Ads for academic jobs carry the ominous line "Not a tenure-track position." There are some exceptions, in the field of environmental protection, for example. Or in agriculture. At the beginning of the 1980s, college-level teaching jobs in agriculture were unfilled in many schools, probably because of relatively low salaries. Industry offered better money for the same skills. There will always be people, however, who want to teach and who are willing to compete for the jobs that do exist.

Teaching in the outdoor fields, in most cases, opens up the same opportunitites and challenges as for other jobs in the same field, all of which are discussed in detail in separate chapters earlier in this book. This is especially true where the teaching appointments are for nine months. The other three months can be used for research or for seasonal jobs, the list of which is circumscribed only by the scope of imagination and the limitations of the field. College professors can be found leading wilderness camping trips, archeological tours, or foreign travel of various kinds. They become summer miners, construction workers, farmhands, fishers, park rangers, or foresters. They turn writer or photographer, two areas that will be covered shortly. A few make institutional films.

It is important, however, to remember that the principal function of a college-level teacher is to present an in-depth analysis of a particular field. Most are scholars in their disciplines and research and writing are important parts of their jobs, especially in four-year colleges and universities. A recent survey indicated that as many as one-quarter of the faculty in science and engineering departments (the main areas in the outdoor fields) that offered doctoral degrees were primarily involved in research and development.

As a part of teaching, faculty members must spend time in preparation and evaluations, as well as time in the classroom. They usually also work directly with students in some advisory capacity. Some faculty members turn to administration and supervision, becoming department chairpersons or deans. Almost every faculty member must spend time serving on various academic committees at times when they would rather be in the laboratory or out in the field.

College faculty members usually have flexible schedules, dividing their time among teaching, research, and administrative responsibilities. The normal teaching load is heavier in junior and community colleges, where less emphasis is placed on scholarly research and publication than in major universities.

Over 90 percent of all full-time college and university faculty work in institutions that have tenure systems (the assurance of continuing employment with freedom from dismissal without cause). Over three-fifths of those faculty members are tenured. Under a tenure system, a faculty member usually receives one-year contracts during a probationary period lasting at least three years and ordinarily no more than seven. Some universities award two- or three-year contracts. After the probationary period, institutions consider faculty members for tenure. Because of declining enrollments and rising budgetary constraints, however, faculty members now find it increasingly difficult to gain tenure. Some colleges and universities are turning more and more to short-term contracts and to part-time faculty members to save money and avoid long-term commitments.

About 675,000 faculty members work in about 3,200 colleges and universities; about 200,000 of them are part-time staff. In addition, there are thousands more part-time instructors, teaching fellows, teaching assistants, and laboratory assistants who aid regular faculty members, usually while studying for their own advanced degrees. No figures are available for the number of these positions that fall in the outdoor career field.

Public institutions, which amount to less than half of all colleges and universities, employ over 70 percent of all full-time faculty. They employ about two-thirds of the full-time faculty in all universities and four-year colleges and over 90 percent in all two-year institutions.

Nearly one-third of full-time faculty teach in universities; almost one-half, in four-year colleges; and over one-fifth, in two-year colleges.

The overwhelming majority of full-time college and university faculty are classified in four academic ranks: instructors, assistant professors, associate professors, and professors. The top three ranks comprise about three-fourths of full-time faculty. A small proportion of faculty are classified as lecturers. Most full-time junior and community college faculty are in institutions that do not use academic ranks.

Most college faculty enter the profession as instructors and must have at least a master's degree. Because competition for positions is so keen, however, some colleges and universities consider only doctoral degree holders for entry level academic appointment. Occasionally they will hire candidates who have fulfilled all of the Ph.D. requirements except completing the dissertation, accepting them with the understanding that the dissertation must be finished by a stated time.

Doctoral programs usually require three to five years of study beyond the bachelor's degree, including the intensive research needed for a dissertation that makes an original contribution to the candidate's field of study. A working knowledge of one or more foreign languages is required, with some institutions offering no-credit courses to give a reading knowledge of the languages to those majoring in other departments. In scientific fields, advanced mathematical and statistical techniques often are required, as well. Because of the time commitment and the obvious cost, students should consider carefully their academic potential and motivation before beginning doctoral studies. This is an important factor for many of the outdoor fields, which require this advanced degree for promotion to certain levels.

Advancement through the academic ranks usually requires a doctorate plus college teaching experience, even in institutions that hire master's degree holders as instructors. Assistant professors usually have a few years' experience as an instructor, while appointment as an associate professor frequently requires three years or more of experience as an assistant professor. For a professorship, extensive teaching experience and published books and articles that evidence expertise in one's discipline usually are essential.

Academic, administrative, or professional contributions affect advancement opportunities in this field. Research, publication, consulting work, and other forms of professional recognition—service on national committees in professional associations, for example—all have a bearing on a college faculty member's chances of rising through the academic ranks.

There was a time when academic life was considered easy, perhaps not really work. Many people agreed with George Bernard Shaw who wrote (in *Maxims for Revolutionists*) most derisively, "He who can, does. He who cannot, teaches." But this is a glib generality. In today's competitive job market a special zeal for learning and the desire and skill to help others learn are necessary for success as a teacher. College faculty must have inquiring, analytical minds in order to devote their lives to the pursuit and dissemination of knowledge. Since they function both as teachers and as researchers, they must be good at communicating information and ideas both orally and in writing. As models for their students, they must exhibit dedication to the principles of academic integrity and intellectual honesty. They share in the growth and development of students and are constantly exposed to new ideas.

Earnings of college and university faculty members vary widely, according to faculty rank and type of institution. In general, faculty members in four-year institutions average higher salaries than those in two-year schools. According to a 1977-78 survey, salaries for full-time faculty on nine-month contracts were $25,000 for professors, $19,000 for associate professors, $15,500 for assistant professors, and $12,500 for instructors.

Ninety percent of full-time faculty members have nine-month contracts, so this means these salaries can be boosted by additional summer earnings from teaching, research, writing, or other jobs such as those mentioned earlier. Royalties and fees for speaking engagements may provide additional earnings. Some faculty members also work as consultants throughout the academic year.

Many college and university faculty members also enjoy fringe benefits offered by few other professions. These include tuition waivers for dependents, housing allowances, travel allowances, and paid leaves of absence. In many institutions, faculty members are eligible for sabbatical leave after six or seven years of employment.

Limited opportunities do exist for teachers in the outdoor field on elementary and secondary levels, mostly in private schools. For example, there are a few schools that build their curricula around sailing, skiing, horsemanship, ranching, wilderness skills, and similar activities. Interested people can dig out these specialty schools by researching the guides like the Porter Sargent *Handbook of Private Schools* or the Bunting and Logan guide to *Private Independent Schools*. (See appendix.) In public schools, the best opportunities are probably in schools with strong science programs and in vocational schools. Information about these is available from local school districts and from state departments of education.

In this area, individual initiative is important. A program often depends on the person. For example, an elementary school in central Pennsylvania had an innovative program in life and environmental sciences. They utilized an old quarry, a swamp, and a creek—all located near the school—as adjunct classrooms. Field trips, sometimes overnight, were common. One gifted and outdoor-loving teacher ran the program. Unfortunately, when he moved to another school district, the program was discontinued.

Anyone with the special interest and training could promote similar programs in any school. Sometimes grants can be found to support such projects. Local organizations from service clubs to the Junior League to nature clubs might be interested in helping.

A few teaching opportunities exist in the Department of the Interior in the Bureau of Indian Affairs. It hires teachers at the kindergarten, elementary, and post-secondary levels. For the adventurous, the posts in Alaska, teaching Eskimo children, might be the most attractive.

And, of course, teachers can always seek jobs at the outposts of civilization and near resort communities. Here, at least, outdoor activities are usually available by simply walking out the door.

Lawyers

Lawyers who specialize in outdoor fields, especially in environmental pollution, have multiplied dramatically in the last two decades. Their interest parallels the general public concern with the environment and the increase in legislation affecting the environment.

It is a legitimate interest, not a "hobby horse," as law schools are adding courses in environmental law to their curricula and publishers are bringing out books on the subject. One organization, the Environmental Law Institute, compiles a monthly record of court cases involving the environment.

Several national non-profit groups have been organized to help people protect the environment by using legal resources and educational measures. One of the largest is the Environmental Defense Fund, which was organized in 1967 to establish "through the cumulative nature of court decisions, a body of law under which the public can assert rights to a viable, minimally-degraded environment." It has had both failures and successes. Notable failures include failure to halt the construction of the Alaskan pipeline and to stop the United States Army from dumping poisonous gas in the Atlantic Ocean. Successes include suits against the Secretaries of the Departments of Health, Education and Welfare and Agriculture to curb the use of DDT, and the Army Corps of Engineers to stop construction of the Cross-Florida Barge Canal.

Lawyers who practice environmental law are known as *pro bon publico* (for the public good) lawyers. To date many of them have been with large firms that permit their members to spend time in public service projects, although it should be pointed out that their services are not free. Funds raised by public subscription go to pay for their time and for court costs. More and more individuals throughout the country, however, are hiring lawyers to protect their rights. Recent examples are the suits brought by a number of families in central Pennsylvania against several government agencies and Metropolitan Edison Company in the wake of the 1978 nuclear incident at the Three Mile Island nuclear power generating plant.

Undoubtedly the most famous pro bono publico lawyer is Ralph Nader, the superstar consumer advocate who runs the Center for the Study of Responsive Law in Washington, D.C. Among his many projects is a summer program in which students from many disciplines, including law, medicine, engineering, the sciences, and public administration, research and write reports on the work of federal agencies.

Federal, state, and local agencies involved with the environment, especially regulatory agencies, all hire lawyers. The Environmental Protection Agency tops the list. Others include the Department of the Interior, the Department of Agriculture, the Department of Housing and Urban Development, the Department of Transportation, the Department of Commerce, and the Tennessee Valley Authority. There are counterparts of these organizations in every state. Similar commissions exist in major cities. And every corporation affected by environmental law retains legal counsel.

Training for a career in environmental law is the same as for any area of law. To practice law in the courts of any state, a lawyer must be admitted to the bar. A written examination is usually required. A few states drop this requirement for graduates of their own schools. Sometimes, lawyers admitted to the bar in one state may be admitted to another without taking an examination if they meet the state's standards of good moral character and have legal experience. Federal courts and agencies set their own qualifications for those practicing before them.

To qualify for the bar examination in most states, an applicant must complete at least three years of college and graduate from one of the 167 law schools approved by the American Bar Association (ABA) or the proper state authorities. A few states accept the study of law in a law office or in combination with study in a law school; only California accepts the study of law by correspondence as qualification for taking the bar exam. Several states require registration and approval of students by the State Board of Examiners, either before they enter law school or during the early years of legal study.

Although there is no nationwide bar exam, forty-three states and the District of Columbia participate in the Multistate Bar Examination. This exam, which covers issues of broad interest since the early 1970s, is required in addition to the state bar exam.

The required college and law school education usually takes seven years of full-time study after high school—four years of undergraduate study followed by three years in law school. Although some law schools accept a very small number of students after three years of college, an increasing number require applicants to have a bachelor's degree. To meet the needs of students who can attend only part-time, a number of law schools have night or part-time divisions that usually require four years of study.

Competition for admission to law school has become intense in recent years. Applicants outnumber available places by about two to one, with the competition being even stiffer in the more prestigious law schools.

Preparation for a career as a lawyer, particularly as an environmental lawyer, begins long before law school. The essential skills—the ability to write, to read and analyze, to think logically, and to communicate verbally—are learned in high school. A college undergraduate program that cultivates these skills while broadening the student's view of the world is best. A major in science and/or engineering is particularly suitable for the would-be environmental lawyer. No law student, however, should specialize too narrowly. Regardless of the major, English, foreign language (particularly Latin), public speaking, government, philosophy, history, economics, and mathematics are highly recommended.

Acceptance by most law schools depends on the applicant's ability to demonstrate an aptitude for the study of law, usually through good grades and the Law School Admission Test (LSAT), administered by the Educational Testing Service.

During the first year or year-and-one-half of law school, students generally study such fundamental subjects as constitutional law, contracts, property law, and judicial procedures. In the remaining time, they may elect specialized courses. Practical experience is often acquired by participation in school-sponsored legal aid or legal clinic activities; in the school's moot court, where students conduct practice trials under the supervision of experienced lawyers and judges; and through writing on legal issues for the school's law journal. Part-time or summer clerkships also provide experience that can be extremely valuable later on. Such training can provide references or lead directly to a job after graduation, and it can help students decide what kind of practice best suits them. Clerkships also may be an important source of financial aid.

Graduates of law school receive the degree of Juris Doctor (J.D.) or Bachelor Law (LL.B.) as the first professional degree. Advanced study is desirable for those planning to specialize, as in environmental law. It is possible to pursue joint degree programs, which generally require an additional year or more in law school.

Most beginning lawyers, unless their families own law firms, start in salaried positions, usually as research assistants. After several years of progressively responsible salaried employment, they go into practice for themselves or join already existing firms as partners. For some lawyers, the ultimate aim is to become judges. A great many go into politics. A lawyer with environmental law training and experience might make a valuable contribution as a responsible office holder.

Competition in law is as fierce as in most of the other fields discussed in this book. The best jobs will go to the students who practice competitive job strategies. One of the most important factors in getting a top job is having top grades. Another is having a degree from a prestigious school. Geographic mobility, experience, and specialization may also help with job-hunting. In environmental law, the competition will be even tougher because the opportunities exist in urban rather than rural areas, where the best opportunities are found for beginning lawyers.

Entry level salaries for lawyers are shocking when the time involved and the cost of training is considered. Some law school graduates are paid as low as $8,000 a year for their first jobs. At the other end of the spectrum, some getting jobs with large corporations make as much as $29,000. The median is probably about $18,000 in private industry and $15,193 or $18,585, depending upon academic and personal qualifications, in federal agencies.

There are more than 480,000 lawyers in the United States, of which 70 percent are in private practice. Most of the balance work for federal, state, and local government. Others are employed by public utilities, transportation firms, banks, insurance companies, real estate agencies, manufacturing firms, welfare and religious organizations, and other business firms and non-profit organizations. About 8,000 teach full- or part-time. No figures are available for the number of lawyers who specialize in environmental law. This means the figure must be very low. It could also follow that it is a growing field with the possibility of filling a great personal need for the person who wants to combine law with the love of the outdoors.

Communicators

The communicators work in the media. They are reporters, writers, radio and television producers and announcers, artists, photographers, advertising copywriters, and public relations workers. Their importance has skyrocketed, developing along with technology. Printing, photography, and broadcasting techniques have been revolutionized by computer and satellite science.

In the outdoor field, no less than in other areas, the media have been instrumental in public education, especially in the areas of conservation and environmental protection. In chapter one, you read about writers and artists from earlier years who molded public opinion by writing about their experiences and their beliefs—people like George Perkins Marsh, Henry David Thoreau, John Muir, John James Audubon and others. In more recent times, communicators have been equally as important. Consider Forest Service Public Information Director Clint Davis, who made Smokey the Bear a household name, or conservationist Ed Dodd, who created the widely syndicated newspaper cartoon strip *Mark Trail*. Biologist Rachel Carson awakened an entire generation to the horrors of environmental plunder when *Silent Spring* was published. Jacques-Yves Cousteau has brought new understanding and appreciation of underwater life with his exquisite and exciting films, which have been seen by millions of television viewers. Dozens of environmental problems have been aired on radio stations and television channels, especially the public ones, and widespread support for viable solutions has resulted.

There is always room for communicators with top skills, although the outdoor area is as crowded as any other in the field. As a result of the Watergate scandals of the early 1970s, journalism and broadcasting especially, have more job-seekers than jobs. Young people are attracted by the glamorous image of media jobs, the opportunities to meet public figures, to attend special events, to be "on stage" whether in print or in person. This glamorous aspect of the job obscures the hard work most of these jobs entail. Journalists spend hours every day on the tedious, but essential task of making contacts, checking facts, following leads. The technical writer spends hours in research and careful writing, trying to make his abstracts and instructions clear and concise. The photographer spends long hours in the darkroom.

This field takes a combination of talent, motivation, imagination, and luck. It also requires a broad education. Not only the craft of the communicator—whether writing, broadcasting, drawing, or photography—is needed, but also knowledge in a scientific or technical field is mandatory.

The ideal preparation is a liberal arts degree with a major in English and a minor in science and engineering, followed by a master's degree in the specific communication field. Summer work might be divided between experience in the outdoor field and some in the communications field. For example, a writer who wants to work on an agriculture publication might spend the summer as a counselor at a farm camp, a summer working as a farmhand on a livestock farm, a summer as an intern on a newspaper, and a summer as a volunteer writer for a regional magazine developing stories on agricultural subjects. Similar scenarios could be developed in any of the fields.

Acute powers of observation and the ability to think clearly and logically are common to all communications jobs. An excellent command of language, both oral and written, is essential for writers and broadcasters. The knack of picking out the unique aspect of any scene is necessary for photographers and artists. Getting along well with people is mandatory. For successful completion, all of these jobs depend on cooperation with a wide variety of people.

Communications workers must perform well under pressure. A reporter who submits a story late may delay a newspaper edition, resulting in a loss of newstand sales. A television announcer who does not react quickly to emergencies on the air can drive viewers away and cause the show's ratings to drop. An artist who produces mediocre work may cause an advertising agency to lose an important account.

The lifestyle of communicators is hectic. Working conditions can be noisy and the hours erratic. Reporters, for instance, have terrible working hours. If they work for morning papers, they report for work in the late afternoon and work until midnight or later. Those who work for afternoon papers work from early morning until mid-afternoon. They frequently work on weekends and holidays, too. Beginning reporters almost always draw these less desirable assignments.

Frequent travel and working in uncomfortable surroundings are common in most of the media field. Sometimes the work can be dangerous, as for example, photographers and reporters covering nuclear disasters, certain assignments for anyone specializing in environmental writing. Overtime work is common, especially for freelance writers, whose lives may be a constant juggling act between unexpected work and not enough time.

None of these discomforts seem, however, to dam the steady stream of young hopefuls who want to enter the field. The lure of possible superstardom, the possibility of big money, the idea of influencing people—these are stronger than any of the negative aspects for those entranced by work in the media. Those who are successful, like Bradford Angier, would not live any other way. He gave up a comfortable desk job to go live in the wilderness and has spent his life writing about the experience. In his autobiography, he says that the combination of developing wilderness survival skills and writing about them has provided him with a happier life than he ever dreamed he would have.

A brief description of the main communications jobs that can be combined with outdoor career areas follows. Anyone interested in this area should consult the resources in the appendix for additional information. Just one general statement about the number of workers in the field. No survey has been done of workers combining communications and outdoor fields, so no accurate statistics are available.

Newspaper Reporters

They are also called journalists, and they represent the free press, one of the most important institutions in a democratic society. They inform the public about local, state, national, and international events, presenting differing points of view on current issues and monitoring the actions of public officials and others who exercise power. They gather information on current events and use it to write stories for daily or weekly newspapers. In covering events, they may interview people, review public records, and do research. They take notes or use tape or cassette recorders while out of the office collecting facts, and they write their stories upon returning to the office. Sometimes, to meet deadlines, they telephone their information or stories to rewriters, who write or transcribe the stories for them. To become a reporter in the outdoor field, beginning reporters might first work as general assignment reporters, making an effort to get assignments in science, outdoor recreation, environmental news, and similar topics. Starting on the sports desk is another way to break into the field. Reporters generally begin working for smaller papers. As their skills develop, they move on to jobs on larger papers. Most editors feel that it takes two to five years to develop dependable reportorial skills. Beginning reporters, according to the American Newspaper Guild, earn from $7,020 to $23,920, with the median between $10,400 and $14,300. Experienced and skilled reporters on medium city dailies make about $30,000. Their counterparts on large city dailies earn much more.

Radio and Television Program Producers, Reporters, and Announcers

They do for broadcasting what reporters do for newspapers. Their technical skills, however, are different. They write for the ear and not the eye and, in addition to writing, they need good speaking voices and delivery skills and an understanding of the potentials and limitations of magnetic tape recording. In radio, on-air personnel may need a Federal Communications Commission (FCC) third class radiotelephone operator's permit; fortunately, the procedure for obtaining one has been vastly simplified in recent years and it is no longer necessary to learn a bewildering amount of broadcast engineering material to qualify for the permit. Technology changes quickly in broadcasting so people on the "editorial side" do not need to bother with it too much except to be aware of the potential for better programs. All stations—radio and television—have chief engineers to worry about the hardware. Specializing in the outdoor field is difficult for beginners, but on commercial stations, sports reporting offers the best entree. Public radio and television provide the best opportunities for reporting on environmental and scientific issues. For example, National Public Radio has one reporter, Ira Flatow, assigned to science and carries regular and special reports by him, and the network also occasionally buys science reports from reporters at its affiliated stations or from freelancers. Public television stations often produce specials on scientific and environmental issues of particular importance to the viewers they serve. An enterprising, experienced producer-announcer might eventually work up a regular program for one of the large public stations. Beginners usually find jobs in small stations, where starting salaries can easily be as low as $8,000. As a rule, radio salaries are lower than television salaries, and public broadcasting pays less than commercial. Experienced producers-announcers may earn between $15,000 and

$25,000, depending on the size and location of the station. There are, of course, the superstars like Barbara Walters, who earn $1,000,000. And this is the "carrot" that makes the field attractive to so many young people and helps them to endure the "stick" of low starting salaries and sometimes poor working conditions, including many assignments that have nothing to do with what they really want to do.

Magazine Staff Writers

Almost all the outdoor career fields have their own publications, and these offer many job possibilities for writers. They range from scientific association journals like *Environmental Science & Technology* to conservation-promoting magazines like *Audubon*. There are also organizations like the National Wildlife Federation that publish not only several major magazines (*Ranger Rick's Nature Magazine* for children is one of the most popular), but also books and directories. Most of them are handsomely produced and well-edited. Most likely, beginners would be hired as editorial assistants and spend a couple of years reading manuscripts, rewriting other people's material, and developing editing skills, Eventually, they would have opportunities to write original material. For some of these publications, technical writing skills (see technical writers) would be necessary. This is excellent training for freelancing. Beginning salaries are low—on some publications, about $8,000. Experienced editor-writer staffers might earn $20,000.

Freelance Writers

News reporting, radio-television work, or magazine staff work offer an excellent background for non-fiction freelance writing in the outdoor field, surely one of the most difficult occupations in the world. Establishing oneself in the field is a long process, and the lack of a steady source of income can cause many problems. But it has, without a doubt, a tantalizing attraction to people with the ability. There are dozens of markets for articles—more than 100 in the environmental field alone, for example. Then there are sports and science magazines. General magazines as varied as *Atlantic, Harpers, Christian Century, National Geographic, Psychology To-*

day, and *Reader's Digest* also carry many articles related to the outdoor field. Most freelancers write for low-paying publications first.
As they become polished craftspeople, they sell to larger, higher-
paying quality magazines. Freelancing is risky, and not an enterprise
to be undertaken lightly. Some resource materials helpful in exploring the field and making decisions are listed in the appendix.

Technical Writers

This is one of the hottest fields in writing now, with about 24,000
people turning out material, mainly for large firms in the electronics,
aviation, aerospace, ordnance, chemical, pharmaceutical, environmental, energy, agricultural, and computer manufacturing industries. The federal government employs 1,700 technical writers for
work in the Departments of Defense, Interior, Agriculture, Health,
and Human Services, Education, and the National Aeronautics and
Space Administration. Technical writers prepare manuals, catalogues, parts lists, instructional materials, research reports, abstracts,
and grant proposals. They may also write speeches and news releases; edit and write technical books; prepare articles for popular
magazines; develop advertising copy, promotional brochures, and
texts for exhibits and displays; and handle technical documentation.
They also are responsible for the preparation of tables, charts, illus-
trations, and other art work, usually working closely with illustrators,
drafters, or photographers in their preparation. They must have a
scientific background and be skilled researchers and interviewers.
Usually they take courses in technical writing and continue to attend
yearly workshops to improve and upgrade their skills. They may
work as freelancers, but at the beginning most have staff jobs with
starting salaries ranging from $8,000 to $10,000. A few writers with
exceptionally good skills and a master's degree may make as much
as $18,000. In the federal government, beginning technical writers
holding bachelor's degrees with science or engineering majors are
paid $10,507. Median salaries for experienced people are $20,000
to $25,000.

Photographers

They use their cameras and film to portray people, places, and
events much as a writer uses words. The possibilities in the outdoor

field are almost endless. For example, they might specialize in scientific or engineering photography, in sports photography, in pictorial journalism (covering environmental, conservation, and recreation subjects), or in photographic oceanography. (See chapter on environmental scientists.) Because procedures involved in still photography are quite different from those in motion picture photography, some photographers specialize in one or the other. The beginner, however, would be wise to have training in both. To be successful, photographers should have good skills and excellent equipment, including lenses, filters, electronic flash, floodlights, reflectors, and other lighting gear. Photographers usually have their own darkrooms, but they may also use commercial laboratories for processing. Photo journalists earn the same as news reporters. Newly hired photographers in the federal government earn from $9,390 to $13,010 a year. Most experienced photographers earn about $20,000. Especially talented photographers who work as freelancers and sell their work to top publications, such as *National Geographic,* or who make films for industry or for educational organizations earn much higher salaries. For example, a photographer who took color slides for a fifteen-minute audio-visual presentation by a conservation group charged $10,000 for his work. The writer working with him earned $8,000.

Artists

In the outdoor career field they are wildlife painters, graphic artists specializing in scientific presentations, scientific illustrators, or layout people working for outdoor publications. Like photography, the field is broad. Top skills are necessary for success. Earnings can be very low to start. The field is difficult to break into and beginners may have to gain experience in another area and work into their outdoor specialty as freelancers or by forming their own firms. For example, wildlife painter Don Bashore is an art director for a commercial television station. Over a decade he has perfected his talent and built up a clientele of collectors. He has displayed his work in one-man museum shows and sells his work regularly at summer outdoor art shows. Eventually he hopes to spend all of his time painting.

Copywriters

Copywriting is a relatively young occupation; the first one was hired ninety years ago. It is a specialized form of idea communication that has evolved to serve the requirements of modern mass marketing. The copywriter's function is to prepare an advertiser's message in such a way that it will be accepted by the people the advertiser wants to reach. He or she works through the media of print, radio, or television. The material can be advertisements, publicity releases, sales presentations, dealer's sales aids, and similar specialized jobs. A copywriter should have a working knowledge of typography and layout because copy is only one part of an ad. Although copywriting is one aspect of public relations, not every public relations worker is a copywriter. The job takes a highly developed and fertile imagination, combined with top writing skills. In the outdoor field, it also requires strong scientific and engineering knowledge, because the writer must understand complex machinery, products, or ideas before he or she can sell them. Entry level salaries range from $8,000 to $10,000. Promotion depends strictly on ability to produce "sell" copy. Successful copywriters earn top money, say $30,000 at a leading agency. But the competition is terrific and the pressure is enormous, perhaps greater than in any of the other communications areas.

Public Relations Workers

In the outdoor field, publicists work for government, private industry, and many non-profit organizations—especially in conservation, environmental protection, and agriculture—to help them build and maintain a positive public image. To achieve this goal, they may handle press, community, or consumer relations; political campaigning; interest-group representation; fund-raising; or employee recruitment. They put together information that keeps the public aware of their employer's policies, activities, and accomplishments, and also information that keeps management aware of public attitudes. After preparing information, they contact people in media to publicize the information. They write slide shows; film, radio, and television scripts; and speeches. They arrange and conduct public meetings of many kinds from simple slide shows to fund-raising campaigns to conventions. They usually also read widely in the field that they are representing and prepare abstracts of the material. Starting salaries for college graduates with bachelor's degrees range from $9,600 to $13,800 in private industry. The federal government pays $10,000. Potential earnings for skilled and experienced workers are high, especially with large organizations. For example, presidents of public relations consulting firms earn $36,000; public information directors in federal government earn $31,200; in state government, $24,000; in local government, $22,700; and in non-profit organizations, $25,000.

Sit patiently and inly ruminate . . .

William Shakespeare

Afterword

Plan for Action:
What to Do Now

Rumination. That is what is called for now. As cows and sheep chew their cud, so must you "chew" your thoughts and feelings about work. If you have read this far you have a good idea about whether or not you are interested in an outdoor career. Now is the time to take seriously the advice given in the beginning chapters of the book.

Get to know yourself. Do the exercises suggested in chapter two. Answer those three important questions: *What do you like to do? What can you do? What would you like to do?* As suggested, do it by making lists or by writing an autobiography or a combination of both. Consult the other books recommended in that chapter. They will help you find answers to the questions.

Talk to your family and friends about your plans. They can help you by providing job leads and by introducing you to people who can answer your questions.

Research various career fields. Spend time with people who

work in the field in which you are interested. Use the various techniques suggested in this book and in the others listed.

If you are still in high school, begin a survey of colleges and universities to discover the ones that are best suited to your particular field. Even if you are already in college, review your course work to be sure you are enrolled in the right classes. Many times you can make changes.

Become familiar with work. Your attitudes are important. How you feel about work is going to influence your judgment and that of the people who want to hire you. Work experience is the factor that will set you apart from other entry level candidates in any field. This does not negate education. Most people will not get far in today's job market without a good education. It is the combination of an education *and* work experience that gives you an advantage when you begin your job search.

Read trade journals and association magazines for the field in which you are interested. They will give you a more accurate image of the field and a familiarity with its special terminology and requirements. Many such publications carry classified advertising about job openings. These can give valuable clues regarding the kind of jobs available, the salary scale, the geographic locations, and other similar information.

All of these suggestions were made earlier in this book. They are repeated now to emphasize their importance. They are the backbone of your competetive job strategies, the techniques that will get you a job in a crowded field.

No book can make decisions for you; but it can provide a framework, based on knowledge, that can help you decide what you want to do.

So ruminate. Digest your subject thoroughly. These exercises are like the vitamin and mineral supplements you add to your diet to perk you up. Rumination will give you an advantage. So take it. Ruminate.

Appendix

It is impossible in the space available in this book to list all the reference sources that you might need in researching the outdoor career field. Instead, a limited list of professional organizations and publications and related information is given, organized in sections relating to chapter headings.

One of the best general reference resources in the outdoor career field is the *Conservation Directory*, published by the National Wildlife Federation, 1412 16th Street N.W., Washington, D.C. 20036. This directory lists hundreds of organizations and their addresses, including government agencies (both state and federal), voluntary organizations, national forests, national parks, national seashores, and national wildlife refuges. It can be ordered from the above address. Request Item No. 79570 TD and send a check or money order for $4.00 for each copy, which price includes handling and book rate postage.

Another good general reference is the *Recreation and Outdoor Life Directory*, published by the Gale Research Company, Book Tower, Detroit, Michigan 48229. It is available in most libraries.

Hundreds of publications on outdoor careers are available from the Superintendent of Documents, United States Government Printing Office,

Washington, D.C. 20402. Write for a list of publications, indicating your field of interest. Also ask to be put on the "new publications" list and you will receive a monthly catalogue.

Chapter 1
From Eden to Antarctica: Rationale for Outdoor Careers

U.S. Workers and Their Jobs: The Changing Picture—A chartbook with brief accompanying text which illustrates patterns of change in the American labor force, including employment, the level of education, and earnings. Prepared by the U.S. Department of Labor, Bureau of Labor Statistics. Bulletin 1919, 1976. Government Printing Office Stock No. 029-001-01917-3. Order from U.S. Superintendent of Documents. $.60.

Carson, Rachel. *Silent Spring*, 1962. Available in many editions, including paperback ones.

Commoner, Barry. *Science & Survival*. The Viking Press, 1963

Muir, John, "John of the Mountains," *The Unpublished Journals of John Muir*, ed. by Linnie Marsh Wolfe. Houghton Mifflin Company, 1938.

——*The Mountains of California*. Century Company, 1894.

——*My First Summer in the Sierra*. Houghton Mifflin Company, 1911.

——*Stickeen: The Story of a Dog*. Houghton Mifflin Company, 1909.

——*The Story of My Boyhood and Youth*. Houghton Mifflin Company, 1913.

——*Travels in Alaska*. Houghton Mifflin Company, 1915.

Smith, Frank E. *The Politics of Conservation*. Pantheon Books/Random House, 1966.

Thoreau, Henry David. *Walden*. 1854. (One of the most interesting contemporary editions is *The Annotated Walden*, edited by Philip Van Doren Stern, and published by Clarkson N. Potter, Inc. 1970.)

Resources for Chapter 2 are included in the text.

Chapter 3
Ways and Means: Preparing Yourself for the Job You Want

For a list of schools and course offerings in any field, write to:

Division of Career Education
Department of Education
200 Independence Avenue S.W.
Washington, D.C. 20201

For assistance with selecting colleges and universities, consult the following volumes found in most libraries:

College Blue Book, five volumes. Published by Macmillan annually. Hardbound. About $80.00.

Peterson's Guide to Undergraduate Study, one volume. Published by Peterson's Guides annually. $12.00.

Peterson's Guide to Graduate Study, five volumes. Published by Peterson's Guides annually. $12.00, each volume.

To apply for work in the Youth Conservation Service, write:
Job Corps
Employment and Training Administration
601 D Street N.W.
Washington, D.C. 20213

To find out about volunteer work with the National Park Service write:
Volunteers in the Parks Service Program
National Park Service
U.S. Department of the Interior
C Street Between Eighteenth and Nineteenth Streets N.W.
Washington, D.C. 20240

To apply for work at Appalachian Mountain Club huts in the White Mountains, write:
Appalachian Mountain Club
5 Joy Street
Boston, Mass. 02108

Some volunteer organizations you might like to join because of your outdoor interests are:
The American Forestry Association
1319 Eighteenth Street N.W.
Washington, D.C. 20036
The American Museum of Natural History
Central Park West at 79th Street
New York, N.Y. 10024
Appalachian Trail Conference, Inc.
Box 236
Harpers Ferry, W.Va. 25425
The Izaak Walton League of America, Inc.
1800 North Kent Street, Suite 806
Arlington, Va. 22209
National Audubon Society
950 Third Avenue
New York, N.Y. 10022
National Wildlife Federation
1412 16th Street N.W.
Washington, D.C. 20036
The Nature Conservancy
Suite 800, 1800 North Kent Street
Arlington, Va. 22209

New York Zoological Society
The Zoological Park
Bronx, N.Y. 10460

The Sierra Club
530 Bush Street
San Francisco, Calif. 94108

Smithsonian Institution
1000 Jefferson Drive S.W.
Washington, D.C. 20560

Financial Aid Information

In addition to information from high school guidance counselors or college
aid officers, students can request the following helps:

Student Consumer's Guide: Six Federal Financial Aid Programs
Published by Bureau of Student Financial Assistance, Box 84, Washington,
D.C. 20044.

*Selected List of Postsecondary Education Opportunities for Minorities and
Women*
Published annually by the United States Department of Education. Includes
list of organizations that offer loan, scholarship, and fellowship assistance.
Available in libraries or guidance offices or can be purchased from the
Superintendent of Documents, United States Government Printing Office,
Washington, D.C. 20402. $3.75

A Student Guide to Fellowships and Internships
Written by students of Amherst College and published by E. P. Dutton. $7.95.

Chapter 4
In a Nutshell: Writing Resumes and Letters

The following books will improve your writing:

Barzun, Jacques. *Simple and Direct: A Rhetoric for Writers.* Harper and Row,
1975.

Strunk, William Jr. and E. B. White. *The Elements of Style*, third edition.
Macmillan, 1979.

Zinsser, William. *On Writing Well.* Harper and Row, 1976.

No Listings for Chapter 5

Chapter 6
Bird in Hand: Who Are the Employers?

Entrepreneurialism

Small Business Administration (SBA)
1030 15th Street, N.W., Washington, D.C. 20416
They publish nearly 200 pamphlets, many of which are free. Form SBA
115-A lists free publications; form SBA 115-B lists the publications for sale.
They also have 96 field offices, whose list will be sent on request, where
management assistance of many kinds, including individual counseling, is
provided. Ask for specifics at the nearest office.

Council of Better Business Bureaus
1150 17th Street, N.W., Washington, D.C. 20046
Send a self-addressed, stamped envelope for book and pamphlet list.

The Internal Revenue Service
Federal Trade Commission, Washington, D.C. 20508
State that you are interested in information about starting a new business
and ask for available information.

Bank of America
Dept. 3120, P.O. Box 37000, San Francisco, Calif. 94137
Ask for list of publications discussing various kinds of business operations.
This is free.

Economic Development Administration
United States Department of Commerce
14th Street and Constitution Avenue, Washington, D.C. 20230
Ask for the list of 12 research and development centers where management
and technical assistance is available.

The American Women's Economic Development Corporation
1270 Avenue of the Americas, New York, New York 10020
Ask for publications and list of services available.

Also consult state and local Departments of Commerce and Chambers of
Commerce and national, state, and local chapters of professional and trade
associations in your particular field. Sometimes colleges and universities,
libraries, and YWCA's also have counselors and/or information about entrepreneurial activities.

Private Sector Employers

The College Placement Annual. Published by The College Placement Council annually. Lists more than 1,000 top United States employers.

The Armed Forces

U.S. Army Recruiting Command, Fort Sheridan, Ill. 60037.

Navy Recruiting Command, Code (40), 4015 Wilson Blvd, Arlington, Va. 22203

USAF Recruiting Service, Directorate of Recruiting Operations, Randolph Air Force Base, Tex. 78148

Director, Personnel Procurement Division, Headquarters, U.S. Marine Corps, Washington, D.C. 20380.

Commandant, (G-PMR), U.S. Coast Guard, Washington, D.C. 20590.

For general information about all federal jobs:

Office of Personnel Management
1900 E Street N.W., Washington, D.C. 20415

Regional Offices/Office of Personnel Management:

New England Region (Formerly Boston Region—comprised of Connecticut, Maine, Massachusetts, New Hampshire, Rhode Island, and Vermont)
John W. McCormack Post Office and Courthouse Building, Boston, Mass. 02109

Eastern Region (Formerly New York Region—comprised of New York, New Jersey, Commonwealth of Puerto Rico, and Virgin Islands)
26 Federal Plaza, New York, N.Y. 10007

Mid-Atlantic Region (Formerly Philadelphia Region—comprised of Delaware, Maryland, Pennsylvania, Virginia, and West Virginia)
William J. Gree, Jr., Federal Building, 600 Arch Street, Philadelphia, Pa. 19106

Southeast Region (Formerly Atlanta Region—comprised of Alabama, Kentucky, Florida, Mississippi, South Carolina, North Carolina, Georgia, and Tennessee)
Richard B. Russell Federal Building, 75 Spring Street S.W., Atlanta, Ga. 30303

Great Lakes Region (Formerly Chicago Region—comprised of Illinois, Indiana, Michigan, Minnesota, Ohio, and Wisconsin)
John C. Kluczynski Federal Building, 29th Floor, 230 South Dearborn Street, Chicago, Ill. 60604

Southwest Region (Formerly Dallas Region—comprised of Arkansas, Louisiana, New Mexico, Oklahoma, and Texas)
1100 Commerce Street, Dallas, Tex. 75242

Mid-Continent Region (Formerly St. Louis Region—comprised of Iowa, Missouri, Kansas, and Nebraska)
1256 Federal Building 1520 Market Street, St. Louis, Mo. 63103

Rocky Mountain Region (Formerly Denver Region—comprised of Colorado, Utah, North Dakota, Montana, South Dakota, and Wyoming)
Building 20, Denver Federal Center, Denver, Colo. 80225

Western Region (Formerly San Francisco Region—comprised of California,

Arizona, Hawaii, Nevada, and the Pacific Ocean area)
525 Market Street, 23rd Floor, San Francisco, Calif. 94105
Northwest Region (Formerly Seattle Region—comprised of Alaska, Idaho, Oregon, and Washington)
Federal Building, 26th Floor, 915 Second Avenue, Seattle, Wash. 98174

Federal Agencies

The following agencies are the ones most likely to have outdoor job openings. For complete listings, consult the *Conservation Directory*, described on the first page of the Appendix.

ACTION/Peace Corps
806 Connecticut Avenue N.W.
Washington, D.C. 20525

ACTION/Vista
806 Connecticut Avenue N.W.
Washington, D.C. 20525

U.S. Department of Agriculture
Fourteenth Street and Independence Avenue S.W.
Washington, D.C. 20250

    Agriculture Extension Service
    Animal and Plant Health Inspection Service
    Economics, Statistics, and Cooperatives Service
    Farmers Home Administration
    Forest Service (Box 2417, Washington, D.C. 20013)
    Food and Nutrition Service
    Foreign Agricultural Service
    Rural Electrification Administration
    Science and Education Administration
    Soil Conservation Service

U.S. Department of Commerce
Fourteenth Street between Constitution Avenue and E Street N.W.
Washington, D.C. 20230

    Bureau of Census
    Industry and Trade Administration
    Maritime Administration
    National Oceanic and Atmospheric Administration (6010 Executive Boulevard, Rockville, Maryland 20852)

Department of Defense
The Pentagon
Washington, D.C. 20301

    U.S. Army Corps of Engineers (Washington, D.C. 20314)

Environmental Protection Agency
40l M Street S.W.
Washington, D.C. 20460

U.S. Department of the Interior
C Street between Eighteenth and Nineteenth Streets N.W.
Washington, D.C. 20240

    Bureau of Land Management
    Bureau of Mines (2401 E Street N.W., Washington, D.C. 20241)
    Bureau of Reclamation
    Geological Survey (National Center, 12201 Sunrise Valley Drive, Reston,
    Va. 22092)
    Heritage Conservation and Recreation Service (includes old Bureau of
    Outdoor Recreation)
    National Park Service
    United States Fish and Wildlife Service

U.S. Department of Labor
200 Constitution Avenue N.W.
Washington, D.C. 20210

    Bureau of Apprenticeship and Training
    601 D Street N.W.
    Washington, D.C. 20213

    Job Corps and Office of Youth Programs
    Employment and Training Administration
    601 D Street N.W.
    Washington, D.C. 20213

    Women's Bureau

National Aeronautics and Space Administration
400 Maryland Avenue S.W.
Washington, D.C. 20546

National Science Foundation
1800 G Street N.W.
Washington, D.C. 20550

Small Business Administration
1441 L Street N.W.
Washington, D.C. 20416

Smithsonian Institution
1000 Jefferson Drive S.W.
Washington, D.C. 20560

U.S. Department of Transportation
400 Seventh Street S.W.
Washington, D.C. 20590

    U.S. Coast Guard
    Federal Highway Administration

Tennessee Valley Authority
400 Commerce Avenue
Knoxville, Tennessee 37902

U.S. Water Resources Council
Suite 800, 2120 L Street N.W.
Washington, D.C. 20037

State Occupational Information Coordinating Committees

These committees can help you find career information tailored to the job situation in your area.

Alabama

Director, Alabama Occupational Information Coordinating Committee, State Department of Education
First Southern Towers, Suite 402
100 Commerce St.
Montgomery, Ala. 36104

Alaska

Coordinator, Alaska Occupational Information Coordinating Committee
Pouch F—State Office Bldg.
Juneau, Alaska 99811

Arizona

Executive Director, Arizona State Occupational Information Coordinating Committee
1535 West Jefferson Ave., Room 345
Phoenix, Ariz. 85007

Arkansas

Director, Arkansas State Occupational Information Coordinating Committee
P.O. Box 5162
Little Rock, Ark. 72205

California

Director, California Occupational Information Coordinating Committee
535 East Main St.
Ventura, Calif. 93009

Colorado

SOICC Director, Office of Occupational Information, Colorado Occupational Information Coordinating Committee
770 Grant St.
Room 222
Denver, Colo. 80203

Connecticut

Executive Director, Connecticut State Occupational Information Coordinating Committee
Hartranft Hall
55 Elizabeth St.
Hartford, Conn. 06053

Delaware

Director, State Occupational Information Coordinating Committee of Delaware
820 North French St.
6th floor
Wilmington, Del. 19801

District of Columbia

Executive Director, D.C. Occupational Information Coordinating Committee
500 C St. NW., Suite 621
Washington, D.C. 20001

Florida

Director, Florida Occupational Information Coordinating Committee
325 John Knox Rd.
Suite L-500
Tallahassee, Fla. 32303

Georgia

Executive Director, State Occupational Information Coordinating Committee
151 Ellis St., NE.
Suite 504
Atlanta, Ga. 30303

Hawaii

Executive Director, Hawaii State Occupational Information Coordinating Committee
1164 Bishop St.
Suite 502
Honolulu, Hawaii 96813

Idaho

Coordinator, State Occupational Information Coordinating Committee
Len B. Jordan Bldg.
650 W. State St.
Boise, Idaho 83720

Illinois

Executive Director, Illinois Occupational Information Coordinating Committee
623 E. Adams St.
P.O. Box 1587
Springfield, Ill. 62705

Indiana

SOICC Contact, Indiana Office of Manpower Development
State Board of Vocational and Technical Education
17 W. Market St.
401 Illinois Bldg.
Indianapolis, Ind. 46204

Iowa

Executive Director, Iowa State Occupational Information Coordinating Committee
523 E. 12th St.
Des Moines, Iowa 50319

Kansas

Director, Kansas Occupational Information Coordinating Committee
Department of Human Resources
634 S. Harrison
Suite C
Topeka, Kans. 66603

Kentucky

Coordinator, Kentucky Occupational Information Coordinating Committee
103 Bridge St.
Frankfort, Ky. 40601

Louisiana

Director, Louisiana State Occupational Information Coordinating Commit-
tee
P.O. Box 44094
Baton Rouge, La. 70804

Maine

Executive Director, State Occupational Information Coordinating Com-
mittee
State House Station 71
Augusta, Maine 04330

Maryland

Executive Director, Maryland Occupational Information Coordinating Committee
Department of Human Resources
110 North Eutaw St.
Baltimore, Md. 21201

Massachusetts

Executive Director, Massachusetts
Occupational Information Coordinating Committee
Park Square Bldg.
Suite 341
31 St. James Ave.
Boston, Mass. 02116

Michigan

Executive Coordinator, Michigan Occupational Information Coordinating
Committee
309 N. Washington, P.O. Box 30015
Lansing, Mich. 48909

Minnesota

SOICC Director, Department of Economic Security
690 American Center Bldg.
150 E. Kellogg Blvd.
St. Paul, Minn. 55101

Mississippi

SOICC Director, Vocational Technical Education
P.O. Box 771
Jackson, Miss. 39205

Missouri

Director, Missouri Occupational Information Coordinating Committee
8300 E. High St.
Jefferson City, Mo. 65101

Montana

Program Manager, Montana State Occupational Information Coordinating
Committee
P.O. Box 1728
Helena, Mont. 59601

Nebraska

Executive Director, State Occupational Information Coordinating Com-
mittee
W. 300 Nebraska Hall
University of Nebraska
Lincoln, Nebr. 68588

Nevada

Director, State Occupational Information Coordinating Committee
Capitol Complex
505 E. King St.
Kinkead Bldg.
Room 603
Carson City, Nev. 89710

New Hampshire

SOICC Director, Department of Employment Security
32 S. Main St.
Concord, N.H. 03301

New Jersey

Acting Staff Director, New Jersey Occupational Information Coordinating
Committee
Department of Labor and Industry, Division of Planning and Research
P.O. Box 2765
Trenton, N.J. 08625

New Mexico

SOICC Director, New Mexico State Occupational Information Coordinating
Committee
Suite C, Harvey Building
839 Paseo de Peralta
Santa Fe, N.M. 87501

New York

SOICC Director, State Department of Labor
Labor Department Bldg. #12
State Campus
Albany, N.Y. 12240

North Carolina

SOICC Director, North Carolina Department of Administration
112 W. Lane St.
Raleigh, N.C. 27611

North Dakota

State Director, State Occupational Information Coordinating Committee
1424 W. Century Ave.
P.O. Box 1537
Bismarck, N. Dak. 58501

Ohio

SOICC Director, State Department Bldg.
S-65 S. Front St., Room 904
Columbus, Ohio 43215

Oklahoma

Executive Director, State Occupational Information Coordinating Committee, School of Occupational and Adult Education, Oklahoma State University
1515 W. 6th St.
Stillwater, Okla 74074

Oregon

Executive Secretary, Oregon Occupational Information Coordinating Committee
875 Union St. NE.
Salem, Oreg. 97311

Pennsylvania

SOICC Director, Pennsylvania Occupational Information Coordinating Committee
Labor and Industry Bldg.
7th and Forster Sts.
Room 1008
Harrisburg, Pa. 17121

Puerto Rico

Executive Director, Puerto Rico Occupational Information Coordinating Committee
414 Barbosa Ave.
Hato Rey, P.R. 00917

Rhode Island

Executive Director, Rhode Island Occupational Information Coordinating Committee
22 Hayes St., Room 315
Providence, R.I. 02908

South Carolina

SOICC Director
1550 Gadsden St.
Columbia, S.C. 29202

South Dakota

Executive Director, South Dakota Occupational Information Coordinating Committee
109 E. Missouri
Pierre, S. Dak. 57501

Tennessee

Director, Tennessee Occupational Information Coordinating Committee
512 Cordell Hull Bldg.
Nashville, Tenn. 37219

Texas

Executive Director, State Occupational Information Coordinating Committee, Texas Employment Commission Bldg.
15th and Congress Ave.
Room 648
Austin, Tex. 78778

Utah

Director, Occupational Information Coordinating Committee, State Board of Education
250 E. 5th St. South
Salt Lake City, Utah 84111

Vermont

Director, Vermont Occupational Information Coordinating Committee
P.O. Box 488
Montpelier, Vt. 05602

Virginia

SOICC Director, Vocational and Adult Education, Department of Education
P.O. Box 6Q
Richmond, Va. 23216

Washington

SOICC Director, Commission for Vocational Education
Bldg. 17
Airdustrial Park
Mail Stop LS-10
Olympia, Wash. 98504

West Virginia

Executive Director, West Virginia State Occupational Information Coordinating Committee, Capitol Complex
Bldg. #6
Room 221
Charleston, W. Va. 25305

Wisconsin

SOICC Director, Wisconsin Occupational Information Coordinating Committee, Educational Sciences Building, Room 952
1025 W. Johnson
Madison, Wis. 53706

Wyoming

Director, Wyoming Occupational Information Coordinating Committee
1520 E. 5th St.
Cheyenne, Wyo. 82002

American Samoa

SOICC State Director for Vocational Education
Government of American Samoa
Pago Pago, American Samoa 96799

Guam

Acting Executive Director, Guam Occupational Information Coordinating
Committee, P.O. Box 2817, Agana, Guam 96910

Northern Mariana Islands

Executive Director, Northern Mariana Islands Occupational Information
Coordinating Committee, P.O. Box 149, Saipan, Northern Mariana Islands
96950

Trust Territory of the Pacific

Chairman, Trust Territory of the Pacific Islands, Occupational Information
Coordinating Committee
Office of Planning and Statistics, Saipan
Mariana Islands 96950

Virgin Islands

Acting Chairman, Virgin Islands Occupational Information Coordinating
Committee, Department of Education
Charlotte Amalie, St. Thomas
Virgin Islands 00801

Labor Market Information

For detailed labor market reports covering current and future employment
in various states, contact the chief of research and analysis in your state.
Titles and addresses include:

Alabama

Chief, Research and Statistics, Department of Industrial Relations
Industrial Relations Bldg.
649 Monroe St.
Montgomery, Ala 36130

Alaska

Chief, Research and Analysis, Employment Security Division
Department of Labor
P.O. Box 3-7000
Juneau, Alaska 99802

Arizona

Chief, Labor Market Information, Research and Analysis
Department of Economic Security
P.O. Box 6123
Phoenix, Ariz. 85005

Arkansas

Chief, Research and Statistics, Employment Security Division
P.O. Box 2981
Little Rock, Ark. 72203

California

Chief, Employment Data and Research Division
Employment Development Department
P.O. Box 1679
Sacramento, Calif. 95808

Colorado

Chief, Research and Analysis, Division of Employment
Department of Labor and Employment
1210 Sherman St.
Denver, Colo. 80203

Connecticut

Director, Research and Information, Connecticut Employment Security Division
200 Folly Brook Blvd.
Weatherfield, Conn. 06109

Delaware

Chief, Office of Research, Planning, and Evaluation
Department of Labor
Bldg. D
Chapman Rd.
Route 273
Newark, Del. 19713

District of Columbia

Chief, Branch of Labor Market Information and Analysis
D.C. Department of Labor
605 G St. NW., Room 1000
Washington, D.C. 20001

Florida

Chief, Research and Statistics, Division of Employment Security
Florida Department of Commerce
Caldwell Bldg.
Tallahassee, Fla. 32304

Georgia

Director, Information Systems, Employment Security Agency
Department of Labor
254 Washington St. SW.
Atlanta, Ga. 30334

Hawaii

Chief, Research and Statistics, Department of Labor and Industrial Relations
P.O. Box 3680
Honolulu, Hawaii 96811

Idaho

Chief, Research and Analysis, Department of Employment
P.O. Box 35
Boise, Idaho 83707

Illinois

Manager, Research and Analysis Division, Bureau of Employment Security
Department of Labor
910 South Michigan Ave.
Chicago, Ill. 60605

Indiana

Chief of Research, Employment Security Division
10 North Senate Ave.
Indianapolis, Ind. 46204

Iowa

Chief, Research and Statistics, Department of Job Service
1000 East Grand Ave.
Des Moines, Iowa 50319

Kansas

Chief, Research and Analysis, Department of Human Resources
401 Topeka Avenue
Topeka, Kans. 66603

Kentucky

Chief, Research and Special Projects, Department of Human Resources
275 E. Main St.
Frankfort, Ky. 40601

Louisiana

Chief, Research and Statistics, Department of Employment Security
P.O. Box 44094
Baton Rouge, La. 70804

Maine

Director, Manpower Research Division, Employment Security Commission
20 Union St.
Augusta, Maine 04330

Maryland
Director, Research and Analysis, Department of Human Resources
1100 North Eutaw St.
Baltimore, Md. 21201

Massachusetts
Director, Information and Research, Division of Employment Security
Hurley Bldg.
Government Center
Boston, Mass. 02114

Michigan
Director, Research and Statistics Division, Employment Security Commission
Department of Labor Bldg.
7310 Woodward Ave.
Detroit, Mich. 48202

Minnesota
Acting Director, Research and Statistics Services, Department of Economic Security
390 North Robert St.
St. Paul, Minn. 55101

Mississippi
Chief, Research and Statistics, Employment Security Commission
P.O. Box 1699
Jackson, Miss. 39205

Missouri
Chief, Research and Statistics, Division of Employment Security
Department of Labor and Industrial Relations
P.O. Box 59
Jefferson City, Mo. 65101

Montana
Chief, Reports and Analysis, Employment Security Division
P.O. Box 1728
Helena, Mont. 59601

Nebraska
Chief, Research and Statistics, Division of Employment
Department of Labor
P.O. Box 94600
Lincoln, Nebr. 68509

Nevada

Chief, Employment Security Research, Employment Security Department, 500 East Third St.
Carson City, Nev. 89713

New Hampshire

Director, Economic Analysis and Reports, Department of Employment Security
32 South Main St.
Concord, N.H. 03301

New Jersey

Director, Division of Planning and Research, Department of Labor and Industry
P.O. Box 2765
Trenton, N.J. 08625

New Mexico

Chief, Research and Statistics, Employment Security Commission
P.O. Box 1928
Albuquerque, N. Mex. 87103

New York

Director, Division of Research and Statistics, Department of Labor
State Campus
Bldg. 1Z
Albany, N.Y. 12240

North Carolina

Director, Bureau of Employment Security Research, Employment Security Commission
P.O. Box 25903
Raleigh, N.C. 27611

North Dakota

Chief, Research and Statistics, Employment Security Bureau
P.O. Box 1537
Bismarck, N.Dak. 58501

Ohio

Director, Division of Research and Statistics, Bureau of Employment Services
145 South Front St.
Columbus, Ohio 43216

Oklahoma

Chief, Research and Planning Division, Employment Security Commission
310 Will Rogers Memorial Office Bldg.
Oklahoma City, Okla. 73105

Oregon
Assistant Administrator, Research and Statistics, Employment Division
875 Union St. NE.
Salem, Oreg. 97311

Pennsylvania
Director, Research and Statistics, Bureau of Employment Security
Department of Labor and Industry
7th and Forster Sts.
Harrisburg, Pa. 17121

Puerto Rico
Chief of Research and Statistics, Bureau of Employment Security
427 Barbosa Ave.
Hato Rey, P.R. 00917

Rhode Island
Supervisor, Employment Security Research, Department of Employment
Security
24 Mason St.
Providence, R.I. 02903

South Carolina
Director, Manpower Research and Analysis, Employment Security Com-
mission
P.O. Box 995
Columbia, S.C. 29202

South Dakota
Chief, Research and Statistics, Employment Security Department
607 North Fourth St.
Box 730
Aberdeen, S. Dak. 57401

Tennessee
Chief, Research and Statistics, Department of Employment Security
Cordell Hull Bldg.
Room 519
Nashville, Tenn. 37219

Texas
Chief, Economic Research and Analysis, Employment Commission
TEC Bldg.
15th and Congress Ave.
Austin, Tex. 78778

Utah

Director, Research and Analysis, Department of Employment Security
P.O. Box 11249
Salt Lake City, Utah 84147

Vermont

Chief, Research and Statistics, Department of Employment Security
P.O. Box 488
Montpelier, Vt. 05602

Virginia

Commissioner, Virginia Employment Commission
P.O. Box 1358
Richmond, Va. 23211

Washington

Chief, Research and Statistics, Employment Security Department
1007 So. Washington St.
Olympia, Wash. 98501

West Virginia

Chief, Labor and Economic Research, Department of Employment Security
112 California Ave.
Charleston, W. Va. 25305

Wisconsin

Director, Research and Statistics, Department of Industry, Labor and Human
Relations
P.O. Box 7944
Madison, Wis. 53701

Wyoming

Chief, Research and Analysis, Employment Security Commission
P. O. Box 2760
Casper, Wyo. 82601

Chapter 7
Life and Living: Biology and Anthropology

American Institute of Biological Sciences
1401 Wilson Boulevard, Arlington, Va. 22209

American Society for Horticultural Science
70 North Saint Asaph Street, Alexandria, Va. 22314

American Physiological Society, Education Office
9650 Rockville Pike, Bethesda, Md. 20014

The American Anthropological Association and The Society for American
Archeology
1703 New Hampshire Avenue N.W., Washington, D.C. 20009

The Archeological Institute of America
53 Park Place, New York, N.Y. 10007

National Science Foundation Division of Social Sciences
1800 G Street N.W., Washington, D.C. 20550

Smithsonian Institution
Washington, D.C. 20560

Veterinarians

There are a number of specialties within the field of veterinary science,
which has about 33,500 veterinarians working in it. Most are in private
practice and specialize. Some treat small animals or pets exclusively. Others
work with cattle, poultry, sheep, swine, or horses. Still others inspect meat,
poultry, and other foods as part of federal and state public health programs.
A smaller group teaches and does research related to animal diseases, foods,
and drugs. The kind of practice is dictated by geographic setting, with veterinarians in rural areas working with farm animals and those in urban and
suburban areas working with pets.

The United States Department of Agriculture and the United States
Public Health Service employ about 2,450. Another 675 are commissioned
officers in the veterinary service of the Army and Air Force. Other employers
are state and local government agencies, international health agencies, colleges of veterinary science, medical schools, research and development laboratories, large livestock farms, animal food companies, and pharmaceutical
companies.

All states and the District of Columbia require veterinarians to have a
license. The requirements include a Doctor of Veterinary Medicine (D.V.M.
or V.M.D.) degree from an accredited college of veterinary medicine and the
successful completion of a written test. Twenty states also have oral state
board proficiency examinations. Some states have reciprocal licensing agreements.

For positions in research and teaching, an additional master's or Ph.D.
degree usually is required in a field such as pathology, physiology, or bac-
teriology.

The D.V.M. or V.M.D. degree requires a minimum of six years of college
consisting of a four-year professional degree program, preceded by at least
two years of pre-veterinary study emphasizing the physical and biological
sciences. Some colleges of veterinary science require three years of pre-
veterinary work. Actually most students complete three or four years of
college before entering the professional program.

In addition to academic instruction, professional training includes considerable practical experience in diagnosing and treating animal diseases,

performing surgery, and performing laboratory work in anatomy, biochemistry, and other scientific and medical subjects.

Admission to veterinary colleges, of which there are twenty-two accredited by the Council on Education of the American Veterinary Medical Association, is highly competitive. Each year there are more qualified applicants than the schools can accept. This means that excellent grades—a B average or better—are necessary. Experience in part-time or summer jobs working with animals helps, too.

Colleges usually give preference to residents of the state in which they are located because the schools are largely state-supported. In the South and West, regional education plans permit cooperating states without veterinary schools to send students to designated regional schools. In other areas, colleges that accept a certain number of students from other states usually give priority to applicants from nearby states that do not have veterinary schools.

In spite of the educational hurdles, the United States Department of Labor predicts that the number of graduates will have doubled by 1990. The growth is attributed to the increase in keeping companion animals such as horses, dogs, and other pets, and the current emphasis on the importance of scientific methods of raising, breeding, and caring for livestock and poultry.

Earnings of veterinarians vary considerably, depending on such factors as location, type of practice, and years of experience, but limited data sets the average income at about $33,000. Newly graduated veterinarians employed by the federal government start at $18,000. The average annual salary of veterinarians employed by the federal government is $27,300. Young people going into the field should keep in mind the high cost of setting up a private practice. They should also realize that the growing number of graduates may create competition in some areas.

Chapter 8
Young MacDonald: Farming and Agribusiness

American Association of Land Grant Colleges and State Universities, Washington, D.C. 20250

Office of Personnel, U.S. Department of Agriculture
Washington, D.C. 20250

Information about opportunities in agricultural finance is available from:

Farm Credit Administration
Washington, D.C. 20578

Farmers Home Administration, U.S. Department of Agriculture
Washington, D.C. 20250

Agriculture, Washington, D.C.

Agriculture Director, American Bankers Association
1120 Connecticut Avenue N.W., Washington, D.C. 20036

For membership information and local chapters write:
National Future Farmers of America Organization
Box 15160
National FFA Center
Alexandria, Va. 22309

Information about careers in veterinary science is also available from:
American Veterinary Medical Association
930 North Meacham Road, Schaumburg, Ill. 60196

Animal and Plant Health Inspection Service, Personnel Division
123 East Grant Street, Minneapolis, Minn. 55403

Food Safety and Quality Service, Personnel Director
123 East Grant Street, Minneapolis, Minn. 55403

Chapter 9
A Tolerable Planet: A Place to Work and Play

Society of American Foresters
5400 Grosvenor Lane, Washington, D.C. 20014

National Forest Products Association
1619 Massachusetts Avenue N.W., Washington, D.C. 20036

American Forest Institute
1619 Massachusetts Avenue N.W., Washington, D.C. 20036

American Forestry Association
1319 18th Street N.W., Washington, D.C. 20036

Forest Service, U.S. Department of Agriculture
Washington, D.C. 20250

Society for Range Management
2760 West Fifth Avenue, Denver, Colo. 80204

Bureau of Land Management
Denver Service Center
Federal Center Building 50, Denver, Colo. 80255

Soil Conservation Service, U.S. Department of Agriculture
Washington, D.C. 20205

National Recreation and Park Association
1601 North Kent Street, Arlington, Va. 22209

American Association for Health, Physical Education, and Recreation
1201 16th Street N.W., Washington, D.C. 20036

American Society of Travel Agents
360 Lexington Avenue, New York, N.Y. 10017

Chapter 10
The Good Earth: The Environmental Sciences

American Geological Institute
One Skyline Place
5205 Leesburg Pike
Falls Church, Va. 22041

Request: *Career in Geology* and *Geology: Science and Profession*

American Association of Petroleum Geologists
Box 979
Tulsa, Okla. 74101

American Geophysical Union
2000 Florida Avenue N.W.
Washington, D.C. 20009

American Institute of Professional Geologists
Box 957
Golden, Colo. 80401

Association of American State Geologists
c/o American Geological Institute (see above)

Association of Earth Science Editors
H. L. James, Secy./Treas.
Montana Bureau of Mines
Butte, Mont. 59701

Association of Engineering Geologists
Floyd T. Johnston, Executive Director
8310 San Fernando Way
Dallas, Tex. 75218

Geochemical Society
c/o Dr. Taro Takahashi, Secretary
Lamont-Doherty Geological Observatory
Palisades, N.Y. 10964

Geological Society of America
3300 Penrose Place
Box 9140
Boulder, Colo. 80301

Geoscience Information Society
c/o American Geological Institute (see above)

Mineralogical Society of America
2000 Florida Avenue N.W.
Washington, D.C. 20009

National Association of Geology Teachers
Business Office
Box 368
Lawrence, Kans. 66044

Paleontological Society
c/o American Geological Institute (see above)

Seismological Society of America
2620 Telegraph Avenue
Berkeley, Calif. 94704

Society of Economic Geologists
Arnold L. Brokaw, Secretary
185 Estes Street
Lakewood, Colo. 80226

Society of Economic Paleontologists and Mineralogists
Box 4756
Tulsa, Okla. 74104

Society of Exploration Geophysicists
Box 3098
Tulsa, Okla. 74101

Society of Mining Engineers
8307 Shaffer Parkway
Caller No. D
Littleton, Colo. 80127

Society of Vertebrate Paleontology
Dr. Bruce MacFadden
Florida State Museum
University of Florida
Gainesville, Fla. 32611

American Meteorological Society
45 Beacon Street
Boston, Mass. 02108

National Center for Atmospheric Research
Box 1470
Boulder, Colo. 80302

Dr. C. Schelske, Secretary
American Society of Limnology and Oceanography
I.S.T. Building

Great Lakes Research Division
University of Michigan
Ann Arbor, Mich. 48109

International Oceanographic Foundation
3979 Rickenbacker Causeway
Miami, Fla. 33149

National Oceanography Association
1900 L. Street N.W.
Washington, D.C. 20036

American Society for Oceanography
854 Main Building
Houston, Texas 77002

Marine Technology Society
1730 M Street N.W.
Washington, D.C. 20036

National Oceanic and Atmospheric Administration
Institute for Oceanography
Gramax Building, 8060 13th Street
Silver Spring, Md. 20910

Interagency Committee on Oceanography
Building 159 E
Washington Navy Yard
Washington, D.C. 20390

Chapter 11
The Problem Solvers: Engineering

American Institute of Aeronautics and Astronautics, Inc.
1290 Avenue of the Americas, New York, N.Y. 10019

American Society of Agricultural Engineers
2950 Niles Road, St. Joseph, Mich. 49850

American Institute of Chemical Engineers
345 East 47th Street, New York, N.Y. 10017

American Chemical Society
1155 16th Street N.W., Washington, D.C. 20036

American Society of Civil Engineers
345 East 47th Street, New York, N.Y. 10017

Institute of Electrical and Electronics Engineers
United States Activities Board
1111 19th Street N.W., Washington, D.C. 20036

American Institute of Industrial Engineers, Inc.
25 Technology Park/Atlanta, Norcross, Ga. 30092

The American Society of Mechanical Engineers
345 East 47th Street, New York, N.Y. 10017

The Society of Mining Engineers of AIME
Caller Number D, Littleton, Colo. 80123

Society of Petroleum Engineers of AIME
6200 North Central Expressway, Dallas, Tex. 75206

American Association of Petroleum Geologists
Box 979, Tulsa, Okla. 74101

American Geological Institute
5205 Leesburg Pike, Falls Church, Va. 22041

United Mine Workers of America
900 15th Street N.W., Washington, D.C. 20005

National Coal Association
1130 17th Street N.W., Washington, D.C. 20036

Mine Safety and Health Administration
4015 Wildson Boulevard, Arlington, VA 22203

Chapter 12
Doing What Comes Naturally: Building with Environment

Information about architecture is available from:
The American Institute of Architects
1735 New York Avenue N.W., Washington, D.C. 20006

The Association of Collegiate School of Architecture, Inc.
1735 New York Avenue N.W., Washington, D.C. 20006

The National Council of Architectural Registration Boards
1735 New York Avenue N.W., Suite 700, Washington, D.C. 20006

Information about community planners is available from:
American Planning Association
1313 East 60th Street, Chicago, Ill. 60637

Information about landscape architecture is available from:
American Society of Landscape Architecture, Inc.
1900 M Street N.W., Washington, D.C. 20036

U.S. Department of Agriculture, Forest Service
Washington, D.C. 20250

Chapter 13
Stopgap Careers: Working Your Way Up the Career Ladder

Information on engineering and science technicians is available from:

Engineers Council for Professional Development
345 East 47th Street, New York, N.Y. 10017

National Association of Trade and Technical Schools
2021 K Street N.W., Washington, D.C. 20006

American Association of Community and Junior Colleges
One Dupont Circle, Suite 410, Washington, D.C. 20036

National Home Study Council
1601 18th Street N.W., Washington, D.C. 20009

Information on surveying is available from:

American Congress on Surveying and Mapping
210 Little Falls Street, Falls Church, Va. 22046

American Society of Photogrammetry
105 North Virginia Avenue, Falls Church, Va. 22046

Chapter 14
The Best of All Possible Worlds: Indoor Skills—Outdoor Fun

Teaching

General information on teaching as a career is available from:

American Federation of Teachers
11 Dupont Circle N.W.
Washington, D.C. 20036

National Science Teachers Association
1742 Connecticut Avenue N.W.
Washington, D.C. 20009

Association for Environmental and Outdoor Education
2428 Walnut Boulevard
Walnut Creek, Calif. 94596

National Association for Environmental Education
1011 S.W. 140 Street
Miami, Fla. 33156

Listings for schools specializing in outdoor subjects are included in the following guides:

Handbook of Private Schools. Revised about every three years by the publisher, Porter Sargent, 11 Beacon Street, Boston, Mass. 02108. About $30.00. Available in some libraries

Private Independent Schools. Revised about every three years by the publisher, Bunting and Lyon, Wallingford, Conn. 06492. Available in some libraries.

Law

Information on the law as a career is available from:

Prelaw Handbook. Published annually by Law School Admission Services, Box 944, Princeton, N.J. 08540. Includes information on law schools and prelaw study. Available in public and school libraries.

Information Services
American Bar Association
1155 East 60th Street
Chicago, Ill. 60637

The Environmental Defense Fund, Inc.
475 Park Avenue South
New York, N.Y. 10016

The Environmental Law Institute
Suite 620, 1346 Connecticut Avenue N.W.
Washington, D.C. 20036

Environmental Action Foundation, Inc.
724 Dupont Circle Building
Washington, D.C. 20036

Association of American Law Schools
1 Dupont Circle NW, Suite 370, Washington, D.C. 20036

National Association for Law Placement
3200 Fifth Avenue, Sacramento, Calif. 95817

Communications

Information on journalism as a career is available from:

American Newspaper Publishers Association Foundation
The Newspaper Center, Box 17407, Dulles International Airport, Washington, D.C. 20041 Ask for: *Your Future in Daily Newspapers* and *Facts About Newspapers.*

The Newspaper Fund, Inc.
Box 300, Princeton, N.J. 08540

National Community College Journalism Association
San Antonio College
1300 San Pedro Avenue, San Antonio, Tex. 78284

The Newspaper Guild
Research and Information Department
1125 15th Street N.W., Washington, D.C. 20005

American Council on Education for Journalism
School of Journalism, University of Missouri
Columbia, Mo. 65205

Association for Education in Journalism
102 Reavis Hall, Northern Illinois University, Dekalb, Ill. 60115

American Newspaper Publishers Association
750 Third Avenue, New York, N.Y. 10017

Women in Communications, Inc.
Box 9561, Austin, Tex. 78766

Information on freelance writing is available from;
Outdoor Writers Association of America, Inc.
308 Outdoors Building, Columbia, Mo. 65201

Society of American Travel Writers
1146 16th Street N.W., Washington, D.C. 20036

Information on technical writing is available from:
Society of Technical Writers and Publishers, Inc.
1010 Vermont Avenue N.W., Washington, D.C. 20005

American Business Communication Association
University of Illinois, 911 South Sixth Street, Champaign, Ill. 61820

Information on public relations is available from:
Public Relations Society of America
845 Third Avenue, New York, N.Y. 10022

PR Reporter
Dudley House, Box 600, Exeter, N.H. 03833

Public Relations News
127 East 80th Street, New York, N.Y. 10021

Information on broadcasting is available from:
National Association of Broadcasters
1771 N Street, N.W., Washington, D.C. 20036

Federal Communication Commission
1919 M Street N.W., Washington, D.C. 20554

Information on photography and art is available from:
National Art Education Association
National Education Association
1201 16th Street N.W., Washington, D.C. 20036

Professional Photographers of America, Inc.
1090 Executive Way, Des Plaines, Ill. 60018

Financial Aid Information

In addition to information from high school guidance counselors or college
aid officers, students can request the following helps:

Student Consumer's Guide: Six Federal Financial Aid Programs
Published by Bureau of Student Financial Assistance, Box 84, Washington,
D.C. 20044.

Selected List of Postsecondary Education Opportunities for Minorities and Women
Published annually by the United States Department of Education. Includes list of organizations that offer loan, scholarship, and fellowship assistance. Available in libraries or guidance offices or can be purchased from the Superintendent of Documents, United States Government Printing Office, Washington, D.C. 20402. $3.75.

Career/Counseling Information for Special Groups

Many groups, especially veterans, youths, handicapped persons, minorities, and women, face special difficulties in job hunting. In a growing number of communities assistance is available to these groups from churches and synagogues, nonprofit organizations (YWCA's, for example), social service agencies, and libraries. The following directories are especially helpful:

Directory of Counseling Services
An annual publication, listing accredited or provisional members of the International Association of Counseling Services, Inc. (IACS), an affiliate of the American Personnel and Guidance Association. 1979-80 edition, $6.00. IACS, Two Skyline Place, Suite 400, 5203 Leesburg Pike, Falls Church, Va. 22041

The National Directory of Women's Employment Programs
Published 1979 by Wider Opportunities for Women, 1649 K. Street, N.W., Washington, D.C. 20006. $7.50 plus $.40 postage.

Finding a Job: A Resource Book for the Middle-Aged and Retired
Published 1978 by Adelphi University. Out-of-print, but available in libraries and counseling centers. Excellent resource.

Free career materials are available from many agencies. Direct requests to:

Youth

Office of Information, Inquiries Unit, Employment and Training Administration, U.S. Department of Labor, Room 10225, 601 D St. NW., Washington, D.C. 20213

Office of Information and Consumer Affairs, Employment Standards Administration, U.S. Department of Labor. Room C-4331, 200 Constitution Ave. NW., Washington, D.C. 20210

Minorities

Office of Information and Consumer Affairs, Employment Standards Administration, U.S. Department of Labor, Room C-4331, 200 Constitution Ave. NW., Washington, D.C. 20210.

Higher Education Scholarship Program, Division of Postsecondary Education, Bureau of Indian Affairs, U.S. Department of the Interior. 1951 Constitution Ave. NW., Washington, D.C. 20245.

Handicapped

President's Committee on Employment of the Handicapped, Room 600, Vanguard Building, 1111 20th St. NW., Washington, D.C. 20036.

President's Committee on Mental Retardation. Washington, D.C. 20201

Office of Information and Consumer Affairs, Employment Standards Administration, U.S. Department of Labor, Room C-4331, 200 Constitution Ave. NW., Washington, D.C. 20210

Rehabilitation Services Administration, U.S. Department of Education, Room 1427, 330 C St. SW., Washington, D.C. 20201

Office of Personnel Management, Federal Job Information Center, P.O. Box 52, Washington, D.C. 20044.

Older Workers

Office of Information, Inquiries Unit, Employment and Training Administration, U.S. Department of Labor, Room 10225, 601 D St. NW., Washington, D.C. 20213.

National Clearinghouse on Aging, U.S. Department of Health and Human Services, Room 4551, 330 Independence Ave, SW., Washington, D.C. 20201.

National Action Forum for Older Women, 200 P Street, N.W., Suite 508, Washington, D.C. 20036

Women

Women's Bureau, U.S. Department of Labor, Room S3002, 200 Constitution Ave. NW., Washington, D.C. 20210

Veterans

Office of Information Inquiries Unit, Employment and Training Administration, U.S. Department of Labor, Room 10225, 601 D St. NW., Washington, D.C. 20213.

Office of Personnel Management, Federal Job Information Center, P.O. Box 52, Washington, D.C. 20044.

Department of Veterans Benefits, 232A, Veterans Administration Central Office, 810 Vermont Avenue, NW., Washington, D.C. 20420

Federal laws, Executive Orders, and selected federal grant programs bar discrimination in employment based on race, color, religion, sex, national origin, age, and handicap. Employers in the private and public sectors, federal contractors, and grantees are covered by these laws. The United States Equal Employment Opportunity Commission is responsible for the administration of these programs. For information and inquiries about how to file a charge of discrimination, write:

Equal Employment Opportunity Commission
2401 E Street, N.W., Washington, D.C. 20506

Index